SpringerBriefs in Information Security and Cryptography

Editor-in-Chief

Yang Xiang, Swinburne University of Technology, Melbourne, Australia

Series Editors

Liqun Chen, Department of Computer Science, University of Surrey, Guildford, UK

Kim-Kwang Raymond Choo, Department of Information Systems, The University of Texas at San Antonio, San Antonio, USA

Sherman S. M. Chow, Chinese University of Hong Kong, Hong Kong, Hong Kong

Robert H. Deng, Singapore Management University, Singapore, Singapore

Dieter Gollmann, FB 4-14, TU Hamburg-Harburg, Hamburg, Germany

Kuan-Ching Li, Department of Computer Science and Information Engineering, Providence University, Taichung, Taiwan

Javier Lopez, University of Malaga, Malaga, Spain

Kui Ren, University at Buffalo, Buffalo, USA

Jianying Zhou, Singapore University of Technology and Design (SUTD), Singapore, Singapore

Pandi Vijayakumar, Information Technology, J. J. College of Engineering and Technology, Tiruchirappalli, Tamil Nadu, India

The series aims to develop and disseminate an understanding of innovations, paradigms, techniques, and technologies in the contexts of information and cybersecurity systems, as well as developments in cryptography and related studies.

It publishes concise, thorough and cohesive overviews of state-of-the-art topics in these fields, as well as in-depth case studies. The series also provides a single point of coverage of advanced and timely, emerging topics and offers a forum for core concepts that may not have reached a level of maturity to warrant a comprehensive monograph or textbook.

It addresses security, privacy, availability, and dependability issues, also welcoming emerging technologies such as artificial intelligence, cloud computing, cyber physical systems, and big data analytics related to cybersecurity research. Among some core research topics:

Fundamentals and theories
- Cryptography for cybersecurity
- Theories of cybersecurity
- Provable security

Cyber Systems and Secure Networks
- Cyber systems security
- Network security
- Security services
- Social networks security and privacy
- Cyber attacks and defense
- Data-driven cyber security
- Trusted computing and systems

Applications and others
- Hardware and device security
- Cyber application security
- Human and social aspects of cybersecurity

Geoffroy Couteau

An Introduction to Silent
Secure Computation

 Springer

Geoffroy Couteau
IRIF, CNRS
Université Paris Cité
Paris, France

ISSN 2731-9555   ISSN 2731-9563 (electronic)
SpringerBriefs in Information Security and Cryptography
ISBN 978-3-032-07088-3   ISBN 978-3-032-07089-0 (eBook)
https://doi.org/10.1007/978-3-032-07089-0

This Springer imprint is published by the registered company Springer Nature Switzerland AG
The registered company address is: Gewerbestrasse 11, 6330 Cham, Switzerland

If disposing of this product, please recycle the paper.

Competing Interests The author has no competing interests to declare that are relevant to the content of this manuscript.

Contents

Chapter 1
Introduction

Secure computation revolves around a fundamental question: Is it possible for multiple individuals to run a joint computation while concealing all information about the data involved in the computation? This question has fascinated cryptographers, complexity theorists, and security enthusiasts ever since it was first scientifically studied in the early 80s. In essence, it asks how finely one can control the information leaked by a conversation. Beyond its scientific and philosophical interest, this abstract question takes an endless number of concrete shapes and relates to natural questionings of our everyday life:

- If I am asked to justify that I am over 18, can I do so without revealing my age?
- Can I find out whether my salary is below that of other employees (e.g., if I fear I am being discriminated against) without disclosing my salary?
- Can I convince the driver that I paid for a public transport pass without letting the public transportation company track my journeys?
- Can I find out which of my contacts are already on a social network without sharing my contact list with the network?
- During a pandemic, can people get notified when they have been in contact with someone sick while protecting patients' privacy and complying with privacy regulations for health data?
- When visiting a website whose funding model relies on publishers showing you targeted ads, is it possible to conceal your browsing history from the publisher?
- If I run a company, can I demonstrate that I did not commit fraud without revealing all my financial data?

Perhaps surprisingly, the existence of general secure computation protocols, which was established in the 80s through the works of Yao and of Goldreich, Micali, and Wigderson, demonstrates that the answer to all of the above questions—and many more—is yes, provided we are willing to assume that some well-studied mathematical

© The Author(s), under exclusive license to Springer Nature Switzerland AG 2026
G. Couteau, *An Introduction to Silent Secure Computation*,
SpringerBriefs in Information Security and Cryptography,
https://doi.org/10.1007/978-3-032-07089-0_1

problems are intractable. This carries an important and counterintuitive conceptual message: the fact that something must be checked or computed on your private data does not entail that anyone should be entitled to hold or see the content of your private data.

1.1 Secure Computation: Why it Solves All Your Problems and Why it Does Not

In the questions listed above, there is a clear common theme: each of them deals with several individuals, some of them holding a piece of data that they wish to keep private to some extent (their age, their salary, their journeys, their contact list, their health information, their browsing history). At the same time, some partial information must be revealed to a subset of the participants: whether the age is above 18, whether one salary is lower than another, etc. We can abstractly model this setting as follows: there is a group of players, denoted $(P_1, \cdots, P_n)$, each holding a private piece of data $(x_1, \cdots, x_n)$. The goal of all participants is to disclose to a subset of them the value $f(x_1, \cdots, x_n)$, where f is some efficiently computable, publicly known, and agreed-upon function that embodies the information that the participants are willing to leak to a subset of them. To compute this function, the participants exchange messages that depend on their private input. The core security requirement is *privacy*: assume a subset of the participants put their information in common. If we denote $S \subset \{1, \cdots, n\}$ this subset, the colluding participants would be $(P_i)_{i \in S}$. Then we say that the protocol is private if every new information that these colluding parties can *efficiently* deduce from the messages they saw throughout the protocol is an information that could have been computed solely from their inputs $(x_i)_{i \in S}$ and the output of the protocol $f(x_1, \cdots, x_n)$. In other words, the participants cannot learn anything new from the protocol: whatever they learn could have been deduced already from what they know and what they are supposed to learn.

Secure computation is the Swiss Army knife of privacy: in contrast with encryption, that has an all-or-nothing flavor (an encrypted data is either entirely concealed if the decryption key is unknown, or entirely revealed if the decryption key is known), it allows to control precisely what information can or cannot be revealed about private data in a given context. Beyond the few questions outlined above, it can play a fundamental role in countless privacy-aware contexts: it is a core component of electronic voting, where one wishes to compute the result of an election while concealing the individual votes of the voters; it can be used to organize auctions where your bid remains private, yet the winner of the auction can be identified; it can be used to aggregate data on energy consumption without revealing any individual's consumption habits; it can be used to outsource an encrypted storage while enabling searching its content, or to enable secure key management; and it opens the door to privacy-preserving machine learning where neural networks can be trained on sensitive data without seeing their content. To anyone privacy-savvy and familiar with the possibilities offered by secure computation, it certainly feels that it could or even *ought to* be everywhere. Then, why is it not? The answer revolves around a combination of factors such as efficiency, design complexity, and legislation.

Why is secure computation not widely deployed? If the same question was asked 15 years ago, the answer would be fairly simple: because it is not efficient enough. Privacy comes at a cost, and if protecting your list of contacts requires terabytes of communication and hours of computation, this is simply not affordable except in rare situations. The grand goal of secure computation, the one that unifies the vast majority of the research done in the area, from the most theoretical to the most applied, is to bring the price to pay for running a secure computation as close as possible to the price of running the computation without security guarantees.

However, starting circa 2011 with the seminal works of Bendlin et al. (2011) and Damgård et al. (2012), the overhead of secure computation protocols over their insecure counterpart has been *vastly* reduced, to the point that in many contexts, the overhead is now small enough as to be an acceptable slowdown over the insecure protocol. Yet, we *still* do not see secure computation protocols at every corner. This stems from a variety of causes, some of which are quite obvious: the significant engineering effort required to implement and deploy secure computation is one, the legal aspects are another—in particular, whether the legislator imposes, or might impose in a near future, that sensitive data should be kept private often conditions whether entities will deploy secure computation mechanisms; in turn, whether there *exists* secure computation mechanisms efficient enough in a context can influence whether the legislator imposes their use. Yet, another major cause of this lack of widespread adoption stems from the sheer hardness of finding the right protocol for a given context—or even, finding out whether an efficient protocol exists for the context at hand. What computational model best represents the function to be computed? How many participants are involved? Do they interact through a slow or a fast network? What is the latency? How powerful are their devices? Do they all have similar computational power? How many of the participants might attempt to cheat? Will they actively cheat, or will they simply attempt to deduce information from their interactions? Can all participants send messages to everyone? Each of these considerations can radically change the landscape of the best available solutions; we will come back to this in Sect. 1.3.

1.2 This Book

An Introduction to Silent Secure Computation is not intended to be used as a textbook. While it provides coverage of some of the basic material related to secure computation that could be part of a cryptography curriculum, it does not have the same focus as a textbook. In particular, it does not contain exercises, and rarely provides in-depth proofs at the level of formalism that would be appropriate for teaching. There are excellent books out there that we would recommend instead for teaching purposes: for an in-depth introduction to the formalism of secure computation and its foundations, we warmly recommend *Foundations in Cryptography, Volume 2* by Oded Goldreich. More broadly, this book is a must-read for any aspiring researcher in secure computation or for a PhD student who, after a few years in the field, would like to strengthen their mastery of the foundations of secure computation. For a more modern coverage that will span many of the cornerstone protocols of secure computation, we recommend *A Pragmatic Introduction to Secure Multi-Party Computation* by David Evans, Vladimir Kolesnikov, and Mike Rosulek. Another great and complementary resource is the book *Secure Multiparty Computation and Secret Sharing* by Ivan Damgård, Jesper Buus Nielsen, and Ronald Cramer: it covers in greater depth the topic of secret sharing, that is at the heart of secure computation, and uncovers some of its deeper mathematical aspects (making it a good topic for a cryptography course aimed at students in mathematics). It also covers in depth the framework of universal composability, which provides a formal methodology to derive the security of a high-level protocol from that of its internal components.

An Introduction to Silent Secure Computation is also not meant to provide an exhaustive coverage of secure computation. As we argued above and will discuss in more depth in the next section, covering all natural settings and solutions would require much more than a book anyway. Rather, we aim to cover a specific subfield of secure computation that emerged circa 2018: the model of secure computation with silent preprocessing, often abbreviated *silent secure computation*.[1] Even within this model, our aim will not be to give an exhaustive coverage, but rather to provide an accessible introduction. The target audience for this book is expected to be any Ph.D. student in cryptography, or any researcher in cryptography who aspires to learn more about some recent developments in secure computation, and might be interested in using some of these approaches in their research, or even to contribute to this line of work. With this in mind, the exposition in this book makes a few strategic choices:

- The book lacks formal proofs for most of the material it introduces. The descriptions are usually given at the level of a technical overview: a sufficiently expert reader could, from the sketch given, reconstruct the proof by themself; the interested reader can also find them in academic papers, usually mentioned in the *historical notes* paragraphs that are spread throughout the book.
- However, the exposition has a strong focus on providing *numbers and estimates*. Unlike a textbook, our goal is less to cover the answer to research questions than it is to explain why these questions are the right questions to ask. The book is filled with back-of-the-envelope calculations and rough runtime estimates that are meant to help the reader always get an intuition of what *efficient* means in the context at hand. The hope is that the reader can form their own opinion on what

---

[1] We warn the reader that the shorter terminology is also a bit more misleading: silent secure computation still requires the participants to speak—they do not remain silent. However, the framework allows the participants to remain silent during the *preprocessing phase* of the protocol: it is a shorthand for the longer (but more accurate) term secure computation with silent preprocessing.

solutions should be deemed "practical" and where more research is required to achieve a satisfying state. More broadly, it should help understand why the model of secure computation with silent preprocessing matters in the first place.

Terminology. Secure computation is sometimes called secure *multi-party* computation, or SMPC, to emphasize the fact that the computation involves private inputs held by multiple participants. The short version *multi-party computation*, abbreviated MPC, is perhaps the most common, though it is sometimes used to refer specifically to secure computation in a model where the participants interact through a complete graph (anyone can communicate with everyone). Equivalent terms, such as private computation or privacy-preserving computation, can also be found (often in older textbooks and articles). While some articles can associate distinct meanings to some of these terminologies (e.g., using "private computation" to refer specifically to protocols protecting the privacy of the input, and "secure computation" to refer to a broader class of security properties in distributed computation, such as properties guaranteeing the correctness of the computation or the fact that all parties will receive an output), there is no universally accepted terminology. In this book, we will use *secure computation* and *multi-party computation* (abbreviated MPC) interchangeably to denote the general area.

1.3 Do We Need One More Book on Secure Computation?

Given the existence of excellent books that cover the foundations and the core secure computation protocols, why do we need one more book on secure computation? While *Foundations in Cryptography, Volume 2* is 21 years old at the time of writing, its content is by no mean outdated and remains very much the reference on the topic, and *A Pragmatic Introduction to Secure Multi-Party Computation* is quite recent—it was published in 2018—and covers many of the core developments in secure computation of the past three decades. What fresh perspective can a new book on secure computation bring to the table? Or, more pragmatically, what is left to cover?

The answer is simple: secure computation is an incredibly vast research domain. It is hard to give a sense of scale to the reader, but we will attempt nonetheless to provide some intuition. Consider the informal definition of secure computation that we outlined: secure computation enables n parties $(P_1, \cdots, P_n)$ with inputs $(x_1, \cdots, x_n)$ to securely compute $f(x_1, \cdots, x_n)$ such that subsets S of colluding parties cannot deduce more information from the transcript of their interactions than what can be deduced from their inputs $(x_i)_{i \in S}$ and the output of the protocol. This seemingly simple definition is only the tip of a gigantic iceberg of subtleties that arise when trying to make the statement more formal. To give a sense of the vastness of the field, we start with a high-level overview of the main security and efficiency features that the designer of a secure computation protocol must decide to target or not before constructing the scheme.

1.3.1   Security Considerations

Corruption threshold. An important consideration lies in the quantification of the participants that can simultaneously collude to gain additional information about the private inputs. The traditional way of defining secure computation imagines an entity, the adversary, that *corrupts* a subset of the parties, meaning that it sees everything they get to see and learn everything they get to know (and possibly more—see later the discussion on active versus passive adversaries). Intuitively, the best possible security is achieved when assuming all-but-one corruption: a subset of up to $n - 1$ parties can collude (be corrupted) to obtain information about the private input of the only non-corrupted party. In this case, every single participant is guaranteed to have their input protected, even if all other participants join forces against them.

However, handling up to $n - 1$ corruptions comes at a cost, the characterization of which has been the subject of an important amount of research. In particular, if we denote t a bound on the maximal number of parties that an adversary is allowed to corrupt simultaneously, it is known (Cleve, 1986) that whenever $t \geq n/2$, secure computation cannot be perfectly private: a computational adversary can always deduce information about the private inputs. In practice, this means that any protocol with $t \geq n/2$ must assume that the adversary has bounded running time (e.g., it is implemented by a polynomial-time algorithm), and given our knowledge of complexity theory, this currently requires assuming that some mathematical problems are intractable. In turn, the cryptographic primitives and protocols built on top of these problems incur some computational overhead due to the need to use complex problems that can plausibly be intractable. In contrast, when $t < n/2$, the seminal protocol of Ben-Or et al. (1988) securely computes any function f with perfect privacy (assuming that the parties can communicate through secure and authenticated point-to-point channels). If $t < n/3$, then the protocol can even achieve much stronger security guarantees, such as ensuring that all honest parties get their output even if the corrupted parties deviate arbitrarily from the specifications of the protocol, or attempt to abort the protocol execution. When $t < n/4$, perfectly private computation remains possible (Ben-Or et al., 1993) even if the network is asynchronous, and arbitrary delays between the message transmissions can occur, while if $t \geq n/4$, this is provably impossible (*i.e.*, there exists functions for which every protocol will fail to be private in this setting).

Therefore, researchers and protocol designers are left with a flexible choice of the corruption threshold they wish to tolerate (from $t < n/4$ to $t < n$ in our examples above) depending on the security guarantees they wish to achieve, the network model, the intractability assumption, and the efficiency of the protocol. These examples are by no means exhaustive: researchers have often focused on concrete small values of t, such as $t = 1$ (Ishai et al., 2010). Others have considered a more general access structure than thresholds (Hirt and Maurer, 1997), allowing for a more fine-grained characterization of which parties can be corrupted. In other settings, when the protocol will be used as an inner component of a larger protocol with more participants, one must also consider the scenario where *all* participants can get simultaneously

corrupted, which is known to introduce additional technicalities (Ishai, 2010). Each
of these settings relies on different sets of techniques and primitives, to the point that
the protocols obtained are often incomparable—and indeed, achieving "best of both
worlds" protocols that would simultaneously guarantee optimal security in multiple
settings (for example, privacy when $t < n/2$ and security with guaranteed output
delivery when $t < n/3$) is a notoriously difficult task, that can even be provably
impossible to achieve in certain settings (Ishai et al., 2006; Katz, 2007). This results
in a flurry of publications and protocols achieving incomparable security and efficiency guarantees.

Corruption model. The previous considerations revolve solely around which participant is corrupted and which is not. Another crucial consideration lies in the corruption
model: what control does the adversary have over the participants it corrupts? There
are two traditional models, which are also the extreme ends of the spectrum: *passive*
adversaries will only observe the information obtained by the corrupted parties, but
will not instruct them to deviate from the specifications of the protocol; the parties will
behave honestly. This model is often called the *honest-but-curious* or *semi-honest*
setting. At the other end of the spectrum, *active* adversaries have full control over
the corrupted parties, and can instruct them to behave maliciously, deviating from
the protocol specifications: this setting is usually called the *malicious* setting. As the
reader might expect at this point, each setting gives rise to different protocol techniques (or, rather, maliciously secure protocol need additional techniques to enhance
the security of semi-honest protocols), and malicious security usually comes at a
cost that researchers have sought to characterize and to minimize over the past few
decades (Goldreich et al., 1987; Ishai et al., 2007, 2008; Genkin et al., 2014, 2015).

In between these two extremes, researchers have also studied other models: the
covert model (Aumann and Lindell, 2007) considers an adversary that can freely
instruct the corrupted participants to deviate from the protocol, as long as they do
not risk getting caught when deviating. Some works consider mixed adversary that
can corrupt some parties actively, and some passively (consider, for example, an
adversary that controls some of the participants and, after the protocols, manages to
hack into the computer of a few other participants and retrieve their local view) (Fitzi
et al., 1998, 1999).

Further security considerations. In addition to who is corrupted and what control
the adversary is given on corrupted parties, countless additional subtleties arise when
trying to precisely pinpoint the power given to the adversary. We provide a few sample points: the corruption can either be *static* (the adversary decides ahead of time
of a subset of participants to corrupt) or *adaptive* (the adversary decides during
the protocol, possibly based on its information gained so far, what participant to
corrupt next). The security analysis of the protocol can be in the *stand-alone* setting,
where we consider a single run of the protocol in isolation, or in a *concurrent* setting,
where the protocol might be ran concurrently with other protocols (and the adversary
can correlate the behavior of the corrupted parties across different sessions). Beyond
enforcing that privacy is guaranteed, we can seek additional security properties, such

as *identifiable aborts* (if a cheater causes the protocol to abort, preventing the honest parties from obtaining their output, then the participants can collectively identify a cheater among them), *fairness* (if a cheater causes a protocol to terminate early, it will obtain its output from the protocol only if the honest participants did), or *guaranteed output delivery* (the corrupted parties cannot prevent the honest participants from obtaining their output). Each such choice gives rise to different approaches, different results, different tradeoffs with other parameters (such as the corruption threshold and model), and different efficiency guarantees.

1.3.2 *Efficiency Considerations*

Beyond the above security considerations, whether a secure computation protocol will exhibit good performance also depends on many other aspects of the context—the function to be computed, the number of participants, their computational power, the communication network, and more. Here again, changing from one setting to the other might completely change the landscape of the best performing solution and the type of techniques that one must use. In fact, most of the considerations listed below are orthogonal (a protocol designer can pick an arbitrary choice for each of them and obtain a plausible, realistic setting), hence the number of settings and solutions grows exponentially with the number of features to consider!

Number of parties. Perhaps the first consideration to have in mind when designing a multi-party protocol is the target number of participants. As a rule of thumb, in the setting of dishonest majority (corruption threshold $t \geq n/2$), there has been historically a dichotomy between two-party protocols and n-party protocols for $n > 2$: some features are considerably simpler to achieve in the two-party setting, and their efficiency drops sharply as soon as we go beyond this setting. A prime example of this behavior is that of constant-round secure computation: the classical protocol of Yao (1986) based on *garbled circuits* yields a two-round two-party protocol (two rounds are easily seen to be optimal), and modern variants of garbled circuit make it fairly efficient (Kolesnikov and Schneider, 2008; Pinkas et al., 2009; Kolesnikov et al., 2014; Zahur et al., 2015; Rosulek and Roy, 2021). As soon as $n > 2$, however, using garbled circuits becomes much harder: the seminal protocol of Beaver et al. (1990) requires a much larger number of rounds (although still constant) and has poor concrete efficiency. Its concrete efficiency was considerably improved in recent years (Ben-Efraim et al., 2016, 2017; Wang et al., 2017; Hazay et al., 2020; Ben-Efraim et al., 2021) but nonetheless lags way behind that of two-party protocols; furthermore, their round complexity remains far from optimal. Achieving round-optimal n-party computation for $n > 2$ was, for a long time, one of the main open problems in secure computation. It was eventually resolved in 2018 by Benhamouda and Lin (2018) and concurrently by Garg and Srinivasan (2018), but these protocols are mostly of theoretical interest, and making this approach concretely efficient remains an active research area. We will come back to the issue of round complexity later on. Another setting that exhibits a similar sharp distinction is precisely the setting of this book: the notion of *pseudorandom correlation generator*, the primitive at the heart of silent secure computation, and the related notion of *homomorphic secret sharing* are prime examples of primitives that admit efficient realizations in the two-party techniques, but for which obtaining n-party generalizations is typically a hard problem. We will come back to this toward the end of this book.

Beyond the sharp distinction between two parties and $n > 2$ parties in the dishonest-majority setting, other protocols exhibit a smoother efficiency degradation as the number of participants increases. Classical protocols based on oblivious transfers, several of which will be described in Chap. 2 of this book, incur an $\Omega(n^2)$ overhead over the cost of securely computing the function with two parties: such protocols are suitable for a small number of parties, but are infeasible when n becomes large. Therefore, a large body of research has been devoted to making this cost linear in n; a classical example (though not the first of the kind) is the seminal work of Damgård et al. (2012). Eventually, as n gets extremely large, even a linear dependency in n becomes unaffordable. In such a setting, where one cannot even afford to let all players participate, a markedly different set of techniques is required, as exemplified with models such as the YOSO model (Gentry et al., 2021), or with protocols using techniques based on packed secret sharing to achieve amortization (Goyal et al., 2021).

Round complexity and latency. The round complexity of a protocol is, informally, the total number of times the parties have to send a message (of any length). For example, if Alice and Bob run a secure protocol where Alice speaks first, then receives a message from Bob (that Bob sends after receiving Alice's message), and finally replies to Bob's message, the round complexity is 3. It is easy to overlook the importance of round complexity, as communication complexity (how much bandwidth the protocol uses) and computational complexity (how many CPU cycles) are perhaps more natural efficiency measures to focus on. However, round complexity turns out to be often the most crucial aspect when protocols are deployed in the real world, due to latency. If a three-party protocol takes place between players in San Francisco, London, and Melbourne, then a single round trip can take up to 200ms, sometimes more. If the protocol involves 10 rounds, this translates to 2s of runtime overhead. Furthermore, unlike bandwidth and computational power, there is a clear limit to how much latency can be improved: one can always add more bandwidth or use more CPUs, but the latency can never decrease below the limits imposed by the speed of light. A round between a player in Paris and a player in San Francisco is bound to require at least 40ms by this physical limit: if the protocol requires 15 rounds, it will never run in under a second.

In a setting such as the Internet, where the location of the participants is unpredictable, reducing the round complexity of protocols is therefore a crucial aspect. Nevertheless, in other settings, such as secure computation happening among close parties over a LAN network, it becomes much less of an issue. We explained earlier that constant-round and round-optimal secure computation protocols are a major and non-trivial research area in the setting of $n > 2$ parties; in contrast, when the number of rounds is allowed to grow with the size of the function, there typically exists much more efficient solutions (we will cover some in Chap. 2 of this book).

Bandwidth restrictions. Another major tradeoff is the computational overhead versus the communication overhead: it is often the case in secure computation that one can achieve savings in one dimension by sacrificing efficiency in the other. An extreme example of this behavior is our work (Couteau, 2019) that shows that, for a certain class of functions and in a certain model, n parties can save a factor k in communication at the cost of a 2^{2^k} increase in computation. These tradeoffs create a spectrum of options to choose from, and the best option depends on how, in a real-world setting, the computational overhead and the communication complexity translate to runtime overhead. Do the players interact over a LAN or a WAN network? If they use a WAN network, is the bandwidth 1Mbps, 10Mbps, or 100Mbps? What machines do the participants use? Do they dedicate a single thread to the computation, or multiple threads? If a powerful machine is used, will they use multiple CPUs in parallel? All this information is necessary to decide which of the two protocols will perform best (when measuring performance as runtime) in a fixed context.

Function representation. Yet another crucial distinction is the computational model in which the function is represented. Traditionally, secure computation has focused on functions represented by a Boolean circuit (see Chap. 2 for a definition of this model), or by arithmetic circuits, a model that generalizes Boolean circuits to sequences of arithmetic operations over a ring (a mathematical structure equipped with additions and multiplications). However, Boolean and arithmetic circuits are a low-level model of computation: translating a function represented by, say, a program in Python to a circuit will generally incur a considerable overhead. Therefore, a significant research effort has been devoted to constructing protocols that handle other models of computation, such as RAM programs (whose study was initiated by Dov Gordon et al. (2012)), or "mixed-mode" protocols that can break the target function in pieces and use different computational models for each of the pieces. At the extreme end of the spectrum, some tailored protocols have been introduced that focus explicitly on a single type of functionality, the most common examples being protocols for privately computing the intersection of sets (Kolesnikov et al., 2016) or for distributively computing cryptographic signatures (Lindell et al., 2017).

Further efficiency considerations. Before we end this section, we stress that the discussion above is by no mean exhaustive, and countless other aspects have been the subject of dedicated research—do all the parties have a similar computational power, or are we, for example, in a client–server model where a weak client interacts with a much more powerful server? What happens if the communication among the participants does not happen synchronously? What happens if the communication graph has a certain topology that the participants do not wish to reveal? Can we handle the case where the participants come and go as they connect or go offline? Can a protocol hide the very fact that the participants are taking part in the protocol?

All of these questions and many more have required the development of tailored techniques.

1.3.3   The Focus of This Book

As a result of the sheer vastness of the area, it is hard to keep track of all the research done on secure computation: to pick a simple data point, looking at the proceedings of the 2025 CRYPTO conference (one of the flagship conference of the International Association for Cryptologic Research, and a top venue for publishing cryptography paper), we counted 56 papers directly related to secure computation (give or take a few, as "related to" involves some judgment) out of 156 papers accepted in total: more than 35% of the program. This makes it infeasible, but also undesirable, to try to cover the whole spectrum of secure computation in a single book. Rather, many of the topics that we outlined briefly would benefit from a dedicated coverage providing an accessible introduction to the techniques and challenges involved in the corresponding subfield of secure computation. This book is precisely a modest contribution along these lines, where we attempt to provide an accessible introduction to the model of silent secure computation.

1.4   Secure Computation with Silent Preprocessing

Silent secure computation takes place in the preprocessing model of secure computation: n participants $(P_1, \cdots, P_n)$, holding private inputs $(x_1, \cdots, x_n)$, interact to evaluate a public function f on their joint inputs. However, prior to this interaction, we assume that the participants already had an occasion to meet and interact, to execute a so-called *preprocessing phase* during which they can interactively and securely generate material that will be later used in the protocol. A crucial aspect of this preprocessing phase is that it should be possible to perform it way ahead of time, before the participants became aware of their private inputs—in fact, in the most stringent variant of the model, before the participants were even decided on the function f to be computed in the future. Imagine a group of hospitals that agree to securely compute statistics on their joint medical data in the future to advance medical research without compromising the privacy of their patients: using secure computation with preprocessing, the hospitals can run the preprocessing phase to speed up the later computation before having even collected the observational data from their patients, and before having decided on what statistics to compute on this data.

Secure computation with preprocessing was born from a seminal paper of Beaver (1995). Ever since its introduction, it has become the leading model for achieving real-world efficient secure computation protocols, and has played a key role in allowing secure computation to transition from a theoretical research area to a situation where secure protocols are routinely implemented, deployed, and used by consumers in their everyday life. As we will cover in depth in this book, however, a major concern of the preprocessing model has long been the cost, and especially the communication overhead, required to run the preprocessing phase: early protocols were often prohibitive on this aspect, requiring the transmission of infeasibly large amount of data even for computing simple functions. The key paradigm shift initiated by the *silent* preprocessing model stems from the observation that, using new cryptographic insights, the communication of the preprocessing phase can often be reduced to a small constant, independent of the size of the function to be computed, and amounting in practice to a few kilobytes or a few megabytes of communication (depending on the setting).

The silent preprocessing model of secure computation, or silent secure compu tation in short, focuses mostly on this preprocessing phase, where the participants securely distribute correlated random strings among themselves (random in the sense that they are independent of the inputs and the function). As such, is it somewhat orthogonal to considerations on round complexity for the protocol itself: the correlated random strings are typically used to speed up protocols that follow the original template of Goldreich et al. (1987), where the round complexity grows with the depth of the function, but can also be (and are) used to speed up constant-round protocols based on garbled circuit, as was done, for example, in the work of Dittmer et al. (2022). However, the round complexity of the preprocessing phase itself is a consideration of fundamental interest. While we will not cover it in great detail in this book, we touch upon the matter toward the end of this book and discuss, in particular, how recent works allow reducing the round complexity to an absolute minimum: a single round of simultaneous communication from the participants.

In the book, our focus is on the setting of maximal corruption: up to $t = n - 1$ participants can be corrupted. As the aim of the book is to provide an accessible introduction to the area, we dedicate most of the coverage to the simplest cases in this setting: two participants and semi-honest corruption. Here again, we briefly touch upon the generalization to more than two participants and to the malicious setting in the last chapter of this book. We typically put a strong emphasis on concrete efficiency rather than aiming for theoretical feasibility results. In an attempt to help the reader get an intuition of the meaningfulness of the results and techniques presented, we provide extensive, concrete runtime estimations, based either on back-of-the-envelope calculations or sometimes on implementations. To give a sense of the scale and of how these numbers translate to runtimes in practical settings of interest, we also sometimes provide concrete illustrations for specific functions. Eventually, the book focuses exclusively on the traditional representation of functions via Boolean or arithmetic circuits: as of the writing of this book, little is known about silent secure computation in other computational models.

With that being said, we end this introduction and wish the reader a good and instructive journey through the thrilling meanders of silent secure computation.

1.5 Notations

In this write-up, λ denotes a security parameter, and we write $n(\lambda) \in \text{poly}(\lambda)$ to indicate that $n(\lambda)$ is polynomial in λ (we also sometimes write this as $n(\lambda) = \text{poly}(\lambda)$). We write $\mu(\lambda) \le \text{negl}(\lambda)$ to indicate that μ goes to zero faster than $1/\lambda^c$ for any constant c, and say that μ is a *negligible* function. Given a distribution $\mathcal{D}$, we write $x \xleftarrow{s} \mathcal{D}$ to indicate that x is sampled from $\mathcal{D}$. Given a set S, we also write $x \xleftarrow{s} S$ as a shorthand to indicate that x is sampled from the uniform distribution over S. For an integer $n \in \mathbb{N}$, we write $[n]$ to denote the set of integers $\{1, \cdots, n\}$. We write vectors as $\vec{x}$, but often identify vectors over $\mathbb{F}_2$ as bitstrings, and write them x, without the arrow. Given two vectors $\vec{x}, \vec{y}, \vec{x} \oplus \vec{y}$ denotes their component-wise XOR (when the vectors are over $\mathbb{F}_2$), and $\vec{x} \odot \vec{y}$ denotes their component-wise product. By default, we view vectors as columns.

Adversaries (modeled as polynomial-size Boolean circuits) are generally denoted $\mathcal{A}$. We use the following template to write probabilities: $\Pr[\text{event} \mid \text{experiment}]$. For example, $\Pr[\mathcal{A}(x) = 0 \mid x \xleftarrow{s} \{0, 1\}^\lambda]$ denotes the probability that the adversary $\mathcal{A}$ outputs 0 when given an input x sampled uniformly from $\{0, 1\}^\lambda$. When the experiment can be concisely described, we sometimes use the more compact notation $\Pr_{\text{experiment}}[\text{event}]$ (e.g., $\Pr_{x \xleftarrow{s} \{0,1\}^\lambda}[\mathcal{A}(x) = 0]$), or even $\Pr[\text{event}]$ when the experiment is clear from the context. For distributions, we use the template $\mathcal{D} = \{\text{sample} \mid \text{experiment}\}$. For example, $\{(a, b, a \cdot b) \mid (a, b) \xleftarrow{s} \mathbb{F}^2\}$ denotes the distribution which samples two random elements (a, b) from a finite field $\mathbb{F}$ and outputs $(a, b, a \cdot b)$.

References

Aumann, Y., & Lindell, Y. (2007). Security against covert adversaries: Efficient protocols for realistic adversaries. In S. P. Vadhan (Ed.), *TCC 2007, LNCS 4392* (pp. 137–156). Springer. https://doi.org/10.1007/978-3-540-70936-7_8

Beaver, D. (1995). Precomputing oblivious transfer. In D. Coppersmith (Ed.), *CRYPTO'95, LNCS 963* (pp. 97–109). Springer. https://doi.org/10.1007/3-540-44750-4_8

Beaver, D., Micali, S., & Rogaway, P. (1990). The round complexity of secure protocols (Extended abstract). In *Proceedings of the 22nd Annual ACM Symposium on Theory of Computing (STOC)* (pp. 503–513). ACM Press. https://doi.org/10.1145/100216.100287

Bendlin, R., Damgård, I., Orlandi, C., & Zakarias, S. (2011). Semi-homomorphic encryption and multiparty computation. In K. G. Paterson (Ed.), *EUROCRYPT 2011, LNCS 6632* (pp. 169–188). Springer. https://doi.org/10.1007/978-3-642-20465-4_11

Ben-Efraim, A., Cong, K., Omri, E., Orsini, E., Smart, N. P., & Soria-Vazquez, E. (2021). Large scale, actively secure computation from LPN and free-XOR garbled circuits. In A. Canteaut & F.-X. Standaert (Eds.), *EUROCRYPT 2021, Part III, LNCS 12698* (pp. 33–63). Springer. https://doi.org/10.1007/978-3-030-77883-5_2

Ben-Efraim, A., Lindell, Y., & Omri, E. (2016). Optimizing semi-honest secure multiparty computation for the internet. In E. R. Weippl et al. (Eds.), *Proceedings of the 2016 ACM SIGSAC Conference on Computer and Communications Security (CCS)* (pp. 578–590). ACM Press. https://doi.org/10.1145/2976749.2978347

Ben-Efraim, A., Lindell, Y., & Omri, E. (2017). Efficient scalable constant-round MPC via garbled circuits. In T. Takagi & T. Peyrin (Eds.), *ASIACRYPT 2017, Part II, LNCS 10625* (pp. 471–498). Springer. https://doi.org/10.1007/978-3-319-70697-9_17

Benhamouda, F., & Lin, H. (2018). k-round multiparty computation from k-round oblivious transfer via garbled interactive circuits. In J. B. Nielsen & V. Rijmen (Eds.), *EUROCRYPT 2018, Part II, LNCS 10821* (pp. 500–532). Springer. https://doi.org/10.1007/978-3-319-78375-8_17

Ben-Or, M., Canetti, R., & Goldreich, O. (1993). Asynchronous secure computation. In *Proceedings of the 25th Annual ACM Symposium on Theory of Computing (STOC)* (pp. 52–61). ACM Press. https://doi.org/10.1145/167088.167109

Ben-Or, M., Goldwasser, S., & Wigderson, A. (1988). Completeness theorems for non-cryptographic fault-tolerant distributed computation (Extended abstract). In *Proceedings of the 20th Annual ACM Symposium on Theory of Computing (STOC)* (pp, 1–10). ACM Press. https://doi.org/10.1145/62212.62213

Cleve, R. (1986). Limits on the security of coin flips when half the processors are faulty (Extended abstract). In *Proceedings of the 18th Annual ACM Symposium on Theory of Computing (STOC)* (pp. 364–369). ACM Press. https://doi.org/10.1145/12130.12168

Couteau, G. (2019). A note on the communication complexity of multiparty computation in the correlated randomness model. In Y. Ishai & V. Rijmen (Eds.), *EUROCRYPT 2019, Part II, LNCS 11477* (pp. 473–503). Springer. https://doi.org/10.1007/978-3-030-17656-3_17

Damgård, I., Pastro, V., Smart, N. P., & Zakarias, S. (2012). Multiparty computation from somewhat homomorphic encryption. In R. Safavi-Naini & R. Canetti (Eds.), *CRYPTO 2012, LNCS 7417* (pp. 643–662). Springer. https://doi.org/10.1007/978-3-642-32009-5_38

Dittmer, S., Ishai, Y., Lu, S., & Ostrovsky, R. (2022). Authenticated garbling from simple correlations. In Y. Dodis & T. Shrimpton (Eds.), *CRYPTO 2022, Part IV, LNCS 13510* (pp. 57–87). Springer. https://doi.org/10.1007/978-3-031-15985-5_3

Fitzi, M., Hirt, M., & Maurer, U. M. (1998). Trading correctness for privacy in unconditional multiparty computation (Extended abstract). In H. Krawczyk (Ed.), *CRYPTO'98, LNCS 1462* (pp. 121–136). Springer. https://doi.org/10.1007/BFb0055724

Fitzi, M., Hirt, M., & Maurer, U. M. (1999). General adversaries in unconditional multi-party computation. In K.-Y. Lam, E. Okamoto, & C. Xing (Eds.), *ASIACRYPT'99, LNCS 1716* (pp. 232–246). Springer. https://doi.org/10.1007/978-3-540-48000-6_19

Garg, S., & Srinivasan, A. (2018). Two-round multiparty secure computation from minimal assumptions. In J. B. Nielsen & V. Rijmen (Eds.), *EUROCRYPT 2018, Part II, LNCS 10821* (pp. 468–499). Springer. https://doi.org/10.1007/978-3-319-78375-8_16

Genkin, D., Ishai, Y., & Polychroniadou, A. (2015). Efficient multi-party computation: From passive to active security via secure SIMD circuits. In R. Gennaro & M. J. B. Robshaw (Eds.), *CRYPTO 2015, Part II, LNCS 9216* (pp. 721–741). Springer. https://doi.org/10.1007/978-3-662-48000-7_35

Genkin, D., Ishai, Y., Prabhakaran, M., Sahai, A., & Tromer, E. (2014). Circuits resilient to additive attacks with applications to secure computation. In D. B. Shmoys (Ed.), *Proceedings of the 46th Annual ACM Symposium on Theory of Computing (STOC)* (pp. 495–504). ACM Press. https://doi.org/10.1145/2591796.2591861

Gentry, C., Halevi, S., Krawczyk, H., Magri, B., Nielsen, J. B., Rabin, T., & Yakoubov, S. (2021). YOSO: You Only Speak Once - Secure MPC with stateless ephemeral roles. In T. Malkin & C. Peikert (Eds.), *CRYPTO 2021, Part II, LNCS 12826* (pp. 64–93). Springer. https://doi.org/10.1007/978-3-030-84245-1_3

Goldreich, O., Micali, S., & Wigderson, A. (1987). How to prove all NP-statements in zero-knowledge, and a methodology of cryptographic protocol design. In A. M. Odlyzko (Ed.), *CRYPTO'86, LNCS 263* (pp. 171–185). Springer. https://doi.org/10.1007/3-540-47721-7_11

Gordon, S. D., Katz, J., Kolesnikov, V., Krell, F., Malkin, T., Raykova, M., & Vahlis, Y. (2012). Secure two-party computation in sublinear (amortized) time. In T. Yu et al. (Eds.), *Proceedings of the 2012 ACM SIGSAC Conference on Computer and Communications Security (CCS)* (pp. 513–524). ACM Press. https://doi.org/10.1145/2382196.2382251

Goyal, V., Polychroniadou, A., & Song, Y. (2021). Unconditional communication-efficient MPC via Hall's Marriage Theorem. In T. Malkin & C. Peikert (Eds.), *CRYPTO 2021, Part II, LNCS 12826* (pp. 275–304). Springer. https://doi.org/10.1007/978-3-030-84245-1_10

Hazay, C., Scholl, P., & Soria-Vazquez, E. (2020). Low cost constant round MPC combining BMR and oblivious transfer. *Journal of Cryptology,33*(4), 1732–1786. https://doi.org/10.1007/s00145-020-09355-y

Hirt, M., & Maurer, U. M. (1997). Complete characterization of adversaries tolerable in secure multi-party computation (Extended abstract). In J. E. Burns & H. Attiya (Eds.), *Proceedings of the 16th Annual ACM Symposium on Principles of Distributed Computing (PODC)* (pp. 25–34). ACM. https://doi.org/10.1145/259380.259412

Ishai, Y., Kumarasubramanian, A., Orlandi, C., & Sahai, A. (2010). On invertible sampling and adaptive security. In M. Abe (Ed.), *ASIACRYPT 2010, LNCS 6477* (pp. 466–482). Springer. https://doi.org/10.1007/978-3-642-17373-8_27

Ishai, Y., Kushilevitz, E., & Paskin, A. (2010). Secure multiparty computation with minimal interaction. In T. Rabin (Ed.), *CRYPTO 2010, LNCS 6223* (pp. 577–594). Springer. https://doi.org/10.1007/978-3-642-14623-7_31

Ishai, Y., Kushilevitz, E., Lindell, Y., & Petrank, E. (2006). On combining privacy with guaranteed output delivery in secure multiparty computation. In C. Dwork (Ed.), *CRYPTO 2006, LNCS 4117* (pp. 483–500). Springer. https://doi.org/10.1007/11818175_29

Ishai, Y., Kushilevitz, E., Ostrovsky, R., & Sahai, A. (2007). Zero-knowledge from secure multiparty computation. In D. S. Johnson & U. Feige (Eds.), *Proceedings of the 39th Annual ACM Symposium on Theory of Computing (STOC)* (pp. 21–30). ACM Press. https://doi.org/10.1145/1250790.1250794

Ishai, Y., Prabhakaran, M., & Sahai, A. (2008). Founding cryptography on oblivious transfer - efficiently. In D. Wagner (Ed.), *CRYPTO 2008, LNCS 5157* (pp. 572–591). Springer. https://doi.org/10.1007/978-3-540-85174-5_32

Katz, J. (2007). On achieving the "best of both worlds" in secure multiparty computation. In D. S. Johnson & U. Feige (Eds.), *Proceedings of the 39th Annual ACM Symposium on Theory of Computing (STOC)* (pp. 11–20). ACM Press. https://doi.org/10.1145/1250790.1250793

Kolesnikov, V., & Schneider, T. (2008). Improved garbled circuit: Free XOR gates and applications. In L. Aceto et al. (Eds.), *ICALP 2008, Part II, LNCS 5126* (pp. 486–498). Springer. https://doi.org/10.1007/978-3-540-70583-3_40

Kolesnikov, V., Kumaresan, R., Rosulek, M., & Trieu, N. (2016). Efficient batched oblivious PRF with applications to private set intersection. In E. R. Weippl et al. (Eds.), *Proceedings of the 2016 ACM SIGSAC Conference on Computer and Communications Security (CCS)* (pp. 818–829). ACM Press. https://doi.org/10.1145/2976749.2978381

Kolesnikov, V., Mohassel, P., & Rosulek, M. (2014). FleXOR: Flexible garbling for XOR gates that beats Free-XOR. In J. A. Garay & R. Gennaro (Eds.), *CRYPTO 2014, Part II, LNCS 8617* (pp. 440–457). Springer. https://doi.org/10.1007/978-3-662-44381-1_25

Lindell, Y. (2017). Fast secure two-party ECDSA signing. In J. Katz & H. Shacham (Eds.), *CRYPTO 2017, Part II, LNCS 10402* (pp. 613–644). Springer. https://doi.org/10.1007/978-3-319-63715-0_21

Pinkas, B., Schneider, T., Smart, N. P., & Williams, S. C. (2009). Secure two-party computation is practical. In M. Matsui (Ed.), *ASIACRYPT 2009, LNCS 5912* (pp. 250–267). Springer. https://doi.org/10.1007/978-3-642-10366-7_15

Rosulek, M., & Roy, L. (2021). Three halves make a whole? Beating the half-gates lower bound for garbled circuits. In T. Malkin & C. Peikert (Eds.), *CRYPTO 2021, Part I, LNCS 12825* (pp. 94–124). Springer. https://doi.org/10.1007/978-3-030-84242-0_5

Wang, X., Ranellucci, S., & Katz, J. (2017). Global-scale secure multiparty computation. In B. M. Thuraisingham et al. (Eds.), *Proceedings of the 2017 ACM SIGSAC Conference on Computer and Communications Security (CCS)* (pp. 39–56). ACM Press. https://doi.org/10.1145/3133956.3133979

Yao, A. C.-C. (1986). How to generate and exchange secrets (Extended abstract). In *Proceedings of the 27th Annual Symposium on Foundations of Computer Science (FOCS)* (pp. 162–167). IEEE Computer Society Press. https://doi.org/10.1109/SFCS.1986.25

Zahur, S., Rosulek, M., & Evans, D. (2015). Two halves make a whole - Reducing data transfer in garbled circuits using half gates. In E. Oswald & M. Fischlin (Eds.), *EUROCRYPT 2015, Part II, LNCS 9057* (pp. 220–250). Springer. https://doi.org/10.1007/978-3-662-46803-6_8

Chapter 2
Secure Computation: A Primer

Traditionally, the goal of cryptography has been to secure *communications*: Alice wants to send a message to Bob, but outside observers should not be able to read the message. In a certain way, this notion lacks granularity: either a participant learns the full message of Alice or none of it. Yet, in many realistic scenarios, it is desirable to have a more fine-grained control over which information is revealed. For example, imagine that Alice and Bob are interacting via a dating app, and wish to discover whether they are romantically interested in each other: it might be that Alice does not want to simply reveal to Bob that she is romantically interested in him. Rather, she could want to let Bob learn her interest *if and only if* Bob is also romantically interested in her. Secure communication does not provide a solution to this problem. One way to formalize this simple task is as follows: Alice has an input bit a and Bob has an input bit b, and both parties want to let the other learn $f(a, b) = a \wedge b$ (the bit equal to 1 in case of mutual romantic interest), *and nothing more*. In other words, our (potential) lovebirds want to exchange private information defined by the computation of a function on their joint private input. The goal of *secure multi-party computation*, often abbreviated MPC (for Multi-party Computation), is to let them do exactly that—and much more.

2.1 Secure Computation

Secure computation (also called multi-party computation, or MPC) is the branch of cryptography that studies the design of methods to execute computations on sensitive data held by multiple parties, without compromising the data privacy. It was introduced in the seminal works of Yao (1982) and of Goldreich et al. (1987). In a secure computation protocol, each participant has an input x_i. It allows all participants to jointly reveal to a subset of them the value $y = f(x_1, \cdots, x_N)$, where f is a public

© The Author(s), under exclusive license to Springer Nature Switzerland AG 2026
G. Couteau, *An Introduction to Silent Secure Computation*,
SpringerBriefs in Information Security and Cryptography,
https://doi.org/10.1007/978-3-032-07089-0_2

function, *while concealing all information about* $(x_1, \cdots, x_N)$ beyond y. The target function f is commonly represented as a *boolean circuit, i.e.,* a directed acyclic graph with indegree two where the internal nodes are called *gates* and compute basic Boolean operations, such as XORs or ANDs.

In the following, we overview some important considerations for secure computation: how do the parties communicate? How many of the parties can collude in an attempt to break security? How do we formalize security? As will become clear to the reader, the answers to these questions come in multiple flavors. Hence, along the way, we will also clarify which of these flavors will be our focus in this book.

2.1.1 Network Hypothesis

Protocols for secure computation commonly assume the availability of two network models: (1) the point-to-point network model, where each pair of parties is connected with a secure and authenticated channel and (2) the broadcast model, where a party can broadcast an authenticated message to everyone (and everyone is guaranteed to receive the same message). In the remainder of this book, we will typically assume that the communication proceeds synchronously, and ignore the issues of network delays, packet loss, and other non-trivial difficulties of distributed computing. Some rationale behind these choices is that they separate the challenges of protecting the privacy of the parties' inputs from the challenges of implementing reliable communication: authentication (which is typically achieved through digital signatures and certificates) and security of the channels (typically achieved through encryption) are themselves the subject of "traditional" cryptography, and considerations on network delays, the difficulty of broadcast, and synchronicity are active research subjects in distributed computing. Nevertheless, we note that there are many examples, in the secure computation community, of efforts in the direction of tackling directly the challenges of securely computing functions over unstable networks.

2.1.2 Corruption Threshold

We informally defined secure computation as a way to compute $y = f(x_1, \cdots, x_N)$ while concealing all remaining information about $(x_1, \cdots, x_N)$. However, this informal definition does not say anything about what happens when multiple parties join their forces (and combine their information) in an attempt to learn new information about the remaining inputs. A slightly less informal restatement addressing this setting could go as follows: even if a subset S up to $|S| = t$ parties combine the information they gathered throughout the protocol (we usually call this information their view of the protocol), they should not learn anything that cannot already be deduced from $(x_i)_{i \in S}$ (their combined inputs) and y (the output).

The value t loosely introduced above is called the *corruption threshold*—the maximum number of parties that can join their forces in an attempt to cheat. The choice of t plays a fundamental role in secure computation, as different choices for t yield to a completely different landscape of secure computation protocols. A particularly important consideration is the distinction between the *honest majority* setting (where $t < N/2$) and the *dishonest-majority* setting ($t \geq N/2$):

- When a (strict) majority of the participants are guaranteed to remain honest throughout the protocol, there exists *unconditionally* secure computation protocol for essentially all functions of interest. In particular, security against the corrupted parties is guaranteed even if they are allowed unbounded running time.
- In contrast, if a majority of the participants can be corrupted, secure computation is known to be impossible to achieve with unconditional security for all but a few restricted type of functions. Hence, protocols in this setting will typically assume that the participants' computational power is bounded, and security is proven by reduction to a cryptographic hardness assumption.

A few comments are in order. First, the statements above hold in a specific security model where the participants do not deviate from the specifications of the protocol (and, in particular, do not quit the protocol before its completion). Considering other types of adversarial behaviors (that might deviate from the specifications, or abort early) complicates the landscape, but related distinctions between low values of t (typically $t < N/2$ or $t < N/3$) and high values of t can be made in other settings. Second, the statement about unconditional secure computation holds under the point-to-point network model, where each pair of parties can interact through a secure and authenticated channel.

In the rest of this book, we will always be interested in the *maximal corruption threshold* setting, i.e., $t = N - 1$. If fact, a significant part of our discussions will focus on the case $N = 2$, where $t = N - 1$ is the only meaningful setting. The protocols we will discuss will therefore ultimately rely on computational hardness assumptions. Before moving on, we are including below a few references on the distinction between honest and dishonest majority (warning: the references prove results about securely computing functions, for a notion of *securely computing* that we have not yet introduced).

2.1.2.1 Historical Notes

The existence of unconditionally secure protocols (for all N-variate functions over a finite domain) for every $t < N/2$ was first established by Ben-Or et al. (1988). The first observation that some functions (e.g., the N-wise OR function) cannot be computed with unconditional security was made in Chaum et al. (1988) (they also observed that other functions, such as the N-wise XOR, admit unconditionally secure protocols for any $t \leq N - 1$). A stronger *zero-one law* was later established in Chor and Kushilevitz (1989) that showed that the only functions computable with unconditional security for $t \geq N/2$ are those of the form $f(x_1, \cdots, x_N) = f_1(x_1) \oplus \cdots \oplus f_N(x_N)$ (where $\oplus$ denotes the XOR). Since all such functions can be securely computed even when $t = n - 1$ (by direct reduction to the protocol of Chaum et al. (1988) for securely computing an N-wise XOR), this yields an interesting phenomenon, where functions can either be computed with unconditional security only when $t < N/2$, or for any $t \leq N - 1$.

2.1.3 Notions of Security

In secure computation, the security of a protocol for computing a function f between N parties $(P_1, \cdots, P_N)$, with respective inputs $(x_1, \cdots, x_N)$, is defined by considering an *adversary* $\mathcal{A}$ that can *corrupt* a subset of the parties. When a party is corrupted, $\mathcal{A}$ sees everything they see: their input, their private coins, and all messages they receive throughout the protocol. The protocol is secure if everything $\mathcal{A}$ can learn about the private inputs $(x_1, \cdots, c_N)$ can be efficiently computed from the inputs $(x_i)_{i \in \mathsf{C}}$ of the corrupted parties C, and the output $y = f(x_1, \cdots, x_N)$ (this is formalized by requiring that the distribution of everything $\mathcal{A}$ sees can be efficiently *simulated* given y and $(x_i)_{i \in \mathsf{C}}$).

2.1.3.1 Semi-honest Versus Malicious Security

The two standard settings are the *honest-but-curious* setting, where the adversary observes the view of all corrupted parties, but the parties follow the specifications of the protocol, and the *malicious* setting, where the adversary fully controls the corrupted parties, and can make them deviate arbitrarily from the specifications of the protocol. The honest-but-curious setting often serves as an important first step in the design of a secure computation protocol, as several techniques and compilers can be used to enhance honest-but-curious protocols to the malicious setting.

In the rest of this book, we will focus exclusively on the semi-honest setting: all definitions and results outlined afterward, unless explicitly stated otherwise, refer to this setting. This is not to say that the setting of malicious security is not of fundamental importance; however, a full coverage of malicious security would require a second book in itself, and considerations for semi-honest security are a necessary first step. Hence, we expect our coverage to be useful even for readers who would be mostly interested in this stronger setting.

2.1.3.2 Functionalities

In the short exposition given above, we focused on the goal of letting all parties obtain the output $y = f(x_1, \cdots, x_N)$ of a function f evaluated on their joint inputs $(x_1, \cdots, x_N)$. More generally, we will often consider the setting where each party can receive a different output. We will say that N parties compute the *functionality* $f : (x_1, \cdots, x_N) \mapsto (y_1, \cdots, y_N)$ on their joint input $(x_1, \cdots, x_N)$ if each party P_i obtains $f_i(x_1, \cdots, x_N) = y_i$ at the end of the protocol. In some settings, the participants will want to compute a *randomized functionality*: on their joint input $\vec{x}$, the joint output $(y_1, \cdots, y_N)$ is randomly sampled by the functionality from a distribution parametrized by the joint inputs $\vec{x} = (x_1, \cdots, x_N)$, and each party P_i receives y_i. Equivalently, a randomized functionality $f = (f_1, \cdots, f_N)$ is a process mapping an input $\vec{x} = (x_1, \cdots, x_N)$ to a sequence $(f_1(\vec{x}), \cdots, f_N(\vec{x}))$ of random variables.

We write $f : (\{0, 1\}^*)^N \rightarrow (\{0, 1\}^*)^*$ to denote the randomized process mapping $(x_1, \cdots, x_N)$ to the random variables $(f_1(\vec{x}), \cdots, f_N(\vec{x}))$ over $\{0, 1\}^*$. While we allow functionalities to take inputs of arbitrary length, we restrict our attention to protocols where all parties hold inputs of the same length $|x_1| = \cdots = |x_N|$.

For future reference, we outline below a formal definition of security in the semi-honest setting via the notion of t-privacy that we define as an asymptotic notion with respect to the input length $\lambda = |x_1| = \cdots = |x_N|$ of the parties. For most of the following sections, and until explicitly mentioned otherwise, sticking with the intuitive notion of "secure against parties that follow the specifications" suffices. The reader can therefore safely skip what follows for now, and returns to it afterward if they want to grasp more of the formalism.

2.1.3.3 Indistinguishability

The notion of t-privacy aims to capture the fact that the joint view of t corrupted participants does not allow them to learn anything about the other parties' inputs, beyond what they can deduce from their outputs. To formalize this notion, we want to say that the distribution of their joint views "looks like" a distribution that would be *independent* of the honest parties' inputs (more precisely, that depends solely on the corrupted parties' outputs). In cryptography, we define "look like" via the notion of indistinguishability between distributions. Because the distribution of the parties' views depends on an asymptotic parameter $\lambda = |x_1| = \cdots = |x_N|$, they are actually *families* of distributions parametrized by λ. Then

Definition 2.1.1 Two distribution families $(\mathcal{D}_\lambda^0, \mathcal{D}_\lambda^1)_{\lambda \in \mathbb{N}}$ are (perfectly, statistically, computationally) indistinguishable if:

- $\mathcal{D}_\lambda^0 = \mathcal{D}_\lambda^1$ for every $\lambda \in \mathbb{N}$ (perfect indistinguishability).
- The statistical distance between $\mathcal{D}_\lambda^0$ and $\mathcal{D}_\lambda^0$ is bounded by a *negligible* function of λ[1] (statistical indistinguishability).

---

[1] A function $g : \mathbb{N} \rightarrow [0, 1)$ is *negligible* if for every constant $c > 0$, there exists a λ' such that for all $\lambda \geq \lambda', g(\lambda) < 1/\lambda^c$.

- For every probabilistic polynomial-time adversary $\mathscr{A}$, for every large enough λ, it holds that

$$\left| \Pr_{x \overset{\$}{\leftarrow} \mathcal{D}_\lambda^0} [\mathscr{A}(x) = 0] - \Pr_{x \overset{\$}{\leftarrow} \mathcal{D}_\lambda^1} [\mathscr{A}(x) = 0] \right| \leq \mathsf{negl}(\lambda),$$

where negl denotes a *negligible* function of λ (computational indistinguishability).

In our definitions below, we will use $\equiv$ as a shorthand to denote either perfect, statistical, or computational indistinguishability, each choice corresponding to a possible flavor of t-privacy (respectively, perfect, statistical, and computational t-privacy). Later in this book, if not specified otherwise, we assume $\equiv$ to refer to computational indistinguishability.

2.1.3.4 Formally Defining Privacy

In the following, we implicitly parametrize all sets, functions, and random variables by a protocol Π. Informally, t-privacy means that the joint view of a coalition of up to t corrupted players contains no information about the inputs of the remaining parties, beyond what can be deduced from the output of the protocol. To formalize this notion, we first define the notion of a view of a player.

Definition 2.1.2 (View) The view of party P_i (on a joint input $\vec{x} = (x_1, \cdots, x_N)$ from all parties), denoted $\mathsf{View}_i(\vec{x})$, is the (joint) distribution of the sequence of messages received by P_i during the execution of the protocol, and the sequence of the results of all coin tosses performed by P_i.

Since some of our definitions will also cover the case of randomized functionalities, whose outputs are sampled from a distribution, we also introduce a notation for the output distribution of a protocol Π:

Definition 2.1.3 (Output Distribution) We let $O_i(\vec{x})$ denote the distribution of the output of P_i after an execution of the protocol Π with a joint input $\vec{x}$.

Given a subset C of $[N]$, we write $\mathsf{View}_C(\vec{x})$ to denote $(\mathsf{View}_i(\vec{x}))_{i \in C}$ and $O_C(\vec{x})$ to denote $(O_i(\vec{x}))_{i \in C}$; we use $O(\vec{x})$ as a shorthand for $O_{[N]}(\vec{x})$. Below, we define the notion of t-privacy for deterministic and for randomized functionalities; we borrow most of the formalism from Asharov and Lindell (2017).

Definition 2.1.4 (t-Privacy for deterministic functionalities Asharov and Lindell (2017)) Let $f : (\{0, 1\}^*)^N \mapsto (\{0, 1\}^*)^N$ be an N-party deterministic functionality and let Π be a protocol. We say that Π is t-private if (1) Π computes f with perfect correctness, and (2) there exists a probabilistic polynomial-time algorithm Sim such that for every $C \subset [N]$ of cardinality at most t and every $\vec{x} \in (\{0, 1\}^*)^N$ where $|x_1| = \cdots = |x_N|$, it holds that $\mathsf{Sim}(C, \vec{x}_C, f_C(\vec{x})) \equiv \mathsf{View}_C(\vec{x})$.

While the above definition considers separately (with (1) and (2)) the issues of correctness and privacy, in the general case of randomized functionalities, the two notions are intertwined:

Definition 2.1.5 (t-Privacy for randomized functionalities (Asharov and Lindell (2017), Definition 2.2)) Let $f : (\{0, 1\}^*)^N \mapsto (\{0, 1\}^*)^N$ be an N-party randomized functionality and let Π be a protocol. We say that Π is t-private if (1) Π computes f with perfect correctness, and (2) there exists a probabilistic polynomial-time algorithm Sim such that for every $C \subset [N]$ of cardinality at most t and every $\vec{x} \in (\{0, 1\}^*)^N$ where $|x_1| = \cdots = |x_N|$, it holds that

$$\{(v, y) \; : \; y \leftarrow f(\vec{x}), v \leftarrow \text{Sim}(C, \vec{x}_C, y_C)\} \equiv (\text{View}_C(\vec{x}), O(\vec{x})),$$

where $(\text{View}_C(\vec{x}), O(\vec{x}))$ denotes the *joint* distribution of the corrupted parties' (final) views and the outputs of all parties in a run of the protocol on common input $\vec{x}$.

A simulator according to the above definitions is simply a machine that produces emulated views for all corrupted parties. However, it is often convenient to view the simulator Sim as an *interactive* machine that pretends to play the role of the honest parties during an execution of the protocol and interacts with the corrupted parties. Under this viewpoint, Sim receives as input $(C, \vec{x}_C, f_C(\vec{x}))$, but also the random tapes of all corrupted parties; this is w.l.o.g. since in the above definition, Sim will sample these random coins itself when emulating the views.

Remark 2.1.6 All definitions above treat the parties' input length $|x_1| = \cdots = |x_N|$ as an asymptotic security parameter. In this write-up, we will often abuse this formalism by considering functionalities f acting on *fixed length* inputs (or even sometimes randomized functionalities that take no inputs), and introduce an auxiliary *security parameter* λ for bounding the running time of the participants and of the simulator. Formally, this means that we will implicitly apply the above definitions of t-privacy to the following modified functionality:

$$f' : ((x_1, 1^{i_1}), \cdots, (x_N, 1^{i_N})) \mapsto \begin{cases} f(x_1, \cdots, x_N) \text{ if } i_1 = \cdots = i_N \\ \bot \text{ otherwise,} \end{cases}$$

where 1^i refers to a dummy string $11 \cdots 1$ of length i. This requirement guarantees that an algorithm that runs in time polynomial in its input length will run in time polynomial in i when given 1^i as input. We will call $\lambda = i_1 = \cdots = i_N$ the *security parameter* of the protocol.

We end here our overview of the formal definition of t-privacy. We stress that our coverage is relatively superficial, and only intended to facilitate a more precise statement of the results discussed later on. For a much more extensive coverage, discussing technical subtleties that we overlooked on purpose in the above definitions, but also extensions to other settings (such as malicious security), we recommend the interested reader to consult Goldreich's book *Foundations of Cryptography, Volume 2* Goldreich (2009).

2.1.3.5 Composition

In this book, we will often discuss the construction of secure computation protocols using smaller protocols as a building block. In discussing their security, we will implicitly assume that the security of the building blocks is *preserved under composition*: that is, assuming that a higher-level protocol is proven secure when the parties are given access to another functionality (the "building block"), we want to deduce that when each invocation of the building block is replaced by a t-private protocol computing this functionality, the higher-level protocol remains secure. Such statements are known as *composition theorems*. In the setting of semi-honest secure computation, that is the focus of this book, suitable composition theorems have indeed been established (see, e.g., (Goldreich, 2009, Sect. 7.3.1) or Canetti (2000)). Stating these theorems require some additional formalism and definitions that we will not cover in this book.

2.1.3.6 Historical Notes

While secure computation was introduced in the work of Yao (1982) (for the two-party case) and of Goldreich et al. (1987) (for the N-party case), the formal treatment of the security definitions for t-privacy only appeared later (though these papers already included sketches of what these definitions should be). The first formal treatment of privacy in secure computation appeared in the work of Beaver (1992; 1991) and of Micali and Rogaway (1992). The definitions were later refined and enhanced with composition theorems in the work of Canetti (2000). Par of the exposition above follows from the one of Goldreich (2009) and from Asharov and Lindell (2017).

2.1.4 Paradigms for Secure Computation

There are currently three main paradigms for the design of secure computation protocols in the dishonest-majority setting with semi-honest security:

- **Secret-sharing-based** protocols build upon the seminal protocol of Goldreich et al. (1987). They are the most lightweight in terms of computation. They usually have communication proportional to the size of the circuit and require several rounds of interaction proportional to the depth of the circuit. Furthermore, they can be efficiently *preprocessed*: all cryptographic operations can be pushed to a one-time *preprocessing phase*, independent of the inputs. The online phase, where the actual computation takes place, is extremely lightweight (a few bits of communications and a few Boolean operations per gate of the circuit).

- **Garbled-circuit-based** protocols build upon the seminal protocol of Yao (1982). They usually require more communication and computation compared to their secret-sharing-based counterpart. However, they only require a constant number of rounds of interaction, making them a good choice over high-latency networks. Some recent protocols (such as Wang et al. (2017)) combine these two paradigms to get the best of both worlds.
- **FHE-based** protocols build upon a cryptographic primitive called *fully homomorphic encryption*, introduced in a 2009 breakthrough Gentry (2009), to achieve an extremely low-communication footprint (proportional only to the size of the inputs and outputs of the function) in a small number of rounds. This comes at the cost of using a considerably larger amount of computation, with heavy cryptographic operations for every gate of the circuit.

2.2 The GMW Protocol

We will start by describing the celebrated GMW protocol, introduced in the seminal work of Goldreich et al. (1987). It is an interesting starting point, because it has a simple description, but it already illustrates several of the techniques used in secure computation and allows us to explain many of the core challenges that drive modern research in the area. To keep notations simple and intuitive, we will focus on the case of two players, Alice and Bob, with respective private inputs a and b (though everything generalizes easily to an arbitrary number of participants). Let f be the two-input function that Alice and Bob wish to securely evaluate on (a, b). We view f as being represented by a Boolean circuit with two types of gates, XOR gates (denoted $\oplus$ and represented by $\mathrel{\rlap{\supset}{\rule{0pt}{0pt}}}$ on the diagram of Fig. 2.1) and AND gates (denoted by $\wedge$ and represented by $\mathrel{\rlap{\supset}{\rule{0pt}{0pt}}}$ on the diagram of Fig. 2.1). It is a standard result that any polynomial-time computable function can be represented by a polynomial-size circuit over the $\{\oplus, \wedge\}$ basis. To provide visual support, we give an example of a simple Boolean circuit in Fig. 2.1.

2.2.1 Description of the Protocol

At a high level, *computing* a function f (such as the one of Fig. 2.1) is done by writing the input bits on the input wires of the circuit (on the left). Then, every time a gate g has values (v_0, v_1) written on its input wires, we write the output $g(v_0, v_1)$ on the output wire of g. These intermediate steps of the computation are propagated this way through the circuit until values are written on all output wires, at which point they form the output of the computation. Our protagonists, Alice and Bob, will

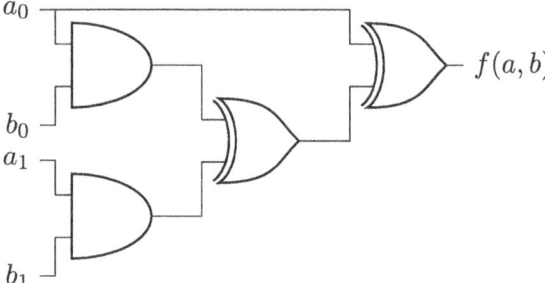

Fig. 2.1 Example of a Boolean circuit computing the function $f(a, b) = f(a_0|a_1, b_0|b_1) = a_0b_0 + a_1b_1 + a_0$ mod 2

follow the same computation path. However, to maintain security, they must manage to perform the propagation of the intermediate steps of the computation without *seeing* the intermediate values (since this would reveal more than just the output of the function).

2.2.1.1 Hiding Intermediate Computations by Secret Sharing

The core technique used to let Alice and Bob manipulate intermediate values of the computation without seeing them is called *secret sharing*. An (n, t)-secret sharing is a method that distributes a secret value (here, some intermediate value of the computation) between N players (here we have Alice and Bob, so $n = 2$) such that (1) if t participants pool their shares together, they can reconstruct the secret, yet (2) if $t - 1$ (or less) participants collude, they do no learn anything (in an information-theoretic sense) about the secret. The value t is called the *threshold*; here, we will use the simplest possible setting, with $N = t = 2$. Typically, to share a bit v between Alice and Bob, we proceed as follows: Alice receives a random bit r, and Bob receives $s = v + r$ mod 2. Observe that neither r nor s leak any information about v (they are both individually distributed as a random bit), yet v can be reconstructed given both shares: $v = r + s$ mod 2.

2.2.1.2 Securely Computing Gates

The GMW protocol maintains the following invariant: at every step of the protocols, the parties hold shares of the values currently written on the wires. The only missing ingredient at this stage is a method to propagate the shared values: given shares of two inputs to a gate, the parties must obtain shares of the gate output. Of course, this should be done without reconstructing the values (or leaking any information whatsoever about them). Now, assume that the input wires of a gate g have values u and v, respectively, and let (u_A, v_A) and (u_B, v_B) denote Alice and Bob's respective shares of u and v (that is, $u_A + u_B = u$ mod 2 and $v_A + v_B = v$ mod 2). The goal is for Alice and Bob to come up with shares of $g(u, v)$. There are two possible gates:

 :   This is the easy case. We have $g(u, v) = u + v = (u_A + v_A) + (u_B + v_B)$ mod 2: Alice and Bob can therefore directly define $u_A + v_A$ and $u_B + v_B$ to be their respective shares of $g(u, v)$. As this does not require any interaction between them, it can of course not leak any information.

 :   This is the hard case. We have $g(u, v) = uv = u_A v_A + u_A v_B + u_B v_A + u_B v B$ mod 2. Here, the computation of $g(u, v)$ contains *cross terms* $u_A v_B$ and $u_B v_A$: Alice and Bob cannot possibly get shares of $g(u, v)$ solely through local computation. To securely evaluate an AND gate, we will need a method to let Alice and Bob obtain *additive shares of the cross terms*: if Alice and Bob get respective shares (s_A, t_A) and (s_B, t_B) of the cross terms $(u_A v_B, u_B v_A)$, they can define their shares of $g(u, v)$ to be $u_A v_A + s_A + t_A$ and $u_B v_B + s_B + t_B$—the reader will easily check that those indeed sum to uv modulo 2.

The *missing ingredient* is, therefore, a protocol that takes as input a bit x from Alice, a bit y from Bob, and outputs shares of the product xy. Let us call this a *secure product*. Propagating shares through an AND gate can be done as explained above, using two invocations of a secure product (on inputs (u_A, v_B) and (v_A, u_B), respectively). We will explain how to get this missing ingredient in the next section; before that, let's wrap up.

2.2.1.3   Full Construction

Without loss of generality, we can consider that Alice and Bob start the protocol with shares of the inputs. For example, if Alice has input bit a_0, she can define her share to be a_0, and Bob defines his share to be 0. (Alternatively, Alice could send a random r to Bob and define her share to be $a_0 + r$ mod 2 if we wanted the shares to be uniformly distributed—but for the inputs, this is unnecessary. We will need uniformly distributed shares for the *intermediate values* since they are the values that should not be known to any party.) Alice and Bob propagate the shares through all the wires, computing the XOR gates locally, and using two invocations of the secure product protocol for each AND gate. Once they obtain shares of the output wires of the circuit, they can simply exchange their shares and reconstruct the output.

Beyond reconstructing the outputs (that both parties must learn anyway), the secure products are the only parts where Alice and Bob communicate. Hence, if this protocol never leaks any information, and if Alice and Bob honestly play throughout the entire protocol as required by the description, they will indeed learn the output $f(a, b)$, and nothing more. In cryptography, we refer to players that follow the rules as being passive or honest-but-curious: they will try to learn information by looking at the transcript of the protocol, but will not actively cheat by deviating from the specifications of the protocol. The (much more demanding) setting where Alice and

Bob could actively cheat is the active or malicious setting, but let us set this harder goal aside for now. We have

Theorem 2.2.1 (GMW—informal) *Assume that there exists a secure product protocol. Then there exists a two-player protocol securely computing any two-input functionality f in the honest-but-curious model. The protocol uses two invocations of a secure product for each AND gate in the boolean circuit representation of f over the* $\{\oplus, \wedge\}$ *basis.*

2.3   Oblivious Transfer, the Missing Ingredient

The GMW protocol requires a secure product: a two-party protocol in the honest-but-curious model where Alice has an input bit x, Bob has an input bit y, and both parties obtain random shares of xy (without learning anything). The *de facto* method to construct a secure product is to rely on an *oblivious transfer* (OT).

2.3.1   *Defining Oblivious Transfer*

An *oblivious transfer* (OT) is a two-party protocol between a sender and a receiver. The sender holds two entries (s_0, s_1), and the receiver holds a *selection bit b*. At the end of the protocol, the receiver should learn s_b. The security requirements are twofold:

- (*Sender security*) the receiver does not learn anything about s_{1-b} (that is, the receiver learns *at most one* of the two entries).
- (*Receiver security*) the sender does not learn anything about b.

Note that relaxing any of these requirements would make OT trivial: without sender security, we could just let the sender send (s_0, s_1) to the receiver, and without receiver security, the receiver could just send b and receive s_b. We represent in Fig. 2.2 an ideal functionality for oblivious transfer. Ideal functionalities are an abstraction of what we want from a primitive: think of them as a trusted third party that would receive inputs and provide outputs through perfectly secure and authenticated channels, and who always behaves exactly as intended.[2]

---

[2] Using an ideal functionality allows us to conveniently abstract out the specific implementation of a protocol when using it in a higher-level protocol. It is a standard theorem in secure computation that if a higher-level protocol is secure in the honest-but-curious model when the parties have access to ideal functionalities for its components, it remains secure when the ideal functionalities are replaced by secure protocol instantiating the components; see also our discussion in Sect. 2.1.3.5.

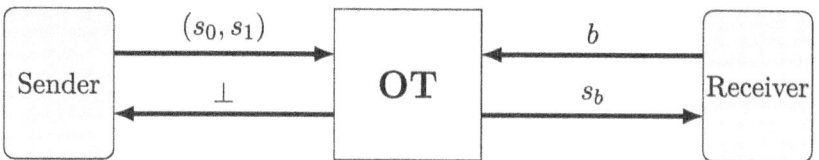

Fig. 2.2 Ideal functionality of the (one-out-of-two) oblivious transfer

2.3.1.1 From OT to Secure Products

Given access to an OT functionality, it is straightforward to implement the secure product functionality. Alice, with input bit x, plays the role of the sender in an OT protocol. She picks a uniformly random bit r_A and sets her inputs to the OT to $(s_0, s_1) \leftarrow (r_A, x + r_A)$ (from now on, additions are modulo 2 unless indicated otherwise). Bob plays the role of the receiver and uses his input y as the selection bit. Observe that Bob's output, denoted r_B, is therefore r_A if $y = 0$ and $r_A + x$ if $y = 1$; that is, it holds that $r_B = r_A + xy$, hence (r_A, r_B) for uniformly random shares of xy.

2.3.1.2 Historical Notes and Remarks

Oblivious transfer was first introduced in the work of Rabin (1981) (a similar concept was introduced earlier by Wiesner (1983) under the name "conjugate coding"). The modern way of defining it is due to Even, Goldreich and Lampel (1982). Oblivious transfer is without a doubt the most fundamental primitive for secure computation with dishonest majority: its existence is both necessary and sufficient for general secure computation in the presence of a dishonest majority (Goldreich and Vainish, 1988; Kilian, 1988; Ishai et al., 2008) (our presentation of GMW demonstrates the sufficiency in the two-party honest-but-curious setting, but this can be generalized to the N-party malicious setting).

2.3.2 Constructing Oblivious Transfer

The existence of OT can be seen as the basic assumption underlying the existence of secure computation for arbitrary functionalities. This is similar to how the existence of one-way functions forms the basic assumption underlying most of symmetric cryptography, as most symmetric primitives (block ciphers, stream ciphers, pseudorandom generators, digital signatures, universal one-way hash functions, commitment schemes, and many more) are equivalent to one-way functions. But more broadly, OT is typically treated as a *resource* for secure computation: the goal of efficient secure computations reduces to the goal of efficiently executing many instances of

OTs, or *consuming* OTs. Therefore, one of the most fundamental (perhaps the most fundamental) questions for the study of efficient secure computation is

How can we generate efficiently a very large number of oblivious transfers?

Due to its fundamental importance for secure computation, countless oblivious transfer protocols have been designed—way too many to cite them all (but the reader might want to check (Naor and Pinkas, 2001; Lai et al., 2021; Döttling et al., 2020; Goyal et al., 2020; Camenisch et al., 2007; Kalai, 2005; Aiello et al., 2001; Berger et al., 1985; Garay and MacKenzie, 2000; Gertner et al., 2000; Cachin et al., 1998; Crépeau and Kilian, 1988; Lipmaa, 2005; Chou and Orlandi, 2015; Choi et al., 2013; Choudhuri et al., 2021; Friolo et al., 2019; Cascudo et al., 2016; Green and Hohenberger, 2011; Lindell and Zarosim, 2009; Wullschleger, 2009; Haitner, 2008; Damgård et al., 2004; Haitner, 2004; Ding et al., 2004; Masny and Rindal, 2019; Blazy and Chevalier, 2015; McQuoid et al., 2021; Micciancio and Sorrell, 2020; Canetti et al., 2020; Kurosawa and Nojima, 2009; Green and Hohenberger, 2008; Hong et al., 2002; Beaver, 1998; Ishai et al., 2011; Garay et al., 2009; Peikert et al., 2008; Ding, 2001; Naor and Pinkas, 1999; Bennett et al., 1992; Bellare and Micali, 1990) for an illustrative sample). OTs can be based on physical assumptions, such as the existence of noisy channels (Crépeau and Kilian, 1988) or tamper-proof hardware tokens (Choi et al., 2014), or on the assumption that the receiver has bounded memory (Ding, 2001). It can be realized using quantum communication channels under symmetric assumptions (Grilo et al., 2021). More commonly, it can be instantiated under a variety of standard cryptographic assumptions, such as assumptions related to discrete logarithms (Bellare and Micali, 1990), lattices (Peikert et al., 2008), factoring (Berger et al., 1985), coding theory (Alekhnovich, 2003), or isogenies (Lai et al., 2021), among others.

For completeness, we describe a simple construction of oblivious transfer due to Bellare and Micali (1990). The protocol integrates some modifications due to Naor and Pinkas (2001). To avoid disrupting the flow of the presentation, we assume some familiarity with cyclic (finite) groups. The parameters define a multiplicative group $\mathbb{G}$ of (known) prime order p, and two generators (g, h) of $\mathbb{G}$. We assume that the receiver does not know the discrete logarithm of h in base g (that is, the unique $x \in \mathbb{Z}_p$ such that $g^x = h$): this can be ensured by letting the sender pick h randomly and relying on a group $\mathbb{G}$ where the discrete logarithm problem is conjectured to be intractable (the existence of such groups is one of the most basic assumptions of cryptography). The protocol also uses a hash function $H : \mathbb{G} \mapsto \{0, 1\}$ (that is modeled as a random oracle in the security analysis). The *Bellare-Micali* protocol involves two messages:

- The receiver, with selection bit b, picks a random $r \overset{s}{\leftarrow} \mathbb{Z}_p$ and set $\mathsf{pk}_b \leftarrow g^r$ and $\mathsf{pk}_{1-b} \leftarrow h/\mathsf{pk}_b$. Observe that by construction, the receiver knows the discrete logarithm of pk_b, but not that of pk_{1-b}. They send pk_0 to the sender.
- The sender with input (s_0, s_1) computes $\mathsf{pk}_1 \leftarrow h/\mathsf{pk}_0$. For $\sigma = 0, 1$, the sender picks $r_\sigma \overset{s}{\leftarrow} \mathbb{Z}_p$ and encrypts s_σ using the *hashed ElGamal* encryption scheme with public key pk_σ, as follows:

$$E_\sigma \leftarrow (g^{r_\sigma}, H(\mathsf{pk}_\sigma^{r_\sigma}) \oplus s_\sigma).$$

They send (E_0, E_1) to the receiver.
- The receiver computes $H((g^{r_b})^r) = H(\mathsf{pk}_b^{r_b})$ and recovers s_b from $H(\mathsf{pk}_b^{r_b}) \oplus s_b$.

The correctness of the protocol can be checked routinely. The protocol is unconditionally secure for the receiver (since c is uniformly distributed over $\mathbb{G}$ for any
value of b). The sender security can be proven (in the random oracle model, which
models the hash function H as a random function—this is a common heuristic in
cryptography) under the decision Diffie–Hellman assumption, a standard cryptographic assumption that states that given (g, g^x, g^y) for random exponents x, y, it
is infeasible to distinguish g^{xy} from a random group element. We note that more
advanced constructions, such as the one of Naor and Pinkas (2001), can get rid of the
random oracle heuristic, at the cost of a slightly more complex protocol (we focus
here on the Bellare-Micali construction since it is among the simplest to describe).

2.4 Considerations on Efficiency

2.4.1 On Communication

If we denote by λ the bit length of the elements of $\mathbb{G}$, the Bellare-Micali OT protocol
communicates $3\lambda + 2$ bits in total. The modern approach to instantiate $\mathbb{G}$ is to use
an appropriate elliptic curve, and a typical value of λ in this setting is $\lambda = 256$.
Hence, the full protocol requires overall 758 bits of communication using a standard
instantiation.

This is arguably not much, but we invite the reader to reflect on the cost of using
such an OT protocol in the GMW protocol: the above cost would translate to about
1500 bits of communication *for each AND gate of the circuit*. But even for simple
functions, Boolean circuits can be *really, really big*. For example, in Kreuter et al.
(2012), the Boolean circuit for computing the edit distance between two strings of
length 4095 bits (a task of interest in scenarios such as privacy-preserving computations on genomic data) has 5901194475 AND gates. Using GMW with the Bellare-
Micali protocol, this translates to an overall communication of around 1 Terabyte.
Needless to say, that is a whole lot of communication.

These back-of-the-envelope calculations show that bandwidth is a scarce resource
for secure computation, as seminal protocols such as GMW require a gargantuan
amount of communication. Whether it is possible to securely compute complex
functions using significantly less computation is a crucial and very active research
topic:

Can we construct secure computation protocols with a low-communication
overhead?

This question can be (and has been, and is) studied from many angles, ranging from very practical considerations to highly theoretical questions: can one construct oblivious transfers with significantly less communication? Can one avoid the "communicate at each gate" bottleneck of the GMW protocol (a goal usually referred to as *breaking the circuit size barrier*)? Can one prove lower bounds on the necessary amount of communication for secure computation?

2.4.2   On Computation

Similar back-of-the-envelope calculations give an intuition of the computational overhead of GMW. In the Bellare-Micali protocol, the sender computation is dominated by four exponentiations in the group $\mathbb{G}$ (two for the receiver). Looking at a benchmark,[3] if we instantiate $\mathbb{G}$ using the elliptic curve curve25519 (Bernstein, 2006) (one of the most standard choices of cryptographic groups), computing four exponentiations over $\mathbb{G}$ requires slightly more than $222\mu s$ over a powerful server (AWS EC2 c5.9xlarge). Using again the circuit of Kreuter et al. (2012) as an example (computing the edit distance between 512-byte strings, a rather simple function on small inputs), this translates to about 740 hours of computation on the server (this count is based solely on exponentiations and ignores many other factors that could contribute to the overall cost).

2.4.3   The Computation/Communication Tradeoff in Modern Protocols

The rough calculations above demonstrate that the seminal approach to secure computation requires a tremendous amount of communication and computation. Where do modern protocols stand in this regard? The (very) high-level summary is that the latest proposals can solve either one of these limitations—*but not both at once*. That is, we have protocols that involve considerably lower amounts of computation, but still suffer from a high communication overhead, or protocols with much lower communication, but very high computational overhead. More concretely:

- The first category follows the high-level template of the GMW paradigm, but includes a fundamental twist: the concept of *oblivious transfer extensions* that we will cover in Sect. 2.5. This method allows to compute all necessary oblivious transfers using a *constant number* of "expensive" OTs (such as those obtained using the Bellare-Micali protocol), followed by cheap computations to *extend* this constant number of OTs into an *arbitrary* number of oblivious transfers. Concretely, this brings computational costs down by five to six orders of magnitude. However

---

[3] www.zka.lc.

(and though it *also* yields some savings in communications), these techniques still require sending of the order of 100 bits of data *for each gate of the circuit*. The need to send data for each gate of the circuit is probably the strongest limitation of this line of work and is known as the *circuit size barrier*. The remainder of this primer will mostly cover this approach.

- The second category departs entirely from the GMW paradigm and emerged as a consequence of the breakthrough result of Gentry in 2009 (Gentry, 2009), who introduced the first *fully homomorphic* encryption (FHE) scheme. Roughly, such a scheme allows computing arbitrary functions on encrypted data. This means that the entire communication complexity can be reduced to just exchanging encryptions of the inputs, then encryptions of the outputs: the rest is just local computation. However, this comes at the cost of running the entire computation over FHE-encrypted data that, to say the least, requires *a lot* of computation. Back in 2009, this was mostly a purely theoretical feasibility result. After one-and-a-half decade of work from hundreds of researchers and companies, the costs became much more manageable, but the most efficient schemes around can still process *at most* a few dozen gates per second—and the room for improvement is becoming tiny.[4] Going back to our example of the edit distance, using a rough figure of 40 gates/second, we are talking about around 60 *months* of computation on a powerful server. Nevertheless, in some scenarios with a very powerful server, a weak client, and a very restricted bandwidth, the FHE-based approach offers some unmatched features.

2.4.4 A Path to Efficient Secure Computation

An immense research and engineering effort is devoted by the cryptographic community to reducing the cost of FHE, and this is by all means a well-motivated problem that deserves a high amount of attention. But for the purpose of someday obtaining *truly efficient* secure computation protocols, the author's thesis is that the first approach is the most promising. Truly efficient solutions would require reducing the cost of FHE-based solutions by, say, at least six orders of magnitude, which seems (in our humble opinion) largely out of reach of current cryptographic techniques. In contrast, "GMW-style" secure computation already achieves competitive computational efficiency, and the core problems to address lie in reducing its communication overhead. As we will show, there have been recent developments that, on the practical side, already reduced the communication complexity of GMW-style secure computation by a large margin (as low as about 4 bits of communication per AND gate of the circuit): this is the model of silent secure computation, the central object of study in this book.

---

[4] One of the latest active trends is to develop specialized hardware tailored to FHE operations that might gain a few more orders of magnitude compared to optimized software implementations, but will likely not become part of your average laptop.

We mention, however, a strong limitation of this approach. From a theoretical point of view, none of the new results in silent secure computation do break the *circuit size barrier*. A parallel line of work has focused on one of the most intriguing problems in the area: can the communication complexity of silent secure computation go beyond the size of the circuit? Looking ahead, we will see that the answer turns out to be yes—but the complexity of the techniques involved currently confines these new approaches to the setting of purely asymptotic results. Hence, while these theoretical developments broaden our understanding of the limits of secure computation, they currently fall short of providing a clear path toward efficient secure computation in settings where the bandwidth is too limited to afford paying a linear amount of communication in the circuit size.

2.5 Extending Oblivious Transfers

As we saw above, secure computation *a la* GMW requires computing a very large number of oblivious transfers: almost 12 billion for the edit distance example that we outlined in Sect. 2.4. In turn, known protocols for oblivious transfer, such as the Bellare-Micali OT, require expensive cryptographic operations. One may ask: could we instead construct OT using cheaper operations? Before we outline the way researchers have approached this problem and the technical barriers it faces, we will take a small detour through the worlds of symmetric cryptography and public-key cryptography that are the key to understanding at a high level the difficulties associated with constructing OTs using only cheap computations.

2.5.1 Symmetric Versus Public-Key Cryptography

It is common to distinguish between two broad categories of cryptographic primitives: *symmetric-key* cryptography and *public-key* cryptography. While this is a very broad and coarse-grained separation, it provides an efficient way to anticipate whether a cryptographic primitive will require some *algebraic structure* that in turn severely constraints the computational efficiency of the constructions.

2.5.1.1 Symmetric Key Cryptography

Historically, symmetric-key cryptography refers to cryptographic primitives that require a pre-established secret to be shared among the participants. This is the cryptography from the pre-1970 era, where Alice wants to send a message m to Bob, and both share a common key K, unknown to the attacker, that can be used for both encryption and decryption. In its modern acceptance, the term covers more broadly a vast network of cryptographic primitives that are *equivalent* to this notion of encryption with a shared secret key, in the sense that the existence of one implies the existence of the other. For example, one-way functions (functions that are easy to evaluate, but hard to invert), digital signatures, pseudorandom number generators, (preimage resistant) hash functions, commitments schemes (that allow locking a secret value inside an opaque box, such that the content of the box cannot be modified after the box is opened), and many more are all known to be (existentially) equivalent to symmetric-key encryption.

All these primitives share a nice unifying feature: *they don't require algebraic structure*. Remember the Bellare-Micali OT construction: we had to introduce a finite cyclic group (which, in the real world, will typically be instantiated with a suitable elliptic curve) endowed with a hard mathematical problem. In contrast, to build (for example) a one-way function, there is no need to invoke any algebraic structure: any "sufficiently complex" function will do. In a sense, anyone can build a one-way function, by composing sufficiently many arbitrary functions (provided, say, that some of them are not too local—their output bits depend on many input bits—and are not too close to linear functions). For example, Oded Goldreich suggested in Goldreich (2000) (perhaps the most celebrated unpublished preprint of cryptography) that evaluating random (hardwired) predicates on random (hardwired) small subsets of the bits of the inputs would likely yield a one-way function.

Their lack of algebraic structure is perhaps the most fundamental aspect that separates them from the rest of cryptography to the point that theoretical cryptographers now typically model "symmetric cryptography" as the set of cryptographic primitives that can be constructed from unstructured functions (formally, whose existence is implied by a random oracle that is a uniformly random—hence unstructured— function that everyone can access through its input–output behavior). This broadens the coverage of symmetric cryptography to include primitives such as collision-resistant hash functions, which also don't require structure, but are not known to be equivalent to symmetric encryption.

Being free to navigate through the vast space of functions without consideration for their algebraic structure, the cryptosystem designers have typically managed to construct symmetric primitives that are very lightweight[5]: modern computers can hash or encrypt several hundreds of megabytes of data per second on one core of a standard laptop.

2.5.1.2   Public-Key Cryptography

This category covers essentially all primitives that do not fit in the previous category. In the 70s, cryptography was revolutionized by the introduction of the first public-key cryptosystems (the RSA cryptosystem (Rivest et al., 1978)) and the first key exchange protocols (the Diffie–Hellman key exchange (Diffie and Hellman, 1976)). These

---

[5] Digital signatures are a slightly different beast: even though they technically don't require any algebraic structure, the most efficient constructions so far had to assume structure. But apart from this outsider, the statement is true of any other symmetric primitive we know of.

schemes emerged from mathematical hardness assumptions tailored to algebraic structures: the hardness of computing the order of the ring $(\mathbb{Z}_n^*, \times)$ of invertible integers modulo a product n of two large primes, or the hardness of computing random discrete logarithms in the multiplicative group $\mathbb{F}_p^*$ of a prime-order field $\mathbb{F}_p$.

Following these breakthrough results, countless advanced cryptographic primitives have been introduced that all rely in one way or the other on mathematical objects with a rich algebraic structure. Unlike symmetric primitives that are (for most of them) known to be equivalent to each other, public-key primitives are typically not known to be equivalent to each other: what unifies them is precisely their apparent need for algebraic structure. This algebraic structure is what *enables* their advanced features—typically, the ability to agree on a shared key unbeknownst to all observers, or the ability to create keys that can encrypt messages, yet cannot decrypt ciphertexts. At the same time, this algebraic structure is what makes them considerably less efficient: the number of elliptic curve operations one can perform on one core of a standard computer is around a thousand per second, five to six orders of magnitude slower than symmetric-key operations.[6]

2.5.1.3   Wrapping-Up: Cheap Versus Expensive Computations

In light of the above, the usual way to categorize which operations are *cheap* versus which operations are *expensive* is to distinguish whether they require symmetric operations (such as evaluating hash functions, encrypting with AES, using a pseudo-random number generator, etc.) or public-key operations (elliptic curve point multiplication, exponentiations in a large finite field or an RSA group, etc.). While this is a relatively coarse-grained notion (using many symmetric operations can become more expensive than using a few public-key operations), the large efficiency gap between the two (at least five orders of magnitude in the benchmark we used) makes this a relatively stable and useful distinction.

Of course, a public-key primitive is only categorized as such because we do not *know* of a way to construct the primitive using only unstructured hardness (as we do for one-way functions or hash functions). Cryptographers have been surprised in the past: digital signatures were long thought to be a typical example of a public-key primitive, as all known constructions required algebraic structure, and some of the first constructions were in a sense dual to public-key encryption (where the public key was used for verification and the secret key for signing a message). This led cryptographers to believe that digital signatures and public-key encryption were of a similar nature. Yet, in a surprising twist of events, digital signatures were shown to be *equivalent to one-way function* in a sequence of papers by Naor and Yung (1989) and by Rompel (1990).

Coming back to the focus of this section, equipped with the above considerations, the question of constructing *cheap* oblivious transfers becomes

---

[6] All benchmarks mentioned are taken from https://www.bearssl.org/speed.html, and ran on the same computer.

Is it possible to build oblivious transfer solely from unstructured primitives? In other terms, does oblivious transfer belong to symmetric cryptography?

2.5.2 On Building Oblivious Transfer from Symmetric Primitives

Unfortunately, the answer to the above question is essentially negative. Of course, one can never hope to *unconditionally* provide a negative answer to any such question: after all, we believe (though we don't have proof of that) that both oblivious transfer and symmetric cryptography *exist* (unconditionally). Therefore, oblivious transfer is logically implied by symmetric cryptography, and we cannot hope to rule out any construction of oblivious transfer from symmetric primitives (after all, the construction that ignores the symmetric primitive and builds an OT from scratch would be a valid construction, provided that OT exists in the first place). However, one can show that *black-box* constructions of oblivious transfers from symmetric primitives are impossible.

Informally, a black-box construction of a primitive A from a primitive B is a construction that ignores specific details about the implementation of B, and relies only on its input–output behavior. This is closely related to the notion of oracle access in complexity theory: a black-box reduction of the existence of A to the existence of B is an efficient oracle algorithm R (the reduction) such that R^B implements the primitive A (*i.e.*, the algorithm R, given oracle access to B, yields an instance of the primitive A). This captures a large majority of all known constructions of cryptographic primitives; for example, all known reductions mentioned above (between one-way functions, digital signatures, hash functions, symmetric encryption, pseudorandom generators, or commitment schemes) are black box.

2.5.2.1 Impossibility of Black-Box Constructions of OT from Symmetric Cryptography

Now, here comes the catch: an oblivious transfer implies a key exchange protocol, *i.e.*, a two-party protocol that allows Alice and Bob to agree on a shared key, without revealing the key to any external (passive) observer. To see this, consider the following construction of a key exchange protocol:

- Alice, playing the role of an OT sender, samples a random key $K \xleftarrow{s} \{0, 1\}^{\lambda}$ and defines $(s_0, s_1) \leftarrow (K, 0^{\lambda})$ to be her two OT inputs (here, λ is the security parameter, used as the key length, and 0^{λ} denotes a string of λ zeroes).
- Bob, playing the role of the receiver, sets his selection bit b to 0.
- At the end of the protocol, Bob receives $s_0 = K$ from the OT. Alice and Bob output K as their shared key.

It is clear that at the end of the above protocol, Alice and Bob agree on the same key. We claim that this protocol is also a *secure* key exchange.

Proof Assume toward contradiction that there is an efficient attacker $\mathcal{A}$ that can recover K (or distinguish it from random) by observing the transcript of the interaction. We use a sequence of game hops, where we gradually change the protocol:

1. In the first game hop, we let Bob use the selection bit 1 instead of 0. By the receiver security of the OT protocol, this change cannot be noticed by $\mathcal{A}$: otherwise, the sender could emulate the attacker (since we assumed the attacker is efficient) and distinguish between the selection bits $b = 0$ and $b = 1$, breaking receiver security.
2. In the second game hop, we replace Alice's input $(K, 0^\lambda)$ by $(0^\lambda, 0^\lambda)$. By the sender security of the OT protocol, this change cannot be noticed by $\mathcal{A}$: otherwise, the receiver with input $b = 1$ could emulate $\mathcal{A}$ locally, and learn something about $s_{1-b} = s_0$ (here, whether $s_0 = 0^\lambda$ or not), contradicting sender security.

Hence, we made two changes to the original protocol and argued that $\mathcal{A}$ cannot notice any of these changes unless we get a contradiction to the OT security. But this implies that $\mathcal{A}$ must still successfully find K in the last game above (otherwise, $\mathcal{A}$ can be used to build an efficient distinguisher between the original game and the last game), which is impossible: the last game is information-theoretically independent of K! This is a contradiction, which concludes the proof.

Hence, if we could base oblivious transfers on symmetric primitives, by the above construction, we could base key exchange on symmetric primitives. However, it was shown by Impagliazzo and Rudich in their seminal paper on black-box impossibility results (Impagliazzo and Rudich, 1989) that this is impossible via black-box reductions. More generally, Impagliazzo and Rudich showed that there can never exist a black-box reduction of a primitive that implies key agreement (such as oblivious transfer) to a primitive implied by a random oracle (such as hash functions, one-way function, symmetric encryption, and many more). Hence, any attempt to build oblivious transfer from symmetric primitives must rely on non-black-box reductions that have proven elusive so far (in this context) and would need to base key agreement on symmetric cryptography, which is one of the most challenging open problems in cryptography, of an overture comparable to that of the famous P versus NP problem.

2.5.3 The Way Around: Many Cheap OTs from Few Expensive OTs

For a long time, the above considerations were seen as a clear indication that one had no hope of constructing cheap oblivious transfer: barring a breakthrough, the use of expensive algebraic structures appears unavoidable. This was eventually challenged in two groundbreaking works. First, in 1996, Beaver showed in Beaver (1996) that assuming only the existence of one-way function, it was possible to generate OTs using only cheap symmetric operations *in an amortized sense*. In simple terms, what Beaver showed is the following: even though generating a *single* OT requires expensive algebraic operations, generating n OT for a large n does not require repeating n times the expensive operations used in the single OT generation! Beaver showed something much more powerful:

Theorem 2.5.1 (Beaver OT extension—informal) *Assuming only the existence of a one-way function, there exists a protocol that uses only λ calls to an oblivious transfer primitive, and allows two parties to execute an arbitrary polynomial number $N(\lambda) = \mathrm{poly}(\lambda)$ of oblivious transfers.*

In other words, Beaver showed that after spending some effort generating a small number of "base" OTs (typically, one can think of λ as being 128), two parties can generate an arbitrary amount of OTs, and this process will involve only cheap symmetric operations (beyond the cost of generating the base OTs). Beaver's *OT extension* protocol was mostly of theoretical interest but showed that the black-box barrier for basing OT on symmetric cryptography was not necessarily a nail in the coffin of efficient MPC, for one could still generate arbitrarily many OTs using a small constant amount of expensive algebraic operations. All that was needed was to design a *practical* OT extension protocol.

2.5.3.1 Practical OT Extension

This is precisely what was achieved in a second groundbreaking work by Ishai, Kilian, Nissim, and Petrank, in 2003 (Ishai et al., 2003).

Theorem 2.5.2 (IKNP OT extension—informal) *Under a suitable hardness assumption about cryptographic hash functions, there exists a protocol that uses only λ calls to an oblivious transfer primitive, and allows two parties to execute an arbitrary polynomial number $N(\lambda) = \mathrm{poly}(\lambda)$ of oblivious transfers. Furthermore, the protocol enjoys the following efficiency features (ignoring the one-time cost of the base OTs):*

- *The computation is dominated by three calls to the underlying hash function per OT.*
- *The communication for executing n OT on strings of length ℓ is $2 \cdot (\ell + \lambda) \cdot n$.*

Later works improved over IKNP in various ways, reducing the communication to $(2\ell + \lambda) \cdot n$ (Kolesnikov and Kumaresan, 2013; Asharov et al., 2013) (in the important case of $\ell = 1$, this is a factor two reduction) or even to $\approx 2n \cdot \lambda / \log \lambda$ when transferring short secrets (Kolesnikov and Kumaresan, 2013), extending to the setting of security against malicious adversaries (Keller et al., 2015; Asharov et al., 2015; Patra et al., 2017), or generalizing the functionality to 1-out-of-n OT (Orrù et al., 2017). Another work (Lindell and Zarosim, 2013) showed that the number λ of base OTs was essentially the best possible, by showing that an OT extension protocol using fewer base OT would imply oblivious transfer (hence can again not be based on symmetric primitives, baring breakthroughs). When referring to OT extensions using the IKNP approach or some of its follow-ups, we will use the terminology *IKNP-style* OT extension.

2.5.3.2 Wrapping-Up: Barriers in GMW-Based Secure Computation

Using oblivious transfer extensions, such as IKNP and its follow-ups, considerably mitigates the computational limitations of OTs: the four exponentiations required by the Bellare-Micali OT protocol are replaced by three invocations of a hash function, which represents a speed up between five and six orders of magnitudes. In our example from Sect. 2.4.2, this translates to a reduction of the computation time from about 740 hours to roughly *one minute*.

The communication is also significantly decreased—e.g., for transferring bit-secrets (as in GMW), about 130 bits of communication are required compared to the 758 bits of Bellare-Micali. Yet, this is by no means an improvement comparable to the efficiency gain: each OT still requires communication of the order of a hundred bits, which translates to Terabytes of communications even for simple functions such as edit distance. This brings us to where GMW and its many variants were until about 2018 or so: OT extension techniques, coupled with the notion of *secure preprocessing* that we will cover in the next section, make it feasible to run reasonably large secure computations on modern hardware in a reasonably short amount of time. However, the amount of communication required makes running these protocols prohibitive in any bandwidth-restricted scenario—in particular, over the Internet.

2.6 Precomputing Oblivious Transfers

We saw above that computing tons of oblivious transfers can be reduced to computing a few hash evaluations per OT. While this represents a tremendous improvement over directly running expensive OTs such as the Bellare-Micali protocol, this can still be too slow for real-world applications. In our example of securely computing the edit distance between two length 4095 strings, we observed that using OT extension reduces the runtime on a standard laptop from hundreds of hours to merely a minute; however, *merely a minute* is too long of a waiting time in an online setting, where many participants could want to run secure computations. Consider, for example, a website that would like to show personalized ads to its users, but without compromising their privacy: this could be done by securely evaluating an algorithm on the private content of the user browsing Cookie. But if running this computation takes one minute, this means that users will need to wait for a full minute before reaching the website, which is an unacceptable slowdown.[7]

In this section, we describe another fundamental observation of Beaver (yes, the same Beaver who introduced OT extension) which, in many settings, can strongly mitigate the overhead of running a secure computation protocol, and enable its use in scenarios where even a few seconds of delay would be too much.

The key insight: preparing the computation ahead of time. In many scenarios, the parties receive their inputs (x, y), and would like to obtain the result *on the spot*, shortly after. In our example of a user accessing a website where an ad provider wants to print a targeted banner, computed securely from the user's browsing history (*i.e.,* without revealing the browsing history), the participants learn their inputs at the last minute (their browsing history depends on recent events) and want to obtain the result of the computation, say, within a matter of milliseconds.

In this context, a natural question to ask is: is it necessary to start the heavy computation only when the parties receive their inputs? In other words, could the parties somehow *pre-execute* part of the computation, before knowing their inputs (and before getting the result becomes urgent)? This question was answered positively by Beaver in 1995, in a seminal paper (Beaver, 1995), that paved the way to efficient secure computation protocols. Beaver's observation was the following: secure computation via GMW boils down to executing many oblivious transfers on entries that depend on partial evaluations of the function on the parties' inputs. Yet, Beaver noticed, the parties can execute *all* their oblivious transfers on *uniformly random* inputs (this can be done long ahead of time, and all these oblivious transfers can be executed in parallel), and later *derandomize* each oblivious transfer, once the inputs to the protocol are known. Furthermore, this derandomization procedure is extremely fast (a few XORs and ANDs), requires little communication (only three bits per OT), and is information-theoretically secure (it does not rely on any unproven assumption).

---

[7] This is one of the reasons why, so far, no legislation prohibits websites from collecting private browsing information, even though secure computation could in principle allow executing any task the websites were running, without collecting any private data.

2.6.1   The Preprocessing Model

Beaver's result suggests the following natural approach to speed up secure computation in practice:

- First, during a **preprocessing phase**, the parties jointly run many oblivious transfer protocols in parallel on uniformly random inputs and store the outputs. This phase might be expensive, but (crucially) it is entirely independent of the inputs to the protocol, and can therefore be executed ahead of time.
- Second, during the **online phase**, when the parties receive their inputs, they execute the GMW protocol. For each OT they need, the parties retrieve a random OT from the preprocessing phase, and derandomize it—this can be viewed as *consuming* a part of the preprocessing material computed ahead of time (since, as we will see shortly, a random OT can only be used once to derandomize an OT). This allows the online phase to run fast (it does not involve any "cryptographic" operations) and use little communication.

This two-phase structure is called the *preprocessing model*. When focusing on optimizations to the online phase, it is also common to abstract out the preprocessing phase by assuming that *somehow*, the parties received random bits sampled with some predefined correlations (random OTs are a particular example of that, but other correlations are possible) from some external trusted dealer (this is to abstract out the fact that this correlated randomness distribution was done securely), and use this material in the online phase. This gives rise to an information-theoretic model of secure computation given access to a trusted source of correlated random coins that is called the *correlated randomness model*.

2.6.2   Beaver's Protocol

We now describe Beaver's derandomization protocol. Assume that, ahead of time, Alice and Bob have obtained the result of an oblivious transfer executed on random inputs: Alice (playing the role of the sender) has two random bits (r_0, r_1), and Bob received (σ, r_σ), where σ is a random selection bit. Once Alice receives her two OT inputs (s_0, s_1), and Bob receives his selection bit b, the protocol proceeds as follows:

- Bob tells Alice whether $\sigma = b$. This is done by sending a single bit $\ell = \sigma \oplus b$. Note that since σ is random and unknown to Alice, this leaks no information about b.
- If $\sigma = b$ ($\ell = 0$), Alice sends $(s_0 \oplus r_0, s_1 \oplus r_1)$ to Bob; else, she sends $(s_0 \oplus r_1, s_1 \oplus r_0)$ (that is, Alice sends $(u_0, u_1) = (s_0 \oplus r_\ell, s_1 \oplus r_{1\oplus\ell})$ to Bob). Observe that in any case, Bob (who knows only r_σ) will only be able to mask one of (s_0, s_1), the one masked by r_σ—that is exactly s_b by construction (since $u_b = s_b \oplus r_{b\oplus\ell} = s_b \oplus r_\sigma$).

It is a simple exercise to check that this protocol is correct and perfectly secure, and we leave it to the interested reader.

2.6.3 Secure Computation with Correlated Randomness

One way to abstract out Beaver's result is as follows: if the parties are given access to a *trusted* source of $2n$ random oblivious transfer, then they can securely compute any Boolean circuit with n AND gates (in the honest-but-curious setting), with *perfect* (information-theoretic) security. This stands in stark contrast with secure computation in the plain model (*i.e.*, without any trusted setup taking place before the execution of the protocol): in the plain model, it is well known that secure two-party computation is *impossible* without assuming computationally bounded parties (see the discussion in Sect. 2.1.2).

The random oblivious transfers form a special case of a source of *correlated randomness*: each random OT (s_0, s_1), (b, s_b) is exactly a uniformly random 4-tuple (s_0, s_1, b, α) of bits sampled conditioned on

$$\alpha = b \cdot (s_0 \oplus s_1) \oplus s_0. \tag{2.1}$$

In other words, (s_0, s_1) and (b, α) are uniformly random pairs of bits sampled conditioned on satisfying the degree-2 correlation given by Eq. 2.1.

Definition 2.6.1 (Correlated randomness model) We call secure computation in the correlated randomness model, a model of information-theoretic secure computation where before the start of the protocol, all participants securely receive random correlated strings from a trusted dealer, of a predefined length and for a predefined correlation.

Using the terminology above, Beaver's result establishes that information-theoretic two-party computation is possible in the correlated randomness model:

Theorem 2.6.2 (Beaver + GMW, informal) *For any boolean circuit C with $2n$ AND gates and m output gates, there exists an information-theoretic two-party computation protocol that securely computes C with semi-honest security in the correlated randomness model, with the following features:*

- *The two players request $2n$ random oblivious transfers from the trusted dealer.*
- *The protocol communicates $4n + 2m$ bits in total.*

While the above theorem is merely a restatement of Theorem 2.2.1 coupled with Beaver's derandomization technique, it highlights an important concept: in secure computation with correlated randomness, we typically distinguish the *amount* of resources consumed by the protocol (*i.e.*, the length of the correlated randomness) and the *type* of correlated randomness (above, random OTs). Our focus so far has been on two-party secure computation of boolean circuits in the honest-but-curious setting. However, as we will see in the next section, many other important settings exist: there can be more than two parties, one might want to achieve security against malicious participants, and the function that the parties want to evaluate might not have a nice representation as a boolean circuit—for example, it can be more suitably represented by an arithmetic circuit over a larger field.

For each of these variants, efficient information-theoretic protocols in the correlated randomness model exist, but the *type* of correlated randomness that they consume differs. Looking ahead, this suggests that the fundamental question we raised in Sect. 2.3.2 (How can we generate efficiently a very large number of oblivious transfers?) should be generalized to the following question:

How can we generate efficiently a large amount of suitable correlated randomness?

Above, "suitable" refers to any type of correlated randomness that the setting at hand might call for. As one would expect, the more one wants to handle complex types of functions or achieve advanced features (e.g., strong security, or handling many participants), the more complex the necessary correlated randomness becomes. Furthermore, *specific applications* of secure computation can often benefit from tailored types of correlated randomness, chosen to optimize the application. The study and design of efficient methods to generate different types of correlated randomness, motivated by different applications in secure computation, is a rich and diverse field. This book will cover some of the ways this field has been explored in an emerging line of work on the topic of *silent secure computation*.

2.7 Extensions of GMW

In this section, we introduce extensions of the GMW protocol to the setting of more than two parties, and for general arithmetic circuits. The seminal GMW protocol of Goldreich et al. (1987) was originally formulated for N parties directly; the extension to arithmetic circuits is straightforward.

Until now, we avoided formal definitions in favor of more intuitive descriptions, to prevent harming readability. However, as we delve further into slightly more complex (or notation-heavy) variants of secure computation, the intuitive descriptions become increasingly less actionable, and introducing more rigor and formalism helps in introducing more complex notions without disrupting too much the flow of the discourse. Therefore, we will introduce, when needed, more formal definitions for the objects we manipulate.

Definition 2.7.1 An arithmetic circuit C with n inputs $(x_1, \cdots, x_n)$ over a finite field $(\mathbb{F}, +, \times)$ is a directed acyclic graph of indegree 2 whose outdegree-0 nodes are called *output gates*. Each internal node (all nodes except indegree-0 nodes) is labeled with either $+$ or $\times$, representing the evaluation of either of the field operations. There are two types of indegree-0 nodes: *input nodes* are labeled with a variable x_i

for $i \leq n$, and *constant nodes* are labeled with a value $c \in \mathbb{F}$. Evaluating C on inputs $(x_1, \cdots, x_n) \in \mathbb{F}^n$ is done by inductively writing on each output wire of a gate the result of the gate operation applied to the value written on the input wires, once it has been defined. The output of the evaluation is the tuple of values written on the output wires.

2.7.1 N-Party MPC of Arithmetic Circuits, Honest-But-Curious Setting

From now on, we will view GMW as an information-theoretic protocol in the correlated randomness model of Beaver (1992; 1995). We now define the notion of a Beaver triple (sometimes also called multiplication triple):

Definition 2.7.2 An N-party Beaver triple over a field $\mathbb{F}$ is obtained by sampling $(u, v) \xleftarrow{s} \mathbb{F}^2$ and distributing uniformly random additive shares of $(u, v, u \cdot v)$ between the N parties. Equivalently, each party $(P_1, \cdots, P_{N-1})$ receives a uniformly random 3-tuple (u_i, v_i, w_i), and P_N receives $(u - \sum_{i<N} u_i, v - \sum_{i<N} v_i, u \cdot v - \sum_{i<N} w_i)$.

For convenience, we will introduce the following shorthand: given $u \in \mathbb{F}$, the notation $\langle u \rangle$ means that the parties hold additive *shares* $(u_1, \cdots, u_N)$ of u. This means that each party P_i holds a value u_i, where the joint distribution of $(u_1, \cdots, u_N)$ is uniformly random conditioned on $u = \sum_{i=1}^{N} u_i$. Note that this implies that for any subset $S \subsetneq [N]$, no coalition $(P_i)_{i \in S}$ of $|S| < N$ parties can learn anything about u from their joint shares $(u_i)_{i \in S}$, yet u can be reconstructed given all N shares. With this notation, we write $(\langle u \rangle, \langle v \rangle, \langle u \cdot v \rangle)$ to denote a Beaver triple without explicitly specifying the share of each party. Then, if the parties are given shares $(\langle u \rangle, \langle v \rangle)$ of elements u, v and if $(\alpha, \beta) \in \mathbb{F}^2$ are public values, we write $\langle \alpha u + \beta v \rangle \leftarrow \alpha \cdot \langle u \rangle + \beta \cdot \langle v \rangle$ to indicate that the parties with shares $(u_i)_i$ and $(v_i)_i$ of u, v can locally (without interaction) compute shares $(\alpha u_i + \beta v_i)_i$ of $\alpha u + \beta v$ (in other words, the sharing function is linear). Eventually, we say that the parties *reconstruct* (or *open*) a shared value u when each party broadcasts their share u_i to every other party, and all parties compute $u \leftarrow \sum_{i=1}^{N} u_i$.

Beaver triples are the main type of correlated randomness that we will use to get information-theoretic N-party secure computation of arithmetic circuits over $\mathbb{F}$ in the honest-but-curious setting (a synonym of t-private). It is a standard exercise to see that given two instances of random oblivious transfers, one can get (without further interaction) a two-party Beaver triple over $\mathbb{F}_2$. This can be generalized to show that a single N-party Beaver triple can be obtained by distributing two random OTs between each pair of participants—but this generalization requires communication.[8]

---

[8] The interested reader can try to show this by themselves—this is not too hard—or jump to Sect. 2.7.2 for a protocol that gives essentially the solution.

Theorem 2.7.3 (GMW + Beaver, generalized) *There exists a $(N-1)$-private information-theoretically secure N-party protocol for computing any functionality $f : (\mathbb{F}^*)^N \mapsto (\mathbb{F}^*)^N$, in the correlated randomness model, with the following features:*

- *If f is computed by an arithmetic circuit C with n $\times$-gates and m output nodes, the parties need n Beaver triples from the trusted dealer.*
- *The total communication of the protocol is $(n+m) \cdot N$ elements of $\mathbb{F}$.*

2.7.1.1 The Protocol

Let $P_1, \cdots, P_N$ be N parties with respective inputs $(x_1, \cdots, x_N)$, and let C_f be an arithmetic circuit computing the function f. The parties will evaluate the circuit gate by gate, starting from the inputs and computing the value of a gate when the values of its two parent nodes (that are either input nodes or gates themselves) have been computed. The protocol maintains the following invariant: after evaluating a gate, each party P_i will hold an additive share v_i of the value v on this gate. Without loss of generality, we assume that the parties always hold shares of the inputs to a gate when evaluating it: if an input to the gate is an input node carrying a field element b_i belonging to party P_i, we define the shares of $(P_1, \cdots, P_i, \cdots, P_n)$ to be $(0, \cdots, b_i, \cdots, 0)$ (while this is technically not a random share, this is sufficient for our purpose).

- Initialization: Before the protocol, all parties ask for $2B$ Beaver triples to the trusted dealer, where B is a bound on the number of AND gates in C_f.
- Evaluating a $+$-gate $+(a, b)$: The parties locally sum their shares of u and v. No communication is required.
- Evaluating a $\times$-gate $\times(a, b)$: The parties must compute additive shares of $u \cdot v$. This is done using the secure product protocol described below. This step consumes a Beaver triple.
- Output: After evaluating the output gate, all parties broadcast their share of the output, and all parties reconstruct the output.

2.7.1.2 Secure Product

On input additive shares $\langle u \rangle$, $\langle v \rangle$ of two field elements a, b, the *secure product* protocol proceeds as follows: the parties

- retrieve a (not previously used) Beaver triple $(\langle u \rangle, \langle v \rangle, \langle u \cdot v \rangle)$;
- compute $\langle u + a \rangle \leftarrow \langle u \rangle + \langle a \rangle$ and $\langle v + b \rangle \leftarrow \langle v \rangle + \langle b \rangle$;
- reconstruct $z_u = u + a$ and $z_v = v + b$ (this step, that is the only one where the parties interact, does not leak any private information because u and v are uniformly random, therefore z_u and z_v perfectly mask a and b);
- compute $\langle a \cdot b \rangle \leftarrow z_u \cdot \langle b \rangle - z_v \cdot \langle u \rangle + \langle u \cdot v \rangle$.

2.7.1.3 Bottom Line

In the N-party honest-but-curious setting, for general arithmetic circuits, Beaver triples form the core resource to enable fast information-theoretic secure computation. Concretely, it allows to implement the N-party secure product functionality, generalizing in a natural way the protocol we described for the two-party secure product functionality over $\mathbb{F}_2$ in Sect. 2.3.1.1. Note that we used oblivious transfers in our description of the protocol of Sect. 2.3.1.1, but we could have equivalently used random OTs, using Beaver's derandomization method. Then, it is a simple exercise to check that the protocol instantiated with two instances of a random OT is syntactically equivalent to the secure product described above, using a two-party Beaver triple over $\mathbb{F}_2$ (since two instances of a random OT immediately yield a two-party $\mathbb{F}_2$-Beaver triple).

Similarly, as for the two-party case, the generalized GMW protocol reduces the question of achieving *efficient* secure multi-party computation to the following question:

Is it possible to generate efficiently a large number of random Beaver triples?

We will cover in the next section what was the state of the art regarding this question until circa 2018.

2.7.2 Generating Beaver Triples

Generating Beaver triple is more involved than generating oblivious transfers and, as we will see, the best solution can vary depending on the field $\mathbb{F}$ and the number N of parties.

2.7.2.1 Over $\mathbb{F}_2$, for Small N

Over $\mathbb{F}_2$, generating an N-party Beaver triple reduces to executing $N \cdot (N - 1)$ oblivious transfers (two OTs for each pair of parties). The reduction works as follows:

- Each party samples a random pair $(u_i, v_i) \xleftarrow{s} \{0, 1\}^2$ of bits. Collectively, these bits form shares $(\langle u \rangle, \langle v \rangle)$ of two values $u = \bigoplus_{i \leq N} u_i$ and $v = \bigoplus_{i \leq N} v_i$. To obtain a Beaver triple, it remains for the parties to construct shares of $u \cdot v$. Expanding the product yields

$$u \cdot v = \bigoplus_{i \neq j} u_i \cdot v_j \oplus \bigoplus_{i \leq N} u_i \cdot v_i.$$

We treat the $u_i \cdot v_j$ with $i \neq j$ and the $u_i \cdot v_i$ separately since the latter is known to party P_i, while the former requires cross-party computation.

- Each pair of parties (P_i, P_j) constructs $(\langle u_i v_j \rangle, \langle u_j v_i \rangle)$ (where $\langle \cdot \rangle$ denote two-party shares) as follows:

  - P_i picks a uniformly random value r that will form their share of $u_i v_j$. Then, it remains for P_j to obtain the corresponding share $r \oplus u_i v_j$.
  - P_i and P_i execute an oblivious transfer protocol, where P_i plays the role of the sender with input $(r, r \oplus u_i)$, and P_j plays the role of the receiver with input v_j. P_j receives an output s; by definition of the OT, s is equal to r if $v_j = 0$, and to $r \oplus u_i$ if $v_j = 1$: in other words, $s = r \oplus u_i v_j$, as desired.
  - P_i and P_j proceed identically, using an OT, to obtain 2-party shares of $u_j v_i$.

- Each party P_i define their share of $u \cdot v$ to be $u_i v_i$ XORed with their shares of the $u_i v_j$ and the $u_j v_i$ for every $j \neq i$. Observe that

$$\langle u \cdot v \rangle = \bigoplus_{i \neq j} \langle u_i \cdot v_j \rangle \oplus \bigoplus_{i \leq N} u_i \cdot v_i,$$

from which correctness follows.

Proving that the protocol satisfies $(N-1)$-privacy (Definition 2.1.4) is a standard exercise, and we leave it to the interested reader.

Lemma 2.7.4 *There is an N-party protocol that securely generates a random Beaver triple over $\mathbb{F}_2$ (in the honest-but-curious setting) using $N \cdot (N-1)$ invocations of an oblivious transfer, and no further communication between the parties.*

2.7.2.2 Over $\mathbb{F}$, for Small N

The above solution has two clear downsides: (1) it is restricted to $\mathbb{F}_2$ and (2) its complexity scales quadratically with the number N of parties (and it is therefore best suited for small values of N). Here, we explain how to lift the first downside. To this end, we introduce the notion of *oblivious linear evaluation* (OLE).

Definition 2.7.5 (OLE, informal) An oblivious linear evaluation (OLE) over a field $\mathbb{F}$ is a two-party protocol between a sender with input $(u, v) \in \mathbb{F}^2$ and a receiver with input $x \in \mathbb{F}$. At the end of the protocol, the receiver should learn $u \cdot x + v$, and the sender does not get anything.

The OLE functionality is summarized in Fig. 2.3. The term oblivious linear evaluation stems from the following interpretation: in an OLE protocol, the sender holds the description of an affine function $f_{u,v} : x \mapsto ux + v$, and the receiver holds an input x. The goal of the protocol is to let the sender *obliviously* evaluate $f_{u,v}$ on x, revealing only the result of the evaluation to the receiver. The term "affine function evaluation" might seem a better choice since $f_{u,v}$ is not a linear function, but here "linear" should be seen as a property of the space of the functions $f_{u,v}$ (that is,

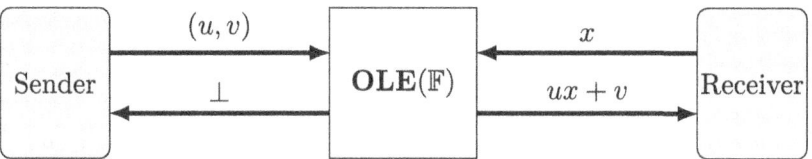

Fig. 2.3 Ideal functionality of the oblivious linear evaluation over $\mathbb{F}$

$\lambda f_{u,v} + f_{u',v'} = f_{\lambda u+v, \lambda u'+v'}$) rather than a property of the functions f themselves (that is, $\lambda f(x) + f(y) = f(\lambda x + y)$)).

Similarly as for random OTs, we say that two parties receive a random OLE if they receive uniformly random (u, v) and (x, w) sampled over $\mathbb{F}$ conditioned on $w = ux + v$.

Remark 2.7.6 OLEs are the natural generalization of OTs over larger fields. In fact, up to a minor syntactical difference, an OLE over $\mathbb{F}_2$, where the receiver gets $ux \oplus v$ is just an oblivious transfer between the sender inputs $(u, u \oplus v)$ using the receiver selection bit x. Therefore, any OLE over $\mathbb{F}_2$ can be locally mapped to an OT by the sender via the reversible mapping $(u, v) \mapsto (u, u \oplus v)$, and conversely.

A useful variant of OLE, that we will rely upon later on in this book, is the notion of vector-OLE:

Definition 2.7.7 (Vector-OLE, informal) A vector oblivious linear evaluation (vector-OLE, or VOLE) of size n over a field $\mathbb{F}$ is a two-party protocol between a sender with input vectors $(\vec{u}, \vec{v}) \in \mathbb{F}^n \times \mathbb{F}^n$ and a receiver with input $x \in \mathbb{F}$. At the end of the protocol, the receiver should learn $\vec{u} \cdot x + \vec{v}$, and the sender does not get anything.

Vector-OLE has been introduced in Applebaum et al. (2017). They generalize the notion of oblivious transfers of large strings in the same way that OLE generalizes the notion of oblivious transfer between pairs of bits. A vector-OLE of size n can always be realized using n instances of an OLE over $\mathbb{F}$, by letting the receiver use the same input x across all instances. However, vector-OLEs can often be realized more efficiently than n instances of OLE (Applebaum et al., 2017; Applebaum and Konstantini, 2023) and are a useful building block in many applications that motivates defining them independently.

From OLEs to Beaver triples. Using $N \cdot (N-1)$ OLEs over $\mathbb{F}$, N parties can generate a Beaver triple over $\mathbb{F}$. The protocol is an immediate generalization of the OT-based protocol over $\mathbb{F}_2$:

- Each party samples a random pair $(u_i, v_i) \xleftarrow{s} \mathbb{F}^2$. Collectively, these values form shares $(\langle u \rangle, \langle v \rangle)$ of $u = \sum_{i \leq N} u_i$ and $v = \sum_{i \leq N} v_i$. It remains to construct shares of $u \cdot v$. We have

$$u \cdot v = \sum_{i \neq j} u_i \cdot v_j + \sum_{i \leq N} u_i \cdot v_i.$$

- Each pair of parties (P_i, P_j) constructs $(\langle u_i v_j \rangle, \langle u_j v_i \rangle)$ (where $\langle \cdot \rangle$ denote two-party shares) as follows:

    - P_i picks a uniformly random value r that will form their share of $u_i v_j$. It remains for P_j to obtain the corresponding share $r + u_i v_j$: this is done by executing an OLE with input (r, u_i) from the sender, and input v_j from the receiver.
    - P_i and P_j proceed identically, using an OLE, to obtain two-party shares of $u_j v_i$.

- Each party P_i defines their share of $u \cdot v$ to be $u_i v_i$ summed with their shares of the $u_i v_j$ and the $u_j v_i$ for every $j \neq i$. As before,

$$\langle u \cdot v \rangle = \sum_{i \neq j} \langle u_i \cdot v_j \rangle + \sum_{i \leq N} u_i \cdot v_i,$$

from which correctness follows.

Security follows from the same observations as in the case of $\mathbb{F}_2$.

Lemma 2.7.8 *There is an N-party protocol that securely generates a random Beaver triple over $\mathbb{F}$ (in the honest-but-curious setting) using $N \cdot (N - 1)$ invocations of an oblivious linear evaluation, and no further communication between the parties.*

OLEs from OTs. We now show that an OLE over a field $\mathbb{F}$ can be obtained using $\log |\mathbb{F}|$ invocations of an OT. This protocol was first described in Gilboa (1999). Let $(u, v) \in \mathbb{F}^2$ be the sender inputs, and let $x \in \mathbb{F}$ be the receiver input. Assume for simplicity that $\mathbb{F}$ is a prime-order field (and can therefore be identified with the set of integers modulo $|\mathbb{F}|$)—the protocol can be easily generalized to work with general finite fields. We denote by $(x_0, \cdots, x_{t-1})$ the bits of the binary representation of x, where $y = \log |\mathbb{F}|$. The protocol proceeds as follows:

- The sender samples uniformly random shares $(s_0, \cdots, s_{t-1})$ of v over $\mathbb{F}$ (that is, the s_i are random conditioned on $\sum_i s_i = v$).
- The sender and the receiver execute t parallel instances of an oblivious transfer, where in the i-th instance (from 0 to $t - 1$), the sender inputs $(s_i, s_i + 2^i \cdot u)$, and the receiver inputs x_i. Observe that the receiver obtains $s_i + x_i \cdot 2^i \cdot u$.
- The receiver outputs $\sum_{i=0}^{t-1} s_i + x_i \cdot 2^i \cdot u$.

Correctness is straightforward:

$$\sum_{i=0}^{t-1} s_i + x_i \cdot 2^i = \sum_{i=0}^{t-1} s_i + \left(\sum_{i=0}^{t-1} x_i \cdot 2^i \right) \cdot u = v + x \cdot u.$$

Security follows also easily from the security of the OTs and the fact that the s_i are uniformly random shares of v. Combining this protocol with the OLE-based protocol for generating Beaver triples, we get

Lemma 2.7.9 *There is an N-party protocol that securely generates a random Beaver triple over $\mathbb{F}$ (in the honest-but-curious setting) using $N \cdot (N - 1) \cdot \log |\mathbb{F}|$ invocations of an oblivious transfer, and no further communication between the parties.*

Bottom line. It is possible to securely generate Beaver triples over arbitrary fields, and for any number of parties, using only invocations of oblivious transfer protocols. However, the complexity of this approach scales with $\Omega(N^2 \cdot \log |\mathbb{F}|)$. Yet, for not-too-large values of N and $\log \mathbb{F}$, this remains the most computationally efficient way of generating Beaver triples, due to the existence of super-fast OT extension protocols. However, communication-wise, this becomes very quickly prohibitive: assuming 130 bits of communication per OT, if there are $N = 10$ parties and the field $\mathbb{F}$ is chosen to be $\mathbb{F}_{2^{64}}$ (a common choice since it matches the size of machine words), this yields already about 750.000 bits of communication *for each Beaver triple*. When evaluating an arithmetic circuit containing as little as ten million $\times$-gates (which is quite small), this already represents 800 Gigabytes of communication. Below, we will see that there is a better solution when the $\Omega(N^2 \cdot \log |\mathbb{F}|)$ becomes prohibitive.

2.7.2.3   Over $\mathbb{F}$, for Large N

When the size of the field $\mathbb{F}$ grows too much, an alternative solution to the above protocol is to rely on threshold homomorphic encryption. This approach to secure computation dates back to Cramer et al. (2001). The technique has multiple flavors, using different types of homomorphic encryption. The approach we will present below, using the threshold additively homomorphic encryption notion, is somewhat folklore. Depending on the context, other variants might perform better, but our main purpose is to illustrate this type of method. These approaches use a type of cryptographic machinery quite different from the ones we used so far (albeit perhaps closer to the type of primitives one sees in a standard cryptography curriculum).

Definitions. To introduce the construction, we need to recall the notion of public-key encryption over a field $\mathbb{F}$ first:

Definition 2.7.10 (Public-Key Encryption) A public-key encryption scheme Π is a triple of polytime algorithms ($\Pi.\mathsf{KeyGen}, \Pi.\mathsf{Enc}, \Pi.\mathsf{Dec}$), such that

- $\Pi.\mathsf{KeyGen}(1^\lambda)$ generates a pair (pk, sk) of public and private keys. The key pk specifies the ciphertext space $\mathcal{C}$ and the random source $\mathcal{R}$.
- $\Pi.\mathsf{Enc}(\mathsf{pk}, m; r)$, given $m \in \mathbb{F}$ and random coins $r \in \mathcal{R}$, outputs a ciphertext c.
- $\Pi.\mathsf{Dec}(\mathsf{sk}, c)$ outputs a message $m \in \mathbb{F}$.

In addition Π must satisfy the correctness and IND-CPA security properties defined below.

$$\begin{array}{|l|} \hline \mathsf{Exp}_{\mathscr{A}}^{\mathtt{ind-cpa-0}}(1^\lambda): \\ \quad (\mathsf{pk},\mathsf{sk}) \stackrel{\$}{\leftarrow} \Pi.\mathsf{KeyGen}(1^\lambda) \\ \quad (m_0, m_1, \mathsf{st}) \stackrel{\$}{\leftarrow} \mathscr{A}(\mathsf{pk}) \\ \quad r \stackrel{\$}{\leftarrow} \mathcal{R} \\ \quad c \leftarrow \Pi.\mathsf{Enc}(\mathsf{pk}, m_0; r) \\ \quad b \leftarrow \mathscr{A}(\mathsf{pk}, c, \mathsf{st}) \\ \hline \end{array} \qquad \begin{array}{|l|} \hline \mathsf{Exp}_{\mathscr{A}}^{\mathtt{ind-cpa-1}}(1^\lambda): \\ \quad (\mathsf{pk},\mathsf{sk}) \stackrel{\$}{\leftarrow} \Pi.\mathsf{KeyGen}(1^\lambda) \\ \quad (m_0, m_1, \mathsf{st}) \stackrel{\$}{\leftarrow} \mathscr{A}(\mathsf{pk}) \\ \quad r \stackrel{\$}{\leftarrow} \mathcal{R} \\ \quad c \leftarrow \Pi.\mathsf{Enc}(\mathsf{pk}, m_1; r) \\ \quad b \leftarrow \mathscr{A}(\mathsf{pk}, c, \mathsf{st}) \\ \hline \end{array}$$

Fig. 2.4 Experiments for the IND-CPA property of the encryption scheme Π

Definition 2.7.11 (Correctness) Π is *correct* if for any pair $(\mathsf{pk}, \mathsf{sk}) \stackrel{\$}{\leftarrow} \Pi.$ $\mathsf{KeyGen}(1^\lambda)$, message $m \in \mathbb{F}$, and random coin $r \in \mathcal{R}$, it holds that $\Pi.\mathsf{Dec}(\mathsf{sk}, \Pi.$ $\mathsf{Enc}(\mathsf{pk}, m; r)) = m$.

The experiments $\mathsf{Exp}_{\mathscr{A}}^{\mathtt{ind-cpa-0}}(1^\lambda)$ and $\mathsf{Exp}_{\mathscr{A}}^{\mathtt{ind-cpa-1}}(1^\lambda)$ for the IND-CPA property of the encryption scheme Π are represented in Fig. 2.4.

Definition 2.7.12 (IND-CPA Security) Π is IND-CPA *secure* if for any polytime adversary $\mathscr{A}$, it holds that $|\Pr[\mathsf{Exp}_{\mathscr{A}}^{\mathtt{ind-cpa-1}}(1^\lambda) = 1] - \Pr[\mathsf{Exp}_{\mathscr{A}}^{\mathtt{ind-cpa-0}}(1^\lambda) = 1]| = \mathsf{negl}(\lambda)$, where negl denotes a *negligible* function.

An N-party threshold public-key encryption scheme is an encryption scheme where the decryption can be distributed among N parties holding shares sk_i of the secret key sk. Here, for simplicity, we will focus on a notion of additive threshold decryption, where running the partial decryption algorithm with sk_i yields an additive share, over $\mathbb{F}$, of the message m. The definition below is adapted to our setting:

Definition 2.7.13 (Threshold Public-Key Encryption, informal) An N-party threshold public-key encryption scheme Π is a PKE ($\Pi.\mathsf{KeyGen}, \Pi.\mathsf{Enc}, \Pi.\mathsf{Dec}$) satisfying correctness and IND-CPA security, as in Definitions 2.7.11 and 2.7.12, respectively, together with additional algorithms ($\Pi.\mathsf{Share}, \Pi.\mathsf{Rec}$), and a distributed decryption protocol Π_{dec}:

- $\Pi.\mathsf{Share}(\mathsf{sk})$ generates N secret key shares $(\mathsf{sk}_1, \cdots, \mathsf{sk}_N)$.
- $\Pi.\mathsf{Rec}(\mathsf{sk}_1, \cdots, \mathsf{sk}_N)$ reconstructs the secret key sk.
- Π_{dec} is an N-party protocol secure in the *semi-honest* model where all parties hold a ciphertext c as common input, and each party holds a share sk_i of sk. The protocol securely computes the functionality $\Pi.\mathsf{Dec}(\Pi.\mathsf{Rec}(\mathsf{sk}_1, \cdots, \mathsf{sk}_N), c)$.

In addition, the sharing algorithm must satisfy the standard property that for any sk, the distribution of any strict subset of the keys $(\mathsf{sk}_i)_{i \in S}$ with $S \subsetneq [N]$ can be statistically simulated without sk.

Eventually, we will want our threshold public-key encryption scheme to be *additively homomorphic*. We sketch one possible definition below:

Definition 2.7.14 (Additively Homomorphic Encryption, informal)   A PKE
(Π.KeyGen, Π.Enc, Π.Dec) is an additively homomorphic encryption scheme if
there is an efficient randomized algorithm Π.Add where, for any $\alpha \in \mathbb{F}$ and any pair
(c_0, c_1) of ciphertexts, Π.Add(α, c_0, c_1) outputs a new ciphertext c, such that the
following holds:

- (homomorphic correctness) If Π.Dec$(\text{sk}, c_0) = m_0$ and Π.Dec$(\text{sk}, c_1) = m_1$,
  then Π.Dec$(\text{sk}, c) = \alpha \cdot m_0 + m_1$.
- (circuit privacy) The output distribution of Π.Add is statistically independent
  of α.

We also write Π.Add(α, c_0, β) with $\beta \in \mathbb{F}$ to denote the homomorphic computation
of $\alpha m_0 + \beta$ (this can always be done by computing an arbitrary encryption of β
first).

There are several ways to instantiate an N-party threshold additively homomor-
phic encryption scheme. If we replace the field $\mathbb{F}$ by an integer ring $\mathbb{Z}_n$ (where n is
a product of large primes), a common choice is to rely on (threshold variants of) the
Paillier cryptosystem (Paillier, 1999). Otherwise, over arbitrary prime-order fields
$\mathbb{F}$, one can rely on threshold variants of lattice schemes such as the Regev cryptosystem (Regev, 2005). All these works admit efficient threshold variants where
the distributed decryption protocol has a communication comparable to exchanging
$O(n)$ ciphertexts in a constant number of rounds.

Beaver triples from threshold additively homomorphic encryption. Equipped
with the above definition, we can sketch a simple protocol to generate a Beaver triple.
Fix N parties $P_1, \cdots , P_N$ and assume that, in a prior setup phase, they distributively
generated (or received from a trusted dealer) a public key pk as well as shares
$\text{sk}_1, \cdots , \text{sk}_N$ of the corresponding secret key (each party holds one share) for a
threshold additively homomorphic encryption scheme Π. The protocol proceeds as
follows:

- Each party P_i samples $(x_i, y_i) \xleftarrow{s} \mathbb{F}^2$ and broadcasts $c_i \xleftarrow{s} \Pi$.Enc(pk, x_i).
- All parties publicly compute using Π.Add a ciphertext c encrypting the sum $x = \sum_{i=1}^{N} x_i$.
- Each party P_i broadcasts $c'_i \xleftarrow{s} \Pi$.Add(y_i, c_i, z_i).
- All parties publicly compute using Π.Add a ciphertext c' encrypting the sum

$$\sum_{i=1}^{N} \Pi.\text{Dec}(\text{sk}, c'_i) = \sum_i y_i \cdot x + z_i = x \cdot y + \sum_i z_i.$$

- All parties execute the distributed decryption protocol Π_{dec} to obtain $z = x \cdot y + \sum_i z_i$.
- Each party P_i outputs $(x_i, y_i, s_i = -z_i)$, except party P_N who outputs $(x_N, y_N, s_N = z - z_N)$.

Security follows from the IND-CPA security of the scheme, together with the fact that the value $z = x \cdot y + \sum_i z_i$ is perfectly masked to any subset of at most $N - 1$ parties. Correctness can be checked routinely:

$$\sum_{i=1}^{N} s_i = z - \sum_{i=1}^{N} z_i = x \cdot y = \left(\sum_{i=1}^{N} x_i \right) \cdot \left(\sum_{i=1}^{N} y_i \right).$$

Communication-wise, the cost of this protocol is dominated by the communication of $2N$ ciphertexts, plus the cost of the distributed decryption protocol (typically comparable to N ciphertexts). Using the Paillier encryption scheme, one ciphertext has a size comparable to two elements of $\mathbb{Z}_n$. Furthermore, when generating many Beaver triples in parallel using a lattice-based encryption scheme, one can rely on "packing" techniques to achieve an amortized communication of $O(N)$ elements of $\mathbb{F}$ per Beaver triple. Overall, the cost of generating Beaver triples with these methods typically scales as $O(N)$, that is, a factor $N \cdot \log |\mathbb{F}|$ smaller than the OT-based method of Sect. 2.7.2.2. This comes at the cost of using public-key homomorphic encryption, and $O(N)$ public-key operation per party for *each* Beaver triple (while using IKNP-style OT extension, the protocol requires $O(N)$ public-key operation per party *in total*).

Historical notes. Oblivious linear evaluation was originally introduced in the work of Naor and Pinkas (1999). Using threshold additively homomorphic encryption in secure computation was originally introduced in Cramer et al. (2001) (from now on, CDN). Though it was initially described as a method to securely compute multiplication gates, its use for generating Beaver triples for MPC in the correlated randomness model is generally deemed folklore. The idea of using a CDN-style approach in the preprocessing phase was first introduced in Bendlin et al. (2011). Following the seminal SPDZ paper (Damgard et al., 2012), later works (Keller et al., 2018; Gordon et al., 2022) have relied mostly on a variant where the Beaver triples are generated using somewhat homomorphic encryption instead of threshold additive encryption. The CDN approach has recently got some renewed attention (Braun et al., 2023) in the context of the recent YOSO framework for massively large-scale secure computation.

2.7.3 N-Party MPC of Arithmetic Circuits, Malicious Setting

All protocols described so far have been restricted to the honest-but-curious setting, meaning that they are only guaranteed to be secure if the participants follow the specifications of the protocol. A much more challenging goal is that of secure computation in the malicious setting, where participants might behave arbitrarily. This is a fundamental topic, but providing even a superficial coverage of the techniques and challenges involved would take us too far. Hence, before ending this chapter, we will limit ourselves to making two short remarks about malicious security:

- Most maliciously secure protocols proceed by first designing a protocol in the honest-but-curious model, and then designing mechanisms (relying on cryptographic primitives such as *commitments* and *zero-knowledge proofs*) to force the participants to adhere to the specifications (or, equivalently, guaranteeing that any attempt to deviate from the prescribed strategy will be detected by the participants). This is the reason why addressing the design of secure computation protocols in the honest-but-curious setting remains well motivated even if one finds the assumption of honest behavior to be undesirable.
- Maliciously secure MPC protocols in the preprocessing model typically rely on a variant of Beaver triples called *authenticated Beaver triple*, where in addition to shares $(\langle a \rangle, \langle b \rangle, \langle ab \rangle)$ for random $a, b \in \mathbb{F}$, the parties also get $(\langle \Delta \cdot a \rangle, \langle \Delta \cdot b \rangle, \langle \Delta \cdot ab \rangle)$ where Δ is a global authentication value (typically from $\mathbb{F}$ or some extension field thereof) shared between the parties. Roughly, the purpose of Δ will be to check that the parties have honestly computed some target linear relation, by computing the same linear relation on the authenticated values and checking afterward an equation of the form $\Delta \cdot L(\vec{x}) =_? L(\Delta \cdot \vec{x})$. All the methods described in this section can be adapted relatively easily to generate authenticated Beaver triples instead.

With this, we conclude this chapter, that we hope conveyed some intuition about the motivations for using correlated randomness in secure computation and some of the challenges associated with generating this correlated randomness. The next chapter will focus on an alternative approach to correlated randomness generation, whose aim is to enable the generation of a large amount of correlated randomness using a minimal amount of communication.

References

Aiello, W., Ishai, Y., & Reingold, O. (2001). Priced oblivious transfer: How to sell digital goods. In B. Pfitzmann (Ed.), *Advances in Cryptology – EUROCRYPT 2001* (Vol. 2045, pp. 119–135). Springer. https://doi.org/10.1007/3-540-44987-6_8.

Alekhnovich, M. (2003). More on average case vs approximation complexity. In *Proceedings of the 44th Annual Symposium on Foundations of Computer Science (FOCS)* (pp. 298–307). IEEE Computer Society Press. https://doi.org/10.1109/SFCS.2003.1238204.

Applebaum, B., & Konstantini, N. (2023). Actively secure arithmetic computation and VOLE with constant computational overhead. In *Advances in Cryptology – EUROCRYPT 2023, Part II* (pp. 190–219). Springer. https://doi.org/10.1007/978-3-031-30617-4_7.

Applebaum, B., Damgård, I., Ishai, Y., Nielsen, M., & Zichron, L. (2017). Secure arithmetic computation with constant computational overhead. In J. Katz & H. Shacham (Eds.), *Advances in Cryptology – CRYPTO 2017, Part I* (Vol. 10401, pp. 223–254). Springer. https://doi.org/10.1007/978-3-319-63688-7_8.

Asharov, G., Lindell, Y., Schneider, T., & Zohner, M. (2013). More efficient oblivious transfer and extensions for faster secure computation. In A.-R. Sadeghi, V. D. Gligor, & M. Yung (Eds.), *Proceedings of the 2013 ACM SIGSAC Conference on Computer and Communications Security (CCS)* (pp. 535–548). ACM Press. https://doi.org/10.1145/2508859.2516738.

Asharov, G., Lindell, Y., Schneider, T., & Zohner, M. (2015). More efficient oblivious transfer extensions with security for malicious adversaries. In E. Oswald & M. Fischlin (Eds.), *Advances in Cryptology – EUROCRYPT 2015, Part I* (Vol. 9056, pp. 673–701). Springer. https://doi.org/10.1007/978-3-662-46800-5_26.

Asharov, G., & Lindell, Y. (2017). A full proof of the BGW protocol for perfectly secure multiparty computation. *Journal of Cryptology, 30*(1), 58–151. https://doi.org/10.1007/s00145-015-9214-4

Beaver, D. (1992). Efficient multiparty protocols using circuit randomization. In J. Feigenbaum (Ed.), *Advances in Cryptology – CRYPTO'91* (Vol. 576, pp. 420–432). Springer. https://doi.org/10.1007/3-540-46766-1_34.

Beaver, D. (1992). Foundations of secure interactive computing. In J. Feigenbaum (Ed.), *Advances in Cryptology – CRYPTO'91* (Vol. 576, pp. 377–391). Springer. https://doi.org/10.1007/3-540-46766-1_31.

Beaver, D. (1995). Precomputing oblivious transfer. In D. Coppersmith (Ed.), *Advances in Cryptology – CRYPTO'95* (Vol. 963, pp. 97–109). Springer. https://doi.org/10.1007/3-540-44750-4_8.

Beaver, D. (1996). Correlated pseudorandomness and the complexity of private computations. In *Proceedings of the 28th Annual ACM Symposium on Theory of Computing (STOC)* (pp. 479–488). ACM Press. https://doi.org/10.1145/237814.237996.

Beaver, D. (1998). Adaptively secure oblivious transfer. In K. Ohta & D. Pei (Eds.), *Advances in Cryptology – ASIACRYPT'98* (Vol. 1514, pp. 300–314). Springer. https://doi.org/10.1007/3-540-49649-1_24.

Beaver, D. (1991). Secure multiparty protocols and zero-knowledge proof systems tolerating a faulty minority. *Journal of Cryptology, 4*(2), 75–122. https://doi.org/10.1007/BF00196771

Bellare, M., & Micali, S. (1990). Non-interactive oblivious transfer and applications. In G. Brassard (Ed.), *Advances in Cryptology – CRYPTO'89* (Vol. 435, pp. 547–557). Springer. https://doi.org/10.1007/0-387-34805-0_48.

Bendlin, R., Damgård, I., Orlandi, C., & Zakarias, S. (2011). Semi-homomorphic encryption and multiparty computation. In K. G. Paterson (Ed.), *Advances in Cryptology – EUROCRYPT 2011* (Vol. 6632, pp. 169–188). Springer. https://doi.org/10.1007/978-3-642-20465-4_11.

Bennett, C. H., Brassard, G., Crépeau, C., & Skubiszewska, M.-H. (1992). Practical quantum oblivious transfer. In J. Feigenbaum (Ed.), *Advances in Cryptology – CRYPTO'91* (Vol. 576, pp. 351–366). Springer. https://doi.org/10.1007/3-540-46766-1_29.

Ben-Or, M., Goldwasser, S., & Wigderson, A. (1988). Completeness theorems for non-cryptographic fault-tolerant distributed computation (extended abstract). In *Proceedings of the 20th Annual ACM Symposium on Theory of Computing (STOC)* (pp. 1–10). ACM Press. https://doi.org/10.1145/62212.62213.

Berger, R., Peralta, R., & Tedrick, T. (1985). A provably secure oblivious transfer protocol. In T. Beth, N. Cot, & I. Ingemarsson (Eds.), *Advances in Cryptology – EUROCRYPT'84* (Vol. 209, pp. 379–386). Springer. https://doi.org/10.1007/3-540-39757-4_26.

Bernstein, D. J. (2006). Curve25519: New Diffie-Hellman speed records. In M. Yung, Y. Dodis, A. Kiayias, & T. Malkin (Eds.), *Public-Key Cryptography – PKC 2006* (Vol. 3958, pp. 207–228). Springer. https://doi.org/10.1007/11745853_14.

Blazy, O., & Chevalier, C. (2015). Generic construction of UC-secure oblivious transfer. In T. Malkin, V. Kolesnikov, A. B. Lewko, & M. Polychronakis (Eds.), *Applied Cryptography and Network Security - ACNS 2015* (Vol. 9092, pp. 65–86). Springer. https://doi.org/10.1007/978-3-319-28166-7_4.

Braun, L., Damgård, I., & Orlandi, C. (2023). Secure multiparty computation from threshold encryption based on class groups. In *Advances in Cryptology – CRYPTO 2023* (pp. 613–645). Springer.

Cachin, C., Crépeau, C., & Marcil, J. (1998). Oblivious transfer with a memory-bounded receiver. In *Proceedings of the 39th Annual Symposium on Foundations of Computer Science (FOCS)* (pp. 493–502). IEEE Computer Society Press. https://doi.org/10.1109/SFCS.1998.743500.

Camenisch, J., Neven, G., & shelat, a. (2007). Simulatable adaptive oblivious transfer. In M. Naor (Ed.), *Advances in Cryptology – EUROCRYPT 2007* (Vol. 4515, pp. 573–590). Springer. https://doi.org/10.1007/978-3-540-72540-4_33.

Canetti, R., Sarkar, P., & Wang, X. (2020). Efficient and round-optimal oblivious transfer and commitment with adaptive security. In S. Moriai & H. Wang (Eds.), *Advances in Cryptology – ASIACRYPT 2020, Part III* (Vol. 12493, pp. 277–308). Springer. https://doi.org/10.1007/978-3-030-64840-4_10.

Canetti, R. (2000). Security and composition of multiparty cryptographic protocols. *Journal of Cryptology, 13*(1), 143–202. https://doi.org/10.1007/s001459910006

Cascudo, I., Damgård, I., Lacerda, F., & Ranellucci, S. (2016). Oblivious transfer from any nontrivial elastic noisy channel via secret key agreement. In M. Hirt & A. D. Smith (Eds.), *Theory of Cryptography – TCC 2016-B, Part I* (Vol. 9985, pp. 204–234). Springer. https://doi.org/10.1007/978-3-662-53641-4_9.

Chaum, D., Crépeau, C., & Damgård, I. (1988). Multiparty unconditionally secure protocols (extended abstract). In *Proceedings of the 20th Annual ACM Symposium on Theory of Computing (STOC)* (pp. 11–19). ACM Press. https://doi.org/10.1145/62212.62214.

Choi, S. G., Katz, J., Schröder, D., Yerukhimovich, A., & Zhou, H.-S. (2014). (Efficient) universally composable oblivious transfer using a minimal number of stateless tokens. In Y. Lindell (Ed.), *Theory of Cryptography – TCC 2014* (Vol. 8349, pp. 638–662). Springer. https://doi.org/10.1007/978-3-642-54242-8_27.

Choi, S. G., Katz, J., Wee, H., & Zhou, H.-S. (2013). Efficient, adaptively secure, and composable oblivious transfer with a single, global CRS. In K. Kurosawa & G. Hanaoka (Eds.), *Public-Key Cryptography – PKC 2013* (Vol. 7778, pp. 73–88). Springer. https://doi.org/10.1007/978-3-642-36362-7_6.

Chor, B., & Kushilevitz, E. (1989). A zero-one law for boolean privacy (extended abstract). In *Proceedings of the 21st Annual ACM Symposium on Theory of Computing (STOC)* (pp. 62–72). ACM Press. https://doi.org/10.1145/73007.73013.

Chou, T., & Orlandi, C. (2015). The simplest protocol for oblivious transfer. In K. E. Lauter & F. Rodríguez-Henríquez (Eds.), *LATINCRYPT 2015* (Vol. 9230, pp. 40–58). Springer. https://doi.org/10.1007/978-3-319-22174-8_3.

Choudhuri, A. R., Ciampi, M., Goyal, V., Jain, A., & Ostrovsky, R. (2021). Oblivious transfer from trapdoor permutations in minimal rounds. In K. Nissim & B. Waters (Eds.), *Theory of Cryptography – TCC 2021, Part II* (Vol. 13043, pp. 518–549). Springer. https://doi.org/10.1007/978-3-030-90453-1_18.

Cramer, R., Damgård, I., & Nielsen, J. B. (2001). Multiparty computation from threshold homomorphic encryption. In B. Pfitzmann (Ed.), *Advances in Cryptology – EUROCRYPT 2001* (Vol. 2045, pp. 280–299). Springer. https://doi.org/10.1007/3-540-44987-6_18.

Crépeau, C., & Kilian, J. (1988). Achieving oblivious transfer using weakened security assumptions (extended abstract). In *Proceedings of the 29th Annual Symposium on Foundations of Computer Science (FOCS)* (pp. 42–52). IEEE Computer Society Press. https://doi.org/10.1109/SFCS.1988.21920.

Damgård, I., Fehr, S., Morozov, K., & Salvail, L. (2004). Unfair noisy channels and oblivious transfer. In M. Naor (Ed.), *Theory of Cryptography – TCC 2004* (Vol. 2951, pp. 355–373). Springer. https://doi.org/10.1007/978-3-540-24638-1_20.

Damgård, I., Pastro, V., Smart, N. P., & Zakarias, S. (2012). Multiparty computation from somewhat homomorphic encryption. In R. Safavi-Naini & R. Canetti (Eds.), *Advances in Cryptology – CRYPTO 2012* (Vol. 7417, pp. 643–662). Springer. https://doi.org/10.1007/978-3-642-32009-5_38.

Diffie, W., & Hellman, M. E. (1976). New directions in cryptography. *IEEE Transactions on Information Theory, 22*(6), 644–654. https://doi.org/10.1109/TIT.1976.1055638

Ding, Y. Z. (2001). Oblivious transfer in the bounded storage model. In J. Kilian (Ed.), *Advances in Cryptology – CRYPTO 2001* (Vol. 2139, pp. 155–170). Springer. https://doi.org/10.1007/3-540-44647-8_9.

Ding, Y. Z., Harnik, D., Rosen, A., & Shaltiel, R. (2004). Constant-round oblivious transfer in the bounded storage model. In M. Naor (Ed.), *Theory of Cryptography – TCC 2004* (Vol. 2951, pp. 446–472). Springer. https://doi.org/10.1007/978-3-540-24638-1_25.

Döttling, N., Garg, S., Hajiabadi, M., Masny, D., & Wichs, D. (2020). Two-round oblivious transfer from CDH or LPN. In A. Canteaut & Y. Ishai (Eds.), *Advances in Cryptology – EUROCRYPT 2020, Part II* (Vol. 12106, pp. 768–797). Springer. https://doi.org/10.1007/978-3-030-45724-2_26.

Even, S., Goldreich, O., & Lempel, A. (1982). A randomized protocol for signing contracts. In D. Chaum, R. L. Rivest, & A. T. Sherman (Eds.), *Advances in Cryptology – CRYPTO'82* (pp. 205–210). Plenum Press. https://doi.org/10.1007/978-1-4757-0602-4_19.

Friolo, D., Masny, D., & Venturi, D. (2019). A black-box construction of fully-simulatable, round-optimal oblivious transfer from strongly uniform key agreement. In D. Hofheinz & A. Rosen (Eds.), *Theory of Cryptography – TCC 2019, Part I* (Vol. 11891, pp. 111–130). Springer. https://doi.org/10.1007/978-3-030-36030-6_5.

Garay, J. A., & MacKenzie, P. D. (2000). Concurrent oblivious transfer. In *Proceedings of the 41st Annual Symposium on Foundations of Computer Science (FOCS)* (pp. 314–324). IEEE Computer Society Press. https://doi.org/10.1109/SFCS.2000.892120.

Garay, J. A., Wichs, D., & Zhou, H.-S. (2009). Somewhat non-committing encryption and efficient adaptively secure oblivious transfer. In S. Halevi (Ed.), *Advances in Cryptology – CRYPTO 2009* (Vol. 5677, pp. 505–523). Springer. https://doi.org/10.1007/978-3-642-03356-8_30.

Gentry, C. (2009). Fully homomorphic encryption using ideal lattices. In M. Mitzenmacher (Ed.), *Proceedings of the 41st Annual ACM Symposium on Theory of Computing (STOC)* (pp. 169–178). ACM Press. https://doi.org/10.1145/1536414.1536440.

Gertner, Y., Kannan, S., Malkin, T., Reingold, O., & Viswanathan, M. (2000). The relationship between public key encryption and oblivious transfer. In *Proceedings of the 41st Annual Symposium on Foundations of Computer Science (FOCS)* (pp. 325–335). IEEE Computer Society Press. https://doi.org/10.1109/SFCS.2000.892121.

Gilboa, N. (1999). Two party RSA key generation. In M. J. Wiener (Ed.), *Advances in Cryptology – CRYPTO'99* (Vol. 1666, pp. 116–129). Springer. https://doi.org/10.1007/3-540-48405-1_8.

Goldreich, O. (2000). *Candidate one-way functions based on expander graphs*. Cryptology ePrint Archive, Report 2000/063. https://eprint.iacr.org/2000/063.

Goldreich, O. (2009). *Foundations of cryptography: Volume 2, basic applications*. Cambridge University Press.

Goldreich, O., & Vainish, R. (1988). How to solve any protocol problem – an efficiency improvement. In C. Pomerance (Ed.), *Advances in Cryptology – CRYPTO'87* (Vol. 293, pp. 73–86). Springer. https://doi.org/10.1007/3-540-48184-2_6.

Goldreich, O., Micali, S., & Wigderson, A. (1987). How to play any mental game or a completeness theorem for protocols with honest majority. In A. Aho (Ed.), *Proceedings of the 19th Annual ACM Symposium on Theory of Computing (STOC)* (pp. 218–229). ACM Press. https://doi.org/10.1145/28395.28420.

Goldreich, O., Micali, S., & Wigderson, A. (1987). How to prove all NP-statements in zero-knowledge, and a methodology of cryptographic protocol design. In A. M. Odlyzko (Ed.), *Advances in Cryptology – CRYPTO'86* (Vol. 263, pp. 171–185). Springer. https://doi.org/10.1007/3-540-47721-7_11.

Gordon, S. D., Le, P. H., & McVicker, D. (2022). *Linear communication in malicious majority MPC*. Cryptology ePrint Archive, Report 2022/781. https://eprint.iacr.org/2022/781.

Goyal, V., Jain, A., Jin, Z., & Malavolta, G. (2020). Statistical zaps and new oblivious transfer protocols. In A. Canteaut & Y. Ishai (Eds.), *Advances in Cryptology – EUROCRYPT 2020, Part III* (Vol. 12107, pp. 668–699). Springer. https://doi.org/10.1007/978-3-030-45727-3_23.

Green, M., & Hohenberger, S. (2008). Universally composable adaptive oblivious transfer. In J. Pieprzyk (Ed.), *Advances in Cryptology – ASIACRYPT 2008* (Vol. 5350, pp. 179–197). Springer. https://doi.org/10.1007/978-3-540-89255-7_12.

Green, M., & Hohenberger, S. (2011). Practical adaptive oblivious transfer from simple assumptions. In Y. Ishai (Ed.), *Theory of Cryptography – TCC 2011* (Vol. 6597, pp. 347–363). Springer. https://doi.org/10.1007/978-3-642-19571-6_21.

Grilo, A. B., Lin, H., Song, F., & Vaikuntanathan, V. (2021). Oblivious transfer is in MiniQCrypt. In A. Canteaut & F.-X. Standaert (Eds.), *Advances in Cryptology – EUROCRYPT 2021, Part II* (Vol. 12697, pp. 531–561). Springer. https://doi.org/10.1007/978-3-030-77886-6_18.

Haitner, I. (2004). Implementing oblivious transfer using collection of dense trapdoor permutations. In M. Naor (Ed.), *Theory of Cryptography – TCC 2004* (Vol. 2951, pp. 394–409). Springer. https://doi.org/10.1007/978-3-540-24638-1_22.

Haitner, I. (2008). Semi-honest to malicious oblivious transfer – the black-box way. In R. Canetti (Ed.), *Theory of Cryptography – TCC 2008* (Vol. 4948, pp. 412–426). Springer. https://doi.org/10.1007/978-3-540-78524-8_23.

Hong, D., Chang, K.-Y., & Ryu, H. (2002). Efficient oblivious transfer in the bounded-storage model. In Y. Zheng (Ed.), *Advances in Cryptology – ASIACRYPT 2002* (Vol. 2501, pp. 143–159). Springer. https://doi.org/10.1007/3-540-36178-2_9.

Impagliazzo, R., & Rudich, S. (1989). Limits on the provable consequences of one-way permutations. In *Proceedings of the 21st Annual ACM Symposium on Theory of Computing (STOC)* (pp. 44–61). ACM Press. https://doi.org/10.1145/73007.73012.

Ishai, Y., Kilian, J., Nissim, K., & Petrank, E. (2003). Extending oblivious transfers efficiently. In D. Boneh (Ed.), *Advances in Cryptology – CRYPTO 2003* (Vol. 2729, pp. 145–161). Springer. https://doi.org/10.1007/978-3-540-45146-4_9.

Ishai, Y., Kushilevitz, E., Ostrovsky, R., Prabhakaran, M., Sahai, A., & Wullschleger, J. (2011). Constant-rate oblivious transfer from noisy channels. In P. Rogaway (Ed.), *Advances in Cryptology – CRYPTO 2011* (Vol. 6841, pp. 667–684). Springer. https://doi.org/10.1007/978-3-642-22792-9_38.

Ishai, Y., Prabhakaran, M., & Sahai, A. (2008). Founding cryptography on oblivious transfer – efficiently. In D. Wagner (Ed.), *Advances in Cryptology – CRYPTO 2008* (Vol. 5157, pp. 572–591). Springer. https://doi.org/10.1007/978-3-540-85174-5_32.

Kalai, Y. T. (2005). Smooth projective hashing and two-message oblivious transfer. In R. Cramer (Ed.), *Advances in Cryptology – EUROCRYPT 2005* (Vol. 3494, pp. 78–95). Springer. https://doi.org/10.1007/11426639_5.

Keller, M., Orsini, E., & Scholl, P. (2015). Actively secure OT extension with optimal overhead. In R. Gennaro & M. J. B. Robshaw (Eds.), *Advances in Cryptology – CRYPTO 2015, Part I* (Vol. 9215, pp. 724–741). Springer. https://doi.org/10.1007/978-3-662-47989-6_35.

Keller, M., Pastro, V., & Rotaru, D. (2018). Overdrive: Making SPDZ great again. In J. B. Nielsen & V. Rijmen (Eds.), *Advances in Cryptology – EUROCRYPT 2018, Part III* (Vol. 10822, pp. 158–189). Springer. https://doi.org/10.1007/978-3-319-78372-7_6.

Kilian, J. (1988). Founding cryptography on oblivious transfer. In *Proceedings of the 20th Annual ACM Symposium on Theory of Computing (STOC)* (pp. 20–31). ACM Press. https://doi.org/10.1145/62212.62215.

Kolesnikov, V., & Kumaresan, R. (2013). Improved OT extension for transferring short secrets. In R. Canetti & J. A. Garay (Eds.), *Advances in Cryptology – CRYPTO 2013, Part II* (Vol. 8043, pp. 54–70). Springer. https://doi.org/10.1007/978-3-642-40084-1_4.

Kreuter, B., shelat, a., & Shen, C.-H. (2012). Billion-gate secure computation with malicious adversaries. In T. Kohno (Ed.), *Proceedings of the 21st USENIX Security Symposium* (pp. 285–300). USENIX Association. https://www.usenix.org/conference/usenixsecurity12/technical-sessions/presentation/kreuter

Kurosawa, K., & Nojima, R. (2009). Simple adaptive oblivious transfer without random oracle. In M. Matsui (Ed.), *Advances in Cryptology – ASIACRYPT 2009* (Vol. 5912, pp. 334–346). Springer. https://doi.org/10.1007/978-3-642-10366-7_20.

Lai, Y.-F., Galbraith, S. D., & Delpech de Saint Guilhem, C. (2021). Compact, efficient and UC-secure isogeny-based oblivious transfer. In A. Canteaut & F.-X. Standaert (Eds.), *Advances in*

Cryptology – EUROCRYPT 2021, Part I (Vol. 12696, pp. 213–241). Springer.https://doi.org/10. 1007/978-3-030-77870-5_8.

Lindell, Y., & Zarosim, H. (2009). Adaptive zero-knowledge proofs and adaptively secure oblivious transfer. In O. Reingold (Ed.), *Theory of Cryptography – TCC 2009* (Vol. 5444, pp. 183–201). Springer. https://doi.org/10.1007/978-3-642-00457-5_12.

Lindell, Y., & Zarosim, H. (2013). On the feasibility of extending oblivious transfer. In A. Sahai (Ed.), *Theory of Cryptography – TCC 2013* (Vol. 7785, pp. 519–538). Springer. https://doi.org/ 10.1007/978-3-642-36594-2_29.

Lipmaa, H. (2005). An oblivious transfer protocol with log-squared communication. In J. Zhou, J. Lopez, R. H. Deng, & F. Bao (Eds.), *Information Security - ISC 2005* (Vol. 3650, pp. 314–328). Springer. https://doi.org/10.1007/11556992_23.

Masny, D., & Rindal, P. (2019). Endemic oblivious transfer. In L. Cavallaro, J. Kinder, X. Wang, & J. Katz (Eds.), *Proceedings of the 2019 ACM SIGSAC Conference on Computer and Communications Security (CCS)* (pp. 309–326). ACM Press. https://doi.org/10.1145/3319535.3354210.

McQuoid, I., Rosulek, M., & Roy, L. (2021). Batching base oblivious transfers. In M. Tibouchi & H. Wang (Eds.), *Advances in Cryptology – ASIACRYPT 2021, Part III* (Vol. 13092, pp. 281–310). Springer. https://doi.org/10.1007/978-3-030-92078-4_10.

Micali, S., & Rogaway, P. (1992). Secure computation (abstract). In J. Feigenbaum (Ed.), *Advances in Cryptology – CRYPTO'91* (Vol. 576, pp. 392–404). Springer. https://doi.org/10.1007/3-540-46766-1_32.

Micciancio, D., & Sorrell, J. (2020). Simpler statistically sender private oblivious transfer from ideals of cyclotomic integers. In S. Moriai & H. Wang (Eds.), *Advances in Cryptology – ASIACRYPT 2020, Part II* (Vol. 12492, pp. 381–407). Springer.https://doi.org/10.1007/978-3-030-64834-3_13.

Naor, M., & Pinkas, B. (1999). Oblivious transfer and polynomial evaluation. In *Proceedings of the 31st Annual ACM Symposium on Theory of Computing (STOC)* (pp. 245–254). ACM Press. https://doi.org/10.1145/301250.301312.

Naor, M., & Pinkas, B. (1999). Oblivious transfer with adaptive queries. In M. J. Wiener (Ed.), *Advances in Cryptology – CRYPTO'99* (Vol. 1666, pp. 573–590). Springer. https://doi.org/10. 1007/3-540-48405-1_36.

Naor, M., & Pinkas, B. (2001). Efficient oblivious transfer protocols. In S. R. Kosaraju (Ed.), *Proceedings of the 12th Annual ACM-SIAM Symposium on Discrete Algorithms (SODA)* (pp. 448–457). ACM-SIAM.

Naor, M., & Yung, M. (1989). Universal one-way hash functions and their cryptographic applications. In *Proceedings of the 21st Annual ACM Symposium on Theory of Computing (STOC)* (pp. 33–43). ACM Press. https://doi.org/10.1145/73007.73011.

Orrù, M., Orsini, E., & Scholl, P. (2017). Actively secure 1-out-of-N OT extension with application to private set intersection. In H. Handschuh (Ed.), *Topics in Cryptology – CT-RSA 2017* (Vol. 10159, pp. 381–396). Springer. https://doi.org/10.1007/978-3-319-52153-4_22.

Paillier, P. (1999). Public-key cryptosystems based on composite degree residuosity classes. In J. Stern (Ed.), *Advances in Cryptology – EUROCRYPT'99* (Vol. 1592, pp. 223–238). Springer. https://doi.org/10.1007/3-540-48910-X_16.

Patra, A., Sarkar, P., & Suresh, A. (2017). Fast actively secure OT extension for short secrets. In *Proceedings of the 2017 Network and Distributed System Security Symposium (NDSS)*. The Internet Society. https://doi.org/10.14722/ndss.2017.23089.

Peikert, C., Vaikuntanathan, V., & Waters, B. (2008). A framework for efficient and composable oblivious transfer. In D. Wagner (Ed.), *Advances in Cryptology – CRYPTO 2008* (Vol. 5157, pp. 554–571). Springer. https://doi.org/10.1007/978-3-540-85174-5_31.

Rabin, M. (1981). *How to exchange secrets with oblivious transfer (Technical Report TR-81)*. Aiken Computation Lab: Harvard University.

Regev, O. (2005). On lattices, learning with errors, random linear codes, and cryptography. In H. N. Gabow & R. Fagin (Eds.), *Proceedings of the 37th Annual ACM Symposium on Theory of Computing (STOC)* (pp. 84–93). ACM Press. https://doi.org/10.1145/1060590.1060603.

Rivest, R. L., Shamir, A., & Adleman, L. M. (1978). A method for obtaining digital signatures and public-key cryptosystems. *Communications of the Association for Computing Machinery, 21*(2), 120–126. https://doi.org/10.1145/359340.359342

Rompel, J. (1990). One-way functions are necessary and sufficient for secure signatures. In *Proceedings of the 22nd Annual ACM Symposium on Theory of Computing (STOC)* (pp. 387–394). ACM Press. https://doi.org/10.1145/100216.100269.

Wang, X., Ranellucci, S., & Katz, J. (2017). Authenticated garbling and efficient maliciously secure two-party computation. In B. M. Thuraisingham, D. Evans, T. Malkin, & D. Xu (Eds.), *Proceedings of the 2017 ACM SIGSAC Conference on Computer and Communications Security (CCS)* (pp. 21–37). ACM Press. https://doi.org/10.1145/3133956.3134053.

Wiesner, S. (1983). Conjugate coding. *ACM SIGACT News, 15*(1), 78–88.

Wullschleger, J. (2009). Oblivious transfer from weak noisy channels. In O. Reingold (Ed.), *Theory of Cryptography – TCC 2009* (Vol. 5444, pp. 332–349). Springer. https://doi.org/10.1007/978-3-642-00457-5_20.

Yao, A. C.-C. (1982). Protocols for secure computations (extended abstract). In *23rd Annual Symposium on Foundations of Computer Science (FOCS)* (pp. 160–164). IEEE Computer Society Press. https://doi.org/10.1109/SFCS.1982.38.

Chapter 3
Silent Secure Computation

In this chapter, we provide a step-by-step introduction to the notion of silent secure computation, a recent development in secure computation that aims to significantly mitigate its communication overhead. As the previous chapter made clear, or so we hope, secure computation *a la GMW* in the preprocessing model is one of the most promising paths toward truly efficient MPC protocols. With the combination of IKNP-style OT extensions and preprocessing of the OTs, it exhibits sufficient performances, from a computational point of view, in many real-world applications (including allowing our two lovebirds, Alice and Bob, to discover whether there is a mutual romantic interest—but also including, say, securely running statistical analyses on the joint private data of the patients of several hospitals to evaluate the efficiency of a new medication without compromising the patient's privacy). However, its *communication overhead*—a few hundred bits per AND gate—is prohibitive for most applications, especially in a WAN setting.

The results and techniques that we will introduce in this chapter form the foundations of the *silent preprocessing model* of secure computation. In this model, the entire preprocessing phase boils down to a short interactive phase, with little communication and computation, followed solely by local computations. In the same way that OT extension confines all expensive operations to a one-time generation of a small number of base OTs, silent preprocessing confines the entire *communication* of the preprocessing phase to a one-time small interaction.

Historical notes. The usefulness of silent preprocessing—that is, of methodologies to securely generate correlated pseudorandomness with fewer resources than would be required for securely generating correlated randomness—was first envisioned in Beaver (1996), a work that we discussed earlier in Sect. 2.5.3. However, this visionary work fell short of providing a significant amount of communication savings: its main appeal lies in the use of symmetric-key primitives (namely, a pseudorandom generator) instead of the more expensive public-key primitives required for OT.

G. Couteau, *An Introduction to Silent Secure Computation*,
SpringerBriefs in Information Security and Cryptography,
https://doi.org/10.1007/978-3-032-07089-0_3

The roots of the silent preprocessing model date back to the seminal work of Gilboa and Ishai (1999), where a methodology for compressing linear correlations in the multi-party setting was described. While this original result already enjoys several non-trivial applications to secure computation, general MPC typically requires degree-2 correlations (OT or OLE), or even degree-3 correlations (authenticated Beaver triples, when targeting malicious security). The notion of silent secure computation, as we consider in this book, was originally introduced (under the name of *cryptographic capsules*) by Boyle et al. (2017). The first concretely efficient silent preprocessing protocols, for a specific correlation, were achieved a year later in a work of Boyle et al. (2018). The real breakthrough, achieving concretely efficient silent preprocessing for precomputing oblivious transfers, came in a follow-up work by Boyle et al. (2019) that the same authors further optimized the same year (Boyle, 2019). Concurrently, at the same conference, Schoppmann et al. (2019) also described an improved silent preprocessing protocol for OT correlations, coming up with a subset of the same ideas together with some orthogonal improvements.

A year later, Boyle, Couteau, Gilboa, and Ishai generalized silent preprocessing to the OLE correlation over large fields (Boyle et al., 2020a) and introduced the notion of pseudorandom correlation function (PCF) as a means to achieve *unbounded, on-demand* silent preprocessing (Boyle et al., 2020b). In 2021, Couteau et al. (2021) showed how the use of new and heuristic assumptions could yield considerable efficiency improvements to silent secure computation, and devised a general methodology to identify safe instantiations. While their original heuristic construction was eventually found to be flawed in a follow-up work of Raghuraman et al. (2023), it paved the way to faster protocols from sound assumptions. Boyle et al. (2022) introduced precisely such a protocol, under a new but plausible hardness assumption. In the same work, the authors also described an improved PCF, significantly faster than the original design of Boyle et al. (2020b). The work of Raghuraman et al. (2023) further improved the approach of Boyle et al. (2022) to build a silent preprocessing protocol that remains the fastest to date. Their construction does however not allow building a PCF.

In parallel to these works, an influential line of work initiated in the work of Yang et al. (2020) introduces a method for low-communication generation of correlated pseudorandomness that does not follow the silent preprocessing paradigm (in that it requires interaction during the generation of correlated randomness) but nevertheless borrows much of the tools introduced in this context and leverages a small amount of interaction and communication to achieve high performances. Weng, Yang, Katz, and Wang further refined this approach in Weng et al. (2021), notably devising efficient strategies to achieve security against malicious adversaries. The original work of Boyle et al. (2018) had already outlined how these techniques could be used to obtain efficient zero-knowledge proof systems, and the work of Weng et al. (2021) provided a highly optimized instantiation of this template that initiated the active and flourishing field of VOLE-based zero knowledge. This area, which was born out of the silent preprocessing model and the tools introduced in this context, has rapidly made its way into real-world applications (including commercial products). However, covering recent developments in this fast-moving area would go beyond the purpose of this book. We will therefore restrain ourselves to mentioning a few noteworthy developments in the area (Dittmer et al., 2021; Yang et al., 2021; Baum et al., 2022) that the interested reader is invited to check. For a general introduction to the field, we recommend the survey of Baum et al. (2023).

Recent years have witnessed numerous developments in the silent preprocessing model. Silent preprocessing protocols for the OLE correlation over large fields were shown in the work of Boyle et al. (2020a), but the important case of small fields (and, in particular, that of the Boolean field $\mathbb{F}_2$) remained out of reach for some time. Bombar et al. (2023) came very close to a full solution, obtaining a protocol for OLE correlations over all fields $\mathbb{F}_q$ with $q > 2$, only falling short of handling the important case of $\mathbb{F}_2$. In a follow-up work, the same authors, together with Bui and Servan-Schreiber (2024), showed how to circumvent this limitation by relying on OLEs over $\mathbb{F}_4$ together with a minimal amount of additional communication, and introduced numerous optimizations. Silent protocols for OLEs over $\mathbb{F}_2$ were eventually described in Li et al. (2025), building upon the assumption and framework introduced in Bombar et al. (2023). In parallel, a significant cryptanalytic effort has been devoted to understanding the security of some of the new assumptions introduced in these works, sometimes triggering adjustment of the parameters deemed secure (Liu et al., 2024; Briaud and Øygarden, 2023; Bouillaguet et al., 2025).

Eventually, another line of work has been exploring the design of advanced PCFs using a different framework—in particular, without relying on coding-theoretic assumptions. This line of work was initiated in the work of Orlandi et al. (2021) that introduced a PCF from factoring-related assumptions. A few years later, advanced PCF variants (precomputable PCFs and public-key PCFs) were introduced by Couteau et al. (2023), by the same set of authors together with Bui (2024), and by Couteau et al. (2024). In this book, we will confine ourself to briefly mentioning these notions, the associated challenges, and why they matter for silent secure computation, but we will not provide an extensive treatment of this recent evolution.

3.1 Introduction

The main conceptual message of Chap. 2 is that the task of designing efficient protocols for securely computing a function reduces to the problem of securely and efficiently distributing long correlated random strings among the parties, where the type of correlation is tied to the target functionality and security guarantees. We have seen that for *random oblivious transfers*, using OT extension allows generating an arbitrary amount of correlation with an amortized computational cost of three hash evaluations per OT, and a few hundred bits of communication per OT. Since even simple functions can require a huge number of OTs, the amount of communication forms the core bottleneck of this protocol—computation-wise, it is remarkably efficient.[1] However, the large communication is a big hurdle that severely limits the practicality of these methods.

For Beaver triples, the situation is even less satisfying: one has to choose between a fast protocol using IKNP-style OT extension, at the cost of the (often prohibitive) $\Omega(N^2 \log |\mathbb{F}|)$ of these approaches, or give up on OT extension techniques altogether and use much slower solutions (using public-key cryptography instead of symmetric cryptography) based on additively homomorphic encryption.

3.2   Secure Computation with Silent Preprocessing from PCGs

So far, we have seen that secure computation with preprocessing proceeds in two phases:

1. In the preprocessing phase, the parties generate correlated randomness (e.g., random OTs, Beaver triples, OLEs...), using a protocol of their choice (typically from oblivious transfer or homomorphic encryption).
2. In the online phase, the parties *consume* this correlated randomness using an appropriate protocol, e.g., GMW.

The communication of the preprocessing phase dominates the total communication by a large factor: even in the two-party setting for semi-honest secure computation of Boolean circuits using GMW, one needs a few hundred bits per AND gate of the circuit in the preprocessing phase, and only 3 bits per AND gate in the online phase, using Beaver's protocol (Sect. 2.6.2). For more parties, over arithmetic circuits, or in the malicious setting, the gap grows further.

3.2.1   The Core Insight: Pseudorandomness is Enough

Secure computation with preprocessing pays a huge communication cost to distributively generate long, *truly random* correlated strings. Below, in a big, thick, red box, we outline the core insight at the heart of the new approach we are going to describe. If you take one message from this chapter:

---

[1] In fact, it is possible to instantiate the hash function using a simple tweak on the AES block cipher, which is the universally used standard cipher. Because it is so ubiquitously used, a set of hardware instructions for AES, the AES-NI instruction set, has even been included on recent Intel processors. When using hardware instructions to implement calls to AES, the efficiency becomes incredible—about 1.3 clock cycles on a single processor to encrypt a Byte of data. On such processors, OT extension is insanely fast.

> The long correlated random strings do not have to
> be truly random: they only have to *look* random

Here, by *look random*, we mean the following: it should be infeasible, from the viewpoint of the participants (modeled as polynomial-time algorithms), to distinguish the strings received by the other participants from truly random strings (correlated in the right way with their string). The cryptographic terminology to denote this type of "random-lookingness" is *pseudorandomness*.

3.2.1.1 Pseudorandom Generators

To make it a bit more concrete, let us look at the definition of a pseudorandom generator:

Definition 3.2.1 A pseudorandom generator (*PRG*) is a polynomial-time algorithm $G : \{0, 1\}^\lambda \mapsto \{0, 1\}^m$, with $m \gg \lambda$, such that for any polynomial-time distinguisher $\mathcal{A}$, it holds that

$$|\Pr[\mathcal{A}(y) = 0 \mid x \xleftarrow{s} \{0, 1\}^\lambda, y \leftarrow G(x)] - \Pr[\mathcal{A}(y) = 0 \mid y \xleftarrow{s} \{0, 1\}^m]| \le \mu(\lambda),$$

where μ is a negligible function.

A negligible function is any function that converges toward 0 faster than any inverse polynomial (e.g., $1/2^\lambda$, $\lambda^{-\log \lambda}$...). Concretely, when the probabilities of two events are negligibly close (their absolute difference is a negligible function), this corresponds to saying that the events cannot be distinguished by any polynomial-time adversary. Hence, the above says that no polynomial-time algorithm $\mathcal{A}$ can behave differently (output something different—i.e., notice a difference) in the two following scenarios:

1. it receives the value $y = G(x)$ on a uniformly random *short* input $x \xleftarrow{s} \{0, 1\}^\lambda$ or
2. it receives a uniformly random *long* value $y \xleftarrow{s} \{0, 1\}^m$.

Note that since x is n-bit long, $y = G(x)$ cannot have more than $\lambda \ll m$ bits of entropy: thus, y is the first scenario which is very far from random (it was deterministically computed from a short input), yet all polytime algorithms will still fail to distinguish them from uniformly random inputs.

3.2.1.2 From One-Time Pads to Stream Ciphers

Let us take a short break from secure computation and have a quick look at the easier (and more well-known) task of *secure communication*: Alice wants to transmit a message $M \in \{0, 1\}^m$ to Bob over a public channel while hiding M from a potential eavesdropper. The reader has probably heard of the one-time pad construction of

Vernam: assume Alice and Bob share a pre-established uniformly random key $K \overset{\$}{\leftarrow}$ $\{0, 1\}^m$ of the same length as M. Then Alice can send $C = M \oplus K$ to Bob: this lets Bob retrieve M as $M \leftarrow C \oplus K$, but to any external observer, since K is uniformly distributed, so is C (and, in particular, it carries no information about M). Of course, for long messages, pre-establishing (securely) a uniformly random key K of the same length is impractical. Unfortunately, by a celebrated result of Shannon, this protocol is the best possible: there cannot be any information-theoretically secure protocol using a key K shorter than M.

However, if we do not insist on *information-theoretic* (i.e., perfect) security, but rather are happy to settle for security against polynomial-time adversaries, there is a more efficient variant: Alice and Bob only need to pre-share a *short* random key $k \in \{0, 1\}^\lambda$, and locally construct a "fake long random key" $K = G(k) \in \{0, 1\}^m$ to use in the above protocol. Of course, K is not truly random, but no polytime adversary can distinguish it from random! We leave it to the interested reader—it is a standard exercise—to show that if an adversary could guess with good probability whether, say, M is the all-zero message or the all-one message (assuming M is initially picked to be either of those at random) from the transcript $C = M \oplus G(k)$ of the interaction, then one could use this adversary to construct an algorithm $\mathcal{A}$ contradicting the assumption that G is a pseudorandom generator.

This PRG-based construction of a secure communication protocol is essentially what is known as a *stream cipher*. To put it in perspective with our real target (which is secure computation), one could reformulate the one-time pad as a kind of protocol in the preprocessing model:

1. In the preprocessing phase, the two parties use a protocol to securely generate a long shared key K (this is called a *key exchange* protocol).
2. In the online phase, the parties use the (information-theoretic) one-time pad protocol to exchange M using their shared key K.

Of course, one expects the preprocessing phase of this protocol to dominate the overall cost. But by using a PRG, one gets a much nicer, three-phase protocol:

1. In the preprocessing phase, the two parties use a protocol to securely generate a *short* shared key k.
2. In an offline phase, without any interactions, the parties locally compute the long key $K = G(k)$.
3. In the online phase, the parties use the one-time pad protocol to exchange M using their shared key K.

Observe that, above, the (expensive) preprocessing phase has been replaced by two phases: a much shorter preprocessing phase (to generate a short key k), followed solely by offline computation (that does not require any communication between Alice and Bob).

3.2.1.3   From MPC with Correlated Pseudorandomness
to Pseudorandom Correlation Generators

In one sentence, the goal of the silent preprocessing model is to achieve the same three-phase structure as the protocol above, but for the much harder task of secure computation. In the case of secure communication, the "correlated randomness" is as simple as it gets: Alice and Bob should just receive *the same string*. Hence, any PRG producing random-looking strings suffices. In secure computation, the correlated randomness is not as nice: the participants need to receive distinct, but appropriately correlated random-looking strings (for example, pairs (s_0, s_1) and (b, s_b), respectively, in the case of the random OT correlation).

The notion of pseudorandom correlation generator (PCG), that we will formally introduce later on, aims to achieve just that: a PCG (PCG.Gen, PCG.Expand) yields a way to generate to *distinct, but related* short strings $(k_0, k_1) \leftarrow$ PCG.Gen such that evaluating PCG.Expand(k_0) and PCG.Expand(k_1) yields long, *random-looking but correlated* strings. As we will see, formalizing this notion is not straightforward and requires some care. Building a PCG is an even harder task: it requires a particularly delicate balance to achieve pseudorandomness while preserving some specific correlation—*id est*, to destroy all visible local patterns in the outputs while maintaining a specific global pattern among them.

3.2.2   The Template

Equipped with the above ideas, we put forth the notion of secure computation in the *silent preprocessing model*. Concretely, a protocol in this model has three phases:

1. A one-time short interaction, where the participants generate the short correlated keys output by a pseudorandom correlation generator for their correlation of interest (e.g., random OTs), using a secure protocol to distributively evaluate the Gen algorithm of a PCG.
2. A "silent" computation phase, where the parties go offline and locally expand their short keys into long pseudorandom strings, that are indistinguishable from long random correlated strings, using the PCG.Expand algorithm.
3. A "non-cryptographic" online phase, where the participants use these long correlated strings in the usual way to securely compute the target function, for example, with GMW.[2]

This template is summarized in Fig. 3.1. What remains to do is to formally define pseudorandom correlation generators, in a way that allows us to simultaneously (1)

---

[2] Note, however, that this phase is not information-theoretic anymore, because the correlated randomness used is not truly random, but only pseudorandom. But this is a minor inconvenience; the most important thing is that this phase does not use any heavy cryptographic operations, hence it is highly efficient.

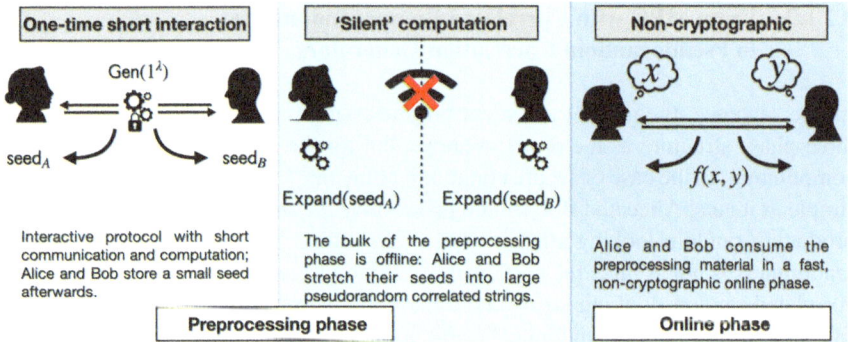

Fig. 3.1 The three steps of an MPC protocol in the silent preprocessing model

get a construction that instantiates this notion (ideally with an efficient construction), and (2) obtain a secure protocol when following the template above with this notion.

3.3 Pseudorandom Correlation Generators: A Definition

We now overview the formal definition of pseudorandom correlation generators. At a high level, a PCG is a pair of algorithms that enables the two steps of the preprocessing phase represented in Fig. 3.1:

- A seed generation algorithm, denoted Gen, outputs two short, correlated seeds. Each party will receive one seed (we use the terms "seed" and "key" interchangeably here).
- An expansion algorithm takes one party's seed and expands it into a long pseudorandom string. When taken together, the two pseudorandom strings should satisfy the prescribed correlation (but appear random beyond that).

This definition abstracts out *how* the participants will run the Gen algorithm (note that one cannot simply let one of the parties run it, because it would reveal to this party the seed of the other party, which would compromise privacy). Looking ahead, Gen will typically be either run by a trusted third party (whose only trusted in generating some short, input-independent correlated seeds) or securely executed through a distributed protocol. The point is that whatever the cost of this distributed protocol, it only depends on Gen's runtime that is *independent* of (or, rather, logarithmic in) the size of the target computation. Then, the expansion procedure is the bulk of the computation (that depends linearly on the amount of correlated randomness to be produced that is proportional to the size of the target function), but it is applied locally: at this stage, the participants do not have to exchange messages, or even to be online.

3.3.1 A Slightly More Formal Overview

More formally, for correctness, we require that the expanded output of a PCG is indistinguishable from truly random correlated strings that are sampled from the ideal correlation. Security, however, turns out to be much harder to formally define. We first explain a failed attempt and then sketch the right definition.

A straightforward (but broken) solution would be the following: a PCG for a target correlation C is secure if for any secure computation protocol Π in the correlated randomness model, the protocol Π' obtained by replacing the (true) correlated random string by short correlated seeds (locally expanded by the parties) is secure. Alas, in the paper where we introduced the notion of PCG (Boyle et al., 2019), we showed that this ideal security requirement would be impossible to meet: one can craft artificial protocols that are secure in the correlated randomness model, yet provably become insecure as soon as the true correlated randomness is replaced by short seeds.[3]

Instead, in Boyle et al. (2019), we introduced a weaker (but achievable) indistinguishability-based security notion. The notion requires that an adversary, given access to one of the short seeds k_σ, cannot distinguish the pseudorandom string $R_{1-\sigma}$ from a pseudorandom string that is chosen at random conditioned on (R_0, R_1) being appropriately correlated (where $R_\sigma = \mathsf{PCG}(k_\sigma)$ is the expansion of the short seed k_σ). In other words, an adversary given access to a short seed cannot learn more about the other party's pseudorandom string than what is obvious given access to its own pseudorandom *output string*. What makes this notion a useful notion for PCGs is that

1. It is achievable: many constructions of PCGs, starting with Boyle et al. (2018, 2019) were provably shown to achieve it (under standard cryptographic assumptions related to decoding problems in suitable linear codes).
2. It can provably replace *securely* the correlated randomness in any protocol Π proven secure in the *corruptible correlated randomness model*, a weakening of the correlated randomness model that, informally, allows the adversary to choose themself what the correlated randomness of the corrupted participants will be (and the correlated randomness of the remaining parties is sampled afterward to be consistent with the choice of the adversary). This model avoids the impossibility result of Boyle et al. (2019).[4] More importantly, essentially all known protocols

---

[3] To give a rough intuition of this impossibility result, the idea is to have a protocol that instructs the participants to reveal all their private inputs if their opponents ever manage to produce a succinct description of their correlated randomness. Since truly random strings cannot be compressed beyond their entropy, this remains secure in the correlated randomness model, but leaks all inputs whenever we use a PCG, since its purpose is exactly to distribute succinct representations of the correlated randomness!

[4] That's because, in the corruptible correlated randomness model, the adversary can freely decide that the corrupted parties will receive strings with a succinct description; therefore, the protocol given as a counter-example in the correlated randomness model cannot be secure in the corruptible correlated randomness model.

ever designed in the correlated randomness model are secure in the corruptible correlated randomness model! This includes, in particular, GMW and its many variants.

Equipped with the above intuition, we now outline the full formal definition of PCGs. The definition comes from Boyle et al. (2019), and builds upon an earlier definition of pseudorandom VOLE generator that we had introduced in Boyle et al. (2018) (retrospectively, a pseudorandom VOLE generator is a PCG for a specific correlation, the vector-OLE correlation that is a variant of the OLE correlation covered in Sect. 2.7.2.2).

3.3.2 Formal Definition of PCGs

To formally define PCGs, we first introduce the concept of a *correlation generator* as a PPT algorithm outputting correlated strings. We will use a correlation generation generator to define an ideal target correlation $(\mathcal{R}_0, \mathcal{R}_1)$. For simplicity, we assume that $(\mathcal{R}_0, \mathcal{R}_1)$ are two bitstrings of the same length n, though in some of the useful instances we will discuss, they are more naturally interpreted as vectors over some finite ring.

Definition 3.3.1 (*Correlation Generator*) A PPT algorithm $\mathcal{C}$ is called a *correlation generator*, if $\mathcal{C}$ on input 1^n outputs a pair of strings in $\{0, 1\}^n \times \{0, 1\}^n$.

Our security definition requires the target correlation to satisfy a technical requirement, which roughly says that it is possible to efficiently sample from the conditional distribution of $\mathcal{R}_0$ given $\mathcal{R}_1 = r_1$ and vice versa.

Definition 3.3.2 (*Reverse-sampleable Correlation Generator*) Let $\mathcal{C}$ be a correlation generator. We say $\mathcal{C}$ is *reverse-sampleable* if there exists a PPT algorithm RSample such that for $\sigma \in \{0, 1\}$ the correlation obtained via

$$\{(\mathcal{R}'_0, \mathcal{R}'_1) \,|\, (\mathcal{R}_0, \mathcal{R}_1) \xleftarrow{s} \mathcal{C}(1^n), \mathcal{R}'_\sigma := \mathcal{R}_\sigma, \mathcal{R}'_{1-\sigma} \xleftarrow{s} \mathsf{RSample}(\sigma, \mathcal{R}_\sigma)\}$$

is computationally indistinguishable from $\mathcal{C}(1^n)$.

To illustrate the above notion, observe that the random OT correlation is reverse-sampleable: consider a random OT correlation, defined as a pair $((s_0, s_1), (b, s_b))$, where $s_0, s_1, b \xleftarrow{s} \{0, 1\}$. The reverse sampling algorithm $\mathsf{RSample}(\sigma, y_\sigma)$ works as follows: if $\sigma = 0$, parse y_σ as $y_\sigma = (s_0, s_1)$, sample $b \xleftarrow{s} \{0, 1\}$, and output (b, s_b); otherwise (i.e. if $\sigma = 1$) parse y_σ as $y_\sigma = (b, s)$, sample $s' \xleftarrow{s} \{0, 1\}$, and output $((1 - b) \cdot s + b \cdot s', b \cdot s + (1 - b) \cdot s')$. This immediately generalizes to the reverse-sampleability of the n-fold random OT correlation, where the parties receive n pairs of random OT correlations.

The following definition of *pseudorandom correlation generators* generalizes an earlier definition of pseudorandom VOLE generator in Boyle et al. (2018).

Definition 3.3.3 (*Pseudorandom Correlation Generator (PCG)* (Boyle et al., 2019))
Let $n = n(\lambda) \in \text{poly}(\lambda)$ be a polynomial, and let $\mathcal{C}$ be a reverse-sampleable correlation generator. A *PCG for* $\mathcal{C}$ is a pair of algorithms (PCG.Gen, PCG.Expand) with the following syntax:

- PCG.Gen(1^λ) is a PPT algorithm that given a security parameter λ outputs a pair of seeds (k_0, k_1);
- PCG.Expand(σ, k_σ) is a polynomial-time algorithm that given party index $\sigma \in \{0, 1\}$ and a seed k_σ outputs a bitstring $\mathcal{R}_\sigma \in \{0, 1\}^n$.

The algorithms (PCG.Gen, PCG.Expand) should satisfy the following:

- **Pseudorandomness.** The correlation obtained via

$$\{(\mathcal{R}_0, \mathcal{R}_1) \mid (k_0, k_1) \xleftarrow{s} \text{PCG.Gen}(1^\lambda), (\mathcal{R}_\sigma \leftarrow \text{PCG.Expand}(\sigma, k_\sigma))_{\sigma=0,1}\}$$

is computationally indistinguishable from $\mathcal{C}(1^n)$.
- **Security.** For any $\sigma \in \{0, 1\}$, the following two distributions are computationally indistinguishable:

$$\{(k_{1-\sigma}, \mathcal{R}_\sigma) \mid (k_0, k_1) \xleftarrow{s} \text{PCG.Gen}(1^\lambda), \mathcal{R}_\sigma \leftarrow \text{PCG.Expand}(\sigma, k_\sigma)\} \text{ and}$$

$$\{(k_{1-\sigma}, \mathcal{R}_\sigma) \mid (k_0, k_1) \xleftarrow{s} \text{PCG.Gen}(1^\lambda), \mathcal{R}_{1-\sigma} \leftarrow \text{PCG.Expand}(\sigma, k_{1-\sigma}),$$
$$\mathcal{R}_\sigma \xleftarrow{s} \text{RSample}(\sigma, \mathcal{R}_{1-\sigma})\}$$

where RSample is the reverse sampling algorithm for correlation $\mathcal{C}$.

In words, security in Definition 3.3.3 means that from the view point of party 0 holding a key k_0, the string $\mathcal{R}_1$ obtained by the other party is indistinguishable from a uniformly random string reverse-sampled from $\mathcal{R}_1 \leftarrow \text{PCG.Expand}(0, k_0)$, i.e., a string sampled uniformly at random conditioned on satisfying the target correlation with $\mathcal{R}_0$ (and a similar security condition holds in the other direction).

Note that the above definition is trivial to achieve in general: We can let PCG.Gen on input 1^λ return $(R_0, R_1) \leftarrow \mathcal{C}(1^{n(\lambda)})$, and simply define Expand to be the identity. Typically, we will be interested in non-trivial constructions of PCGs, in which PCG.Expand stretches a short seed to a long output. As a simple example, a standard pseudorandom generator $G : \{0, 1\}^\lambda \rightarrow \{0, 1\}^{n(\lambda)}$ naturally defines the following PCG for the target correlation $\mathcal{C}(1^n) = (r, r)$, where $r \xleftarrow{s} \{0, 1\}^{n(\lambda)}$: PCG.Gen output a pair of identical random seeds and PCG.Expand applies G locally on each seed. In the following, we will consider more involved constructions of PCGs for useful target correlations where neither of the outputs determines the other. These include Oblivious Transfer (OT) correlations, Oblivious Linear Evaluation (OLE) correlations, and (authenticated) multiplication triples.

3.3.3 Historical Notes

The notion of pseudorandom correlation generators has its roots in the work of
Beaver (1996), where the potential of the notion was first envisioned, but could not
be realized without an amount of communication scaling with the target number
of correlations. The first design of a PCG (beyond the simple equality correlation)
dates back to Gilboa and Ishai's work Gilboa and Isha (1999), who gave an efficient
multi-party PCG for any *linear* additive correlations, where a linear correlation refers
to a correlation where the strings $(\mathcal{R}_1, \ldots, \mathcal{R}_N)$ received by the parties are in the
kernel of a linear function L: $L(\mathcal{R}_1, \ldots, \mathcal{R}_N) - 0$ (for example, this is the case of
the equality correlation, where two parties receive $\mathcal{R}_0 - \mathcal{R}_1$, since $\mathcal{R}_0 - \mathcal{R}_1 = 0$).

Linear correlations enjoy various applications but are not sufficient for the application to silent secure computation, where the target correlations (random OTs, OLEs,
Beaver triples...) are all at least degree-2 polynomials. What we mean there is that
the strings $(\mathcal{R}_0, \mathcal{R}_1)$ output by the correlation generator $\mathcal{C}$ can be parsed as vectors
over a field $\mathbb{F}$ satisfying $P(\mathcal{R}_0, \mathcal{R}_1) = 0$ over $\mathbb{F}$, where P is a (vector of multivariate)
degree-2 polynomial(s). For example, if $\mathcal{C}$ generates n copies of an OLE correlation,
one party gets n pairs $(u_i, v_i) \in \mathbb{F}^2$ and the other party gets $(x_i, w_i) \in \mathbb{F}_2$, which are
zeroes of $P(\vec{u}, \vec{v}, \vec{x}, \vec{w}) = \vec{w} - (\vec{u} \odot \vec{x} + \vec{v})$, where $\odot$ denotes the component-wise
product.

The first PCG for a degree-2 correlation was achieved in Boyle et al. (2018), albeit
still for a correlation that does not suffice for general circuits (but rather for circuits
with high fan-in multiplications). The work also introduced a security notion for
their pseudorandom correlation generator, which later formed the basis of the general
definition we presented in this section. Eventually, the first "full-fledged" PCG for a
secure-computation-complete correlation, the OT correlation, was presented in Boyle
et al. (2019), together with a formal definition of the general notion, and the proof that
it suffices to instantiate the silent preprocessing framework for any protocol proven
secure in the corruptible correlated randomness model.

3.4 Pseudorandom Correlation Generators: A Template

The purpose of this section is to outline a general template for building pseudorandom correlation generators. This template emerged progressively and was refined
throughout many of the author's works (Boyle et al., 2017, 2018, 2019; Boyle,
2019; Boyle et al., 2020a, b; Couteau et al., 2021; Boyle et al., 2022; Bombar et al.,
2023) and captures all known efficient constructions of PCGs for concrete correlations of interest to date. We will attempt to provide a step-by-step, intuitive exposition
of how one arrives at this template, and formally introduces along the way the necessary building blocks. For the sake of concreteness, we will focus in this overview
on the notion of two-party additive correlation:

Definition 3.4.1 A two-party additive correlation of length m is a correlation with the following structure: the two parties receive uniformly random additive *shares* of $C(r_i)$ for $i = 1$ to m, where C is a public function defining the correlation, and $(r_1, \ldots, r_m)$ are uniformly random inputs.

For example, Beaver triples are an additive correlation, where the function C is given by $C : (a, b) \to (a, b, a \cdot b)$. Random OTs and OLEs are not immediately additive correlations (they are isomorphic to random shares of random products $a \cdot b$ over some field, where a and b are given to the two players instead of being shared between them), but they are in a sense simpler (because part of the correlation is given to the parties instead of being shared between them), and PCGs for these correlations will follow a similar template.

The purpose of a PCG for an additive correlation C is to generate two short keys (k_0, k_1) which, once expanded, yield pseudorandom shares of $(C(r_1), \ldots, C(r_m))$, where $(r_1, \ldots, r_m)$ itself is a pseudorandom string. Notice how pseudorandomness appears in two places: internally, to generate $(r_i)_{i \leq m}$, and externally, to yield pseudorandom shares of the evaluation of C on $r_1 \cdots r_m$. Looking ahead, the template combines two distinct ingredients for each notion of pseudorandomness, which we now outline.

3.4.1 PCGs from Shares of a Function

Fix for now a pseudorandom generator G that will be made explicit later on. At a high level, G will be a suitable PRG that generates $(r_1, \ldots, r_m)$ from a short seed k. What we mean by "suitable" depends heavily on how we instantiate the external component. We first cover this external component: a method to distribute the shares of $(C(r_1), \ldots, C(r_m))$ from short keys. With a slight abuse of notation, we will write $G_k(i)$ to denote the function that has k hardcoded in its description, and that returns on input i the i-th component of the output $G(k)$. This is equivalent to viewing $G(k)$ as the *truth table* of the function $G_k : i \to G_k(i) = G(k)_i$.

The template will rely on a method to distribute short keys (k_0, k_1) to the parties that encode the secret function

$$F_k = C \circ G_k.$$

This encoding will be a pair of functions (Gen, Eval), where Gen generates the short keys (k_0, k_1) encoding the secret function F_k, and Eval is an evaluation algorithm that outputs a string y_σ given an input i and a key k_σ for $\sigma \in \{0, 1\}$. We will want this encoding to satisfy three fundamental properties:

- It has to be *succinct*: the size of the keys given by the parties should be not much larger than the description length of $F_k = C \circ G_k$ (which is essentially the length of k, since C and G are already public information).
- It has to be *private*: given its part k_σ of the encoding, the party P_σ should not be able to infer anything about the secret input k.

- It has to *preserve evaluation*: given their respective keys, the parties should be able to compute additive shares of the evaluation of $C \circ G_k$ on any input i. That is, for any i, it must hold that $\mathsf{Eval}(\mathsf{k}_0, i) + \mathsf{Eval}(\mathsf{k}_1, i) = F_k(i) = (C \circ G)(k)_i = C(r_i)$.

Note that any two of the above requirements are easy to satisfy via trivial construction: one gets privacy and evaluation preservation by distributing shares of the entire truth table of the function (hence Eval simply requires a lookup to the table share), but this does not satisfy succinctness. Defining the encodings to be simply k yields succinctness while preserving evaluation (the parties can compute $C \circ G_k$ in the clear), but breaks security. Of course, satisfying succinctness and privacy without preserving evaluation is also trivial (just define the keys to be the empty string). The definition becomes, however, non-trivial as soon as one insists on achieving all three properties at once.

It is not too hard to see that if we find an encoding of $C \circ G_k$ that satisfies the three properties above, we are done: $\mathsf{PCG.Gen}$ will simply sample a random key k and output the encoding $(\mathsf{k}_0, \mathsf{k}_1)$ of the function $F_k = C \circ G_k$. Then, $\mathsf{PCG.Expand}(\sigma, \mathsf{k}_\sigma)$ computes and returns $\mathsf{Eval}(\mathsf{k}_\sigma, i)$ for $i = 1$ to m. Because the encoding is evaluation preserving, the outputs of $\mathsf{PCG.Expand}$ form additive shares of $((C \circ G)(k)_1, \ldots, (C \circ G)(k)_m) = (C(r_1), \cdots C(r_m))$. Security follows from the privacy of the encoding, and non-triviality from the succinctness. This was for the intuition—now, let's make this more formal.

3.4.2 Function Secret Sharing

The above way of encoding a secret function $C \circ G_k$ is called function secret sharing. In full generality, an N-party FSS scheme splits a *function* $f : \{0, 1\}^\ell \to \mathbb{G}$ from a function class $\mathcal{F}$ into N additive shares $f_i : \{0, 1\}^\ell \to \mathbb{G}$, each represented by a key k_i, where every strict subset of the keys k_i hides f. The correctness requirement is that the N functions f_i represented by the keys add up to f. Namely, there is a function Eval (defining the function f_i represented by k_i), such that for every $x \in \{0, 1\}^\ell$ we have $f(x) = \sum_i \mathsf{Eval}(k_i, x)$. The challenge is to design efficient FSS schemes in which the key size grows polynomially with the input length ℓ. The short keys k_i can be viewed as *compressed* additive shares of the truth table of f. This is only possible for classes $\mathcal{F}$ of *structured* functions f that have a short (polynomial-size) description, and inevitably require one to settle for *computational* hiding of f. Later, we will focus mostly on the two-party setting, which is the one we use for our target application to PCGs—and also the one for which suitable efficient constructions are known.

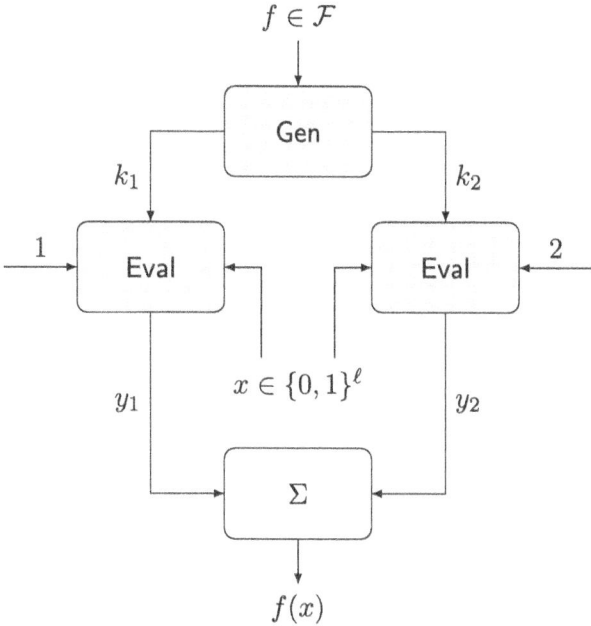

Fig. 3.2 Representation of a two-party function secret sharing scheme for a function class $\mathcal{F} = \{f : \{0, 1\}^\ell \to \mathbb{G}\}$. Σ denotes the sum over $\mathbb{G}$

3.4.2.1 Modeling Function Families

Formally, a *function family* is defined by a pair $\mathcal{F} = (P_{\mathcal{F}}, E_{\mathcal{F}})$, where $P_{\mathcal{F}} \subseteq \{0, 1\}^*$ is an infinite collection of function descriptions $\hat{f}$, and $E_{\mathcal{F}} : P_{\mathcal{F}} \times \{0, 1\}^* \to \{0, 1\}^*$ is a polynomial-time algorithm defining the function described by $\hat{f}$. Concretely, each $\hat{f} \in P_{\mathcal{F}}$ describes a corresponding function $f : D_f \to R_f$ defined by $f(x) = E_{\mathcal{F}}(\hat{f}, x)$. We assume for simplicity that $D_f = \{0, 1\}^\ell$ for a positive integer ℓ and always require R_f to be a finite Abelian group, denoted by $\mathbb{G}$. For simplicity, we will typically identify f with its description $\hat{f}$ and write $f \in \mathcal{F}$ instead of $\hat{f} \in P_{\mathcal{F}}$, and assume when passing f as input that this also includes an explicit description of both D_f and R_f, as well as a parameter $|f|$ that denotes the size (in bits) of the description of f.

3.4.2.2 Defining Function Secret Sharing

The definition given below follows the exposition given in Boyle et al. (2016, 2015), but simplifies some of the formalism for clarity of the exposition. A visual representation of the FSS algorithms is given on (Fig. 3.2).

Definition 3.4.2 (*FSS: Syntax*) An N-party function secret sharing (FSS) *scheme* is a pair of PPT algorithms (Gen, Eval) with the following syntax:

- Gen(1^λ, f), on input 1^λ and a function $f : \{0, 1\}^\ell \to \mathbb{G}$, outputs an N-tuple of keys $(k_1, \ldots, k_N)$.
- Eval(i, k_i, x) is a polynomial-time *evaluation algorithm*, which on input $i \in [N]$ (party index), key k_i and input $x \in \{0, 1\}^\ell$, outputs a group element $y_i \in \mathbb{G}$.

When N is omitted, it is understood to be 2.

Definition 3.4.3 (FSS: *Requirements*) Let $\mathcal{F}$ be a function family and define Leak(f) to be $(1^\ell, |f|, \mathbb{G})$ for any $f : \{0, 1\}^\ell \to \mathbb{G}$.[5] Let N (the number of parties) and t (the secrecy threshold) be positive integers. An N-party t-secure FSS for $\mathcal{F}$ with leakage Leak is a pair (Gen, Eval) as in Definition 3.4.2, satisfying the following requirements:

- **Correctness:** For all $f : \{0, 1\}^\ell \to \mathbb{G}$ in $\mathcal{F}$, and every $x \in \{0, 1\}^\ell$, it holds that

$$\Pr \left[\sum_{i=1}^{N} \mathsf{Eval}(i, k_i, x) = f(x) \right] = 1,$$

where the probability is taken over the random sampling of $(k_1, \ldots, k_N) \xleftarrow{s} $ Gen(1^λ, f).
- **Secrecy:** For every set of corrupted parties $S \subset [N]$ of size t, there exists a PPT simulator Sim such that for every sequence $f_1, f_2, \ldots$ of polynomial-size functions from $\mathcal{F}$, the outputs of the following experiments Real and Ideal are computationally indistinguishable:

  - Real(1^λ): $(k_1, \ldots, k_N) \leftarrow $ Gen(1^λ, f_λ); Output $(k_i)_{i \in S}$.
  - Ideal(1^λ): Output Sim(1^λ, Leak(f_λ)).

When t is omitted, it is understood to be $N - 1$.

3.4.2.3 PCG from FSS

Equipped with this formal definition, let us state the core theorem that underlies our template:

Theorem 3.4.4 *Let $C : \mathbb{F} \mapsto \mathbb{G}$ (where $\mathbb{F}$ is some field and $\mathbb{G}$ is some Abelian group) be a function and let $G : \{0, 1\}^\ell \mapsto \mathbb{F}^m$ be a PRG. Let $\mathcal{F} = \{C \circ G_k : [m] \mapsto \mathbb{G}\}$ be the family of functions $F_k = C \circ G_k$ indexed by the hardcoded input k (we view C and*

---

[5] Leak models the leakage that the adversary is allowed to get about the secret function f; more general notions of allowed leakage can be considered, see Boyle et al. (2016) for more discussions on this aspect.

G as public functions, and k as the secret description of $C \circ G_k$). Let (Gen, Eval) be a two-party function secret sharing for the class of functions $\mathcal{F}$. Consider the following construction:

- PCG.Gen(1^λ): sample $k \xleftarrow{s} \{0, 1\}^\lambda$ and output $(k_0, k_1) \leftarrow$ Gen($1^\lambda, k$);
- PCG.Expand(σ, k_σ): for $i = 1$ to m, compute $y_i \leftarrow$ Eval(σ, k_σ, i). Output $\mathcal{R}_\sigma \leftarrow (y_1, \ldots, y_m)$.

The construction (PCG.Gen, PCG.Expand) is a secure PCG for the two-party additive correlation defined by C.

The proof of this theorem is omitted from this book: it is rather elementary but slightly tedious.

3.5 Instantiating the Template I: A Step-by-Step FSS Construction

So far, we have established the following: if we have a PRG G and an FSS scheme for the function class $\mathcal{F} = \{C \circ G_k\}$, then we can build a PCG for the additive correlation defined by C. This begs the question: for what function classes $\mathcal{F}$ do we have efficient FSS constructions? In particular, what kind of PRGs G and correlations C yield functions $C \circ G_k$ for which efficient FSS schemes exist?

Here, we would like to stress the keyword "efficient." Under suitable cryptographic assumptions, it has been shown in the work of Boyle et al. (2015) (which introduced the notion of FSS) that FSS can be constructed for *all* polytime-computable functions. However, this construction employs very heavy machinery—in particular, it requires very strong forms of fully homomorphic encryption, which is extremely expensive (and if the reader remembers our discussions from Sect. 2.4.2, this is exactly the type of primitive that we want to avoid in the GMW paradigm). For a PCG construction to be useful, it must instead build upon a more realistically usable flavor of FSS.

3.5.1 Sharing the All-Zero Function

Our starting point is the standard naive and inefficient approach to FSS: to secretly share a function, it suffices to share its truth table. Then, the question becomes: which functions have truth tables whose random shares can be compressed? A seemingly stupid, but ultimately illuminating example of one such function is the all-zero function (yes, the one that always outputs zero) $Z : [m] \mapsto \{0\}$. The truth table of Z is a length-m vector of zeroes. To randomly share the truth table of Z, it suffices to sample a uniformly random key $K \xleftarrow{s} \{0, 1\}^m$ and to give K to each of the two parties: $K \oplus K$ is the length-m all-zero vector, which is indeed the truth table of Z.

Fortunately, we already know how to compress identical random shares: just use a pseudorandom generator! Let $\mathsf{PRG} : \{0, 1\}^\lambda \mapsto \{0, 1\}^m$ be a PRG. To deal compressed shares of Z to the parties, sample a random short key $s \xleftarrow{s} \{0, 1\}^\lambda$, and give s to both participants. To obtain shares of $Z(i)$ for some $i \in [m]$, the participants reconstruct $K \leftarrow \mathsf{PRG}(s)$ and output the i-th bit of K.[6]

3.5.2   Sharing Point Functions

Of course, the all-zero function is not a useful function. But let us take a tiny step from there: what if our function still evaluates to zero everywhere, except on a *single* point? Such a function is called a point function. We will write $f_{\alpha,\beta} : [m] \mapsto \{0, 1\}^*$ to denote the point function such that $f_{\alpha,\beta}(x) = \beta$ if $x = \alpha$, and $f_{\alpha,\beta}(x) = 0$ otherwise. To succinctly share $f_{\alpha,\beta}$ (without revealing (α, β)), the key idea is to carefully balance between the succinct sharing of the all-zero function (because most of the truth table of $f_{\alpha,\beta}$ contains zeroes anyway) and a naive (non-succinct) sharing of the part of the truth table that contains β.

3.5.2.1   A First Construction

Write the length-m truth table of $f_{\alpha,\beta}$ as a $\sqrt{m} \times \sqrt{m}$ square. We will share $f_{\alpha,\beta}$ row by row. Let (α_0, α_1) denote the coordinates of the nonzero entry in this square (that is, (α_0, α_1) is the decomposition of α in basis $\sqrt{m}$). Each row i with $i \neq \alpha_0$ can be seen as the $\sqrt{m}$-length truth table of an all-zero function: that we already know how to share: sample a short key $k_i \xleftarrow{s} \{0, 1\}^\lambda$ for a PRG PRG, and give the key to both participants. This way, $(\mathsf{PRG}(k_i), \mathsf{PRG}(k_i))$ form two pseudorandom shares of the zero vector.

For the α_0-th row (that we denote r_{α_0}), instead, we sample two different short keys $(k_{\alpha_0}, k'_{\alpha_0})$ and hand one to each participant—notice that from their viewpoint, nothing distinguishes α_0 from the other rows (for each row, they received a uniformly random short key). However, $(\mathsf{PRG}(k_{\alpha_0}), \mathsf{PRG}(k'_{\alpha_0}))$ form shares of $\mathsf{PRG}(k_{\alpha_0}) \oplus \mathsf{PRG}(k'_{\alpha_0})$, which is not the correct row r_{α_0}. Hence, it remains to find a way to correct the value of this row obliviously (i.e., without leaking α_0) without touching the other rows.

To do so, we define $\Delta = r_{\alpha_0} \oplus \mathsf{PRG}(k_{\alpha_0}) \oplus \mathsf{PRG}(k'_{\alpha_0})$, which is the offset between the correct value r_{α_0} and the incorrect value $\mathsf{PRG}(k_{\alpha_0}) \oplus \mathsf{PRG}(k'_{\alpha_0})$, and give it to both participants. Then, the goal is to let the participants obliviously XOR the offset Δ to their α_0-th share, without XORing it to their other shares. To do so, we

---

[6] Of course, because Z does not contain any secret, the participants could also just always define their shares of Z to be the all-zero string and output 0 on each evaluation. But we will use the PRG-based approach as a starting point to build more advanced forms of FSS, so bear with us!

sample $\sqrt{m}$ additional random bits $(b_1, \ldots, b_{\sqrt{m}})$ that we give to the first participant. To the second participant, we give the same bitstring *except that we flip the α_0-th bit*.

Then, to evaluate their share of $f_{\alpha,\beta}(i)$, the first participant computes the i_1-th bit of $b_{i_0} \cdot \Delta \oplus \mathsf{PRG}(k_{i_0})$ (where (i_0, i_1) are the coordinates of $i \in [m]$ in the $\sqrt{m} \times \sqrt{m}$ square). For every $i_0 \neq \alpha_0$, the second participant will output the i_1-th bit of $b_{i_0} \cdot \Delta \oplus \mathsf{PRG}(k_{i_0})$ as well: their outputs are indeed shares of 0. When $i_0 = \alpha_0$, the second participant will instead output the i_1-th bit of $(1 \oplus b_{\alpha_0}) \cdot \Delta \oplus \mathsf{PRG}(k'_{\alpha_0})$. If we XOR the shares of both participants, we get

$$(b_{\alpha_0} \cdot \Delta \oplus \mathsf{PRG}(k_{\alpha_0})) \oplus ((1 \oplus b_{\alpha_0}) \cdot \Delta \oplus \mathsf{PRG}(k'_{\alpha_0}))$$
$$= \Delta \cdot (b_{\alpha_0} \oplus b_{\alpha_0} \oplus 1) \oplus \mathsf{PRG}(k_{\alpha_0}) \oplus \mathsf{PRG}(k_{\alpha_0})$$
$$= \Delta \oplus \mathsf{PRG}(k_{\alpha_0}) \oplus \mathsf{PRG}(k_{\alpha_0})$$
$$= r_{\alpha_0} \text{ by definition of } \Delta,$$

which is again the right value. To make this a bit more visual, the shares received by each participant are represented in Fig. 3.3.

If we denote by λ the length of the short PRG keys (which is typically independent of m), the FSS scheme that we just constructed has keys of size $\Theta(\lambda \cdot \sqrt{m})$ (one can reduce this to $\Theta(\sqrt{\lambda m})$ with a better balancing, using a $\sqrt{m/\lambda} \times \sqrt{\lambda m}$-sized rectangle instead of a square). This is already an important improvement compared to the naive solution of sharing the entire truth table, which yields keys of size $\Theta(m)$.

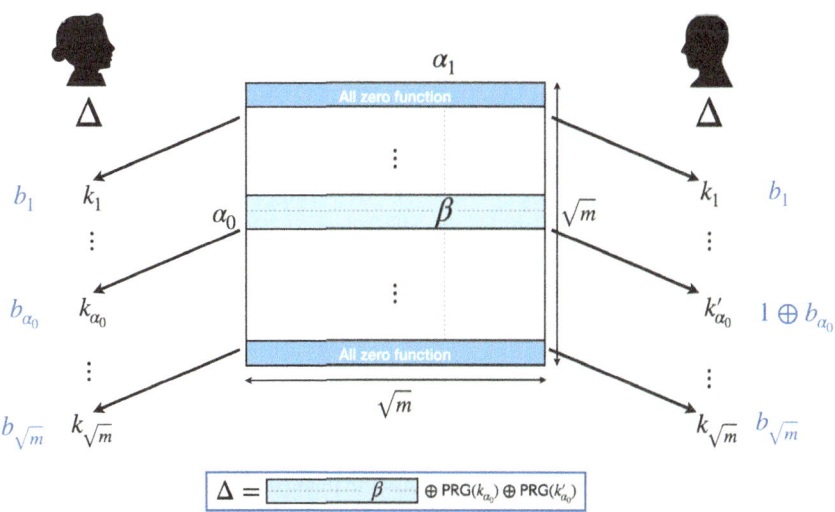

Fig. 3.3 A function secret sharing for the point function $f_{\alpha,\beta}$ with keys of length proportional to $\sqrt{m}$, from any PRG PRG

3.5.2.2 Improved Constructions

We can do even much better: the work of Gilboa and Ishai (2014) followed by subsequent works by Boyle et al. (2015; 2016) showed that using clever variants of the above construction together with more careful balancing strategies, one can recursively compress the length of the shared keys. Concretely, and denoting $n = \log m$ the bitsize of an input to a point function f with domain $[m]$:

- The work of Gilboa and Ishai (2014), which introduced the notion of FSS for point functions, also gave a recursive construction with key size $O(n^{\log_2 3} \cdot \lambda)$.
- This key length was improved to $O(n\lambda)$ bits in Boyle et al. (2015) via a tree-based construction.
- The current best construction (Boyle et al., 2016) has key size $\approx n\lambda + |\beta|$. More precisely, the key size is $\lambda + n(\lambda + 2) - \lfloor \log \lambda/|\beta| \rfloor$ bits.

Formally,

Definition 3.5.1 (*Distributed Point Function*) A *point function* $f_{\alpha,\beta}$, for $\alpha \in [m]$ and $\beta \in \mathbb{G}$, is defined to be the function $f : [m] \to \mathbb{G}$ such that $f(\alpha) = \beta$ and $f(x) = 0$ for $x \neq \alpha$. A *Distributed Point Function* (DPF) is an FSS for the family of all point functions, with the leakage $\mathsf{Leak}(\hat{f}) = (m, \mathbb{G})$.

The theorem below summarizes the state of the art regarding efficient point functions. Remember also that our application to building pseudorandom correlation generators requires running the FSS evaluation algorithm on the entire domain, which can typically be done more efficiently than running the FSS Eval algorithm individually on each entry. We denote by $\mathsf{FullEval}$ an algorithm that outputs the result on Eval on the full domain.

Theorem 3.5.2 (PRG-based DPF (Boyle et al., 2016), Theorems 3.3 and 3.4) *Given a PRG* $\mathsf{PRG} : \{0, 1\}^\lambda \to \{0, 1\}^{2\lambda+2}$, *there exists a DPF for point functions* $f_{\alpha,\beta} : [m] \to \mathbb{G}$ *with key size* $\log m \cdot (\lambda + 2) + \lambda + \lceil \log_2 |\mathbb{G}| \rceil$ *bits. For* $\ell = \lceil \frac{\log |\mathbb{G}|}{\lambda+2} \rceil$, *the key generation algorithm* Gen *invokes* PRG *at most* $2(\log m + \ell)$ *times, the evaluation algorithm* Eval *invokes* PRG *at most* $\log m + \ell$ *times, and the full evaluation algorithm* $\mathsf{FullEval}$ *invokes* PRG *at most* $m(1 + \ell)$ *times.*

3.5.3 Sharing "Matrix × Sparse Vector"

At this stage, the reader might feel like we have not made much progress: to instantiate the template, we need an FSS scheme for a function class that contains $F_k = C \circ G_k$, where C describes a correlation (typically a low-degree multivariate polynomial, for example $C(a, b) = (a, b, a \cdot b)$ for Beaver triples) and G is a pseudorandom generator. So far, the only functions we managed to compress are point functions, i.e., functions with a single nonzero entry, that are way too restricted to capture the functions we care about.

The surprising twist is that, quite on the contrary, FSS for point functions suffices to instantiate the template, provided that C is a sufficiently low-degree polynomial, and for a suitable choice of G. The key insight is that because the **Eval** algorithm of an FSS scheme outputs additive shares, FSS naturally supports composition with linear combinations. This observation will allow us to significantly expand the class of functions, making only a black box use of an FSS scheme for point functions.

Concretely, fix a "sparsity" parameter t, whose value will be discussed later (but the reader can think of it as being some fixed security parameter, with $t \approx 50$ being a reasonable choice). Define a t-*point function* to be a function $f_{\vec{\alpha},\vec{\beta}}$, with $\vec{\alpha} \in [m]^t$ has distinct entries, and $\vec{\beta} \in G^t$, such that $f_{\vec{\alpha},\vec{\beta}}(\alpha_j) = \beta_j$ for $j = 1$ to t, and $f_{\vec{\alpha},\vec{\beta}}(i) = 0$ otherwise (that is, the truth table of $f_{\vec{\alpha},\vec{\beta}}$ is 0 everywhere, except on t points indicated by $\vec{\alpha}$). Because we have FSS for point functions and because the sum of additives shares is also an additive share of the sum, we immediately have

Corollary 3.5.3 (Multi-Point Function Secret Sharing)   *Given a PRG* $\mathsf{PRG} : \{0, 1\}^\lambda \to \{0, 1\}^{2\lambda+2}$, *there exists an FSS scheme for t-point functions $f_{\vec{\alpha},\vec{\beta}}$:* $[m] \to G$ *with key size* $t \cdot (\log m \cdot (\lambda + 2) + \lambda + \lceil \log_2 |G| \rceil)$ *bits. For $\ell = \lceil \frac{\log |G|}{\lambda+2} \rceil$, the key generation algorithm* **Gen** *invokes* **PRG** *at most $2t(\log m + \ell)$ times, the evaluation algorithm* **Eval** *invokes* **PRG** *at most $t \cdot (\log m + \ell)$ times, and the full evaluation algorithm* **FullEval** *invokes* **PRG** *at most $t \cdot m \cdot (1 + \ell)$ times.*

The construction is immediate: write $f_{\vec{\alpha},\vec{\beta}}$ as the sum of point functions $\sum_{j=1}^t f_{\alpha_j,\beta_j}$. The key generation algorithm generates t independent key pairs, one for each f_{α_j,β_j}, and the evaluation algorithm, on input i, runs **Eval** with each of the t keys to get shares $(y_1, \ldots, y_t)$ of the $f_{\alpha_j,\beta_j}(i)$. The output share is just the sum over G of the y_j's.

To put it differently, when two parties (P_0, P_1) evaluate an FSS for a t-point function on its entire domain $[m]$, they obtain pseudorandom additive shares $(\vec{e}_0, \vec{e}_1)$ of a length-m sparse vector $\vec{e}$ that has exactly t nonzero entries. The FSS keys, that have total length $O(t \cdot \lambda \cdot \log m)$, form a succinct encoding of shares of $\vec{e}$ that does not reveal anything about $\vec{e}$, beyond the fact that it is a t-sparse vector. Furthermore, because the shares are additive, when the output group G is a ring $\mathcal{R}$, the participants can post-process their share of $\vec{e}$ by multiplying it with a public matrix H: their post-processed shares $(H \cdot \vec{e}_0, H \cdot \vec{e}_1)$ form additive shares of $H \cdot \vec{e}_0 + H \cdot \vec{e}_1 = H \cdot \vec{e}$ by linearity. Summing up, we have

Corollary 3.5.4 (Matrix × Sparse Vector Function Secret Sharing) *Given a matrix $H \in \mathcal{R}^{\ell \times m}$ and a t-sparse vector $\vec{e} \in \mathcal{R}^m$, let $F_{H,\vec{e}} : [m] \mapsto \mathcal{R}$ that, on input $i \in [m]$, output the i-th entry of $H \cdot \vec{e}$. Let $\mathcal{F} = \{F_{H,\vec{e}}\}$ denote the class of all such functions. Then assuming the existence of a PRG* $\mathsf{PRG} : \{0, 1\}^\lambda \to \{0, 1\}^{2\lambda+2}$, *there exists an FSS scheme for the function class $\mathcal{F}$ with leakage* $\mathsf{Leak}(F_{H,\vec{e}}) = (t, \mathcal{R}, H)$, *with key size $O(t \cdot \lambda \cdot \log m)$.*

As long as t is not too large, this yields a significant compression compared to sharing the m-sized truth table of $F_{H,\vec{e}}$ directly. Before we finally move on to the choice of the PRG G that will fit in the class for which we have efficient FSS, let us make one final step.

Observation 3.5.5 *We can further expand the function class to the class of functions $F'_{H,\vec{e}}$ that, on input $i \in [m]$, outputs the i-th entry of $P(H \cdot \vec{e})$, where P is a multi-output low-degree multivariate polynomial over $\mathcal{R}$ (that is, each output of P is a low-degree multivariate polynomial over $\mathcal{R}$), by observing that computing $P(H \cdot \vec{e})$ reduces to computing a linear function on $\vec{e}^{\otimes \deg P}$, that denotes $\vec{e}$ tensored with itself $\deg P$ times, and that $\vec{e}^{\otimes \deg P}$ is a $t^{\deg P}$-sparse vector. In particular, this captures the class of functions $Q \circ F_{M \cdot \vec{v}}$ that, on input $i \in [m]$, outputs $Q(F_{M \cdot \vec{v}}(i))$ (where Q is a multi-output low-degree multivariate polynomial). The FSS scheme for this extended function class $\mathcal{F}'$ has key size $O(t^{\deg Q} \cdot \lambda \cdot \log m)$.*

For simplicity, let us focus on the case where P is a degree-2 polynomial (the general case follows similarly). Given a vector $\vec{u}$, a degree-2 polynomial in $\vec{u}$ can be written as a linear function L of the tensor product $\vec{u} \cdot \vec{u}^{\mathsf{T}}$ of $\vec{u}$ with itself.[7] Hence, we can rewrite $P(H \cdot \vec{e})$ as $L(H \cdot (\vec{e} \cdot \vec{e}^{\mathsf{T}}) \cdot H^{\mathsf{T}})$, for a suitable linear function L. Because the map $X \to H \cdot X \cdot H^{\mathsf{T}}$ is itself linear, this computation boils down to evaluating a suitable linear function $L_{\vec{H}}$ of the matrix $E = \vec{e} \cdot \vec{e}^{\mathsf{T}}$.

Now, observe that since $\vec{e}$ is a t-sparse vector, E is a t^2-sparse matrix: the two parties can obtain shares of E using a sum of t^2 point functions with domain $[m^2]$, and locally evaluate the linear function $L_{\vec{H}}$ on their shares afterward, obtaining shares of $P(H \cdot \vec{e})$. This yields an FSS scheme for the class of functions $F'_{H,\vec{e}}$ with key size $O(t^2 \cdot \lambda \cdot \log m)$. Generalizing this approach to degree-d multivariate polynomials yields a scheme with key size $O(t^d \cdot \lambda \cdot \log m)$, which remains much smaller than m for small values of d.

3.5.4 Concluding Words

It took us a bit of time, but we hope that we made it clear to the reader that arriving at FSS for functions like $Q \circ F_{H,\vec{e}}$ only takes elementary steps—we did not use any heavy cryptographic machinery or advanced mathematical reasoning. Now, getting back to our original goal: what we want FSS for is the function $F_k = C \circ G_k$, where $G_k(i)$ output the i-th entry of the PRG evaluation $G(k)$, and C is our correlation. For most applications, C will be a low-degree polynomial—for example, a degree-two polynomial in the case of Beaver triples. This is perfect: we can set the low-degree polynomial Q in our construction above to be exactly the correlation C we care about. The function $F_{H,\vec{e}}$ outputs the i-th entry of $H \cdot \vec{e}$: if only the map $\vec{e} \to H \cdot \vec{e}$ could turn out to be a PRG, we would be done! Because the description of $\vec{e}$ can be encoded using $O(t \cdot \log m)$ bits (remember, it's a t-sparse vector) and $H \cdot \vec{e}$ is

---

[7] That is, the square matrix containing all degree-2 monomials in the entries of $\vec{u}$. If we want P to also contain degree-1 or constant monomials, we can append a 1 to $\vec{u}$—we ignore this minor technicality to avoid making notations heavier.

a length-ℓ vector, for a large enough ℓ, this mapping is indeed expanding. But is it pseudorandom? This will be the focus of the next section.

3.6 Instantiating the Template II: Coding Theory to the Rescue

Before we continue, we're going to need a bit of background on coding theory. We will keep it relatively short—there are countless resources out there providing an extensive treatment of the subject—but understanding notions such as *parity-check matrices* and the *minimum distance* of a code is a must to understand the design principles behind PCG constructions.

3.6.1 Preliminaries on Coding Theory

A code, or error-correcting code, is (according to Wikipedia) "a technique used for controlling errors in data transmission over unreliable or noisy communication channels." Concretely, it is a method that associates a *codeword* to every possible message, such that even if some of the codeword entries are corrupted by some noise during the transmission, retrieving the original message remains possible. A linear code is a code such that the mapping between messages and codewords is a linear map. Linear codes capture many (if not most) of the codes used in the wild. Formally:

Definition 3.6.1 (*Linear Codes*) Let $\mathbb{F}$ be a field, and (k, n) be integers with $k < n$. A linear code $\mathcal{C}$ with dimension k and codeword length n over $\mathbb{F}$ is a linear subspace of $\mathbb{F}^n$:

$$\mathcal{C} := \{\vec{c} = G \cdot \vec{x} \mid \vec{x} \in \mathbb{F}^k\},$$

where $G \in \mathbb{F}^{n \times k}$ is called the *generator matrix* of $\mathcal{C}$. We say that $\mathcal{C}$ is an $[n, k, d]_q$-code if $|\mathbb{F}| = q$ and $d = \min_{\vec{x} \in \mathbb{F}^k \setminus \{0\}^k} \mathsf{HW}(G \cdot \vec{x})$, where HW denotes the Hamming weight (number of nonzero entries). The value d is called the *minimum distance* of $\mathcal{C}$. Equivalently, d is the smallest Hamming distance between any pair of codewords.

We say that the generator matrix G is in *systematic form* if

$$G = \begin{bmatrix} I_k \\ G' \end{bmatrix},$$

where I_k is the $k \times k$ identity matrix. The systematic form of a generator matrix G can be obtained by performing elementary row operations (assuming the columns of G are linearly independent).

Parity-check matrix. Let $m \leftarrow n - k$. A parity-check matrix of a code $\mathcal{C}$ is a maximal rank matrix such that $H \cdot G = 0$. Formally:

Definition 3.6.2 (*parity-check matrix*)   We say that a matrix H is a *parity-check matrix* of a code $\mathcal{C}$ if $\mathcal{C} = \ker(H) = \{\vec{c} \mid H \cdot \vec{c} = 0\}$. It is not too hard to see that $H \in \mathbb{F}^{m \times n}$. The code generated by H^{T} is called the *dual code* of $\mathcal{C}$ and is denoted $\mathcal{C}^{\perp}$.

One can verify that the minimum distance d of a code $\mathcal{C}$ also corresponds to the smallest number of linearly dependent columns in a parity-check matrix of $\mathcal{C}$.

3.6.2   The Hardness of Syndrome Decoding

The historical purpose of a code is to enable error correction: given a corrupted codeword $\vec{c} + \vec{e}$, where $\vec{e}$ is some noise added by the transmission channel, it should be possible to retrieve the original message $\vec{x}$ provided that the amount of noise is not too large. Concretely, let us assume that the channel corrupts t entries in $\vec{c}$, where an entry c_i of $\vec{c}$ is said to be *corrupted* when it is replaced by $x_i + e_i$, where e_i is a uniformly random element of $\mathbb{F}^*$. This corresponds to adding a t-sparse vector to $\vec{c}$. Because the Hamming distance between any two codewords is at least d, it is easy to see that whenever $t < d/2$, it is possible to uniquely decode a corrupted codeword $\vec{c}' = \vec{c} + \vec{e}$, by returning the message $\vec{x}$ corresponding to the element of $\mathcal{C}$ that is the closest to $\vec{c}'$. This is called "minimum distance decoding," and is equivalent to the maximum likelihood decoding (i.e., returning the most likely message given a codeword) whenever the channel corrupts strictly less than $d/2$ entries with high probability.

The above, however, only says that decoding is possible *in principle* whenever the amount of noise is not too large, but it says nothing about whether it is possible to *efficiently* decode a corrupted codeword: in general, finding the element of $\mathcal{C}$ closest to $\vec{c}'$ with a brute-force search could take up to $|\mathbb{F}|^t \cdot \binom{n}{t}$ time! Of course, brute force is far from the best strategy: starting with the seminal work of Prange in the 60s (Prange, 1962), coding theorists have developed much better algorithms for decoding corrupted codewords over general linear codes. At a high level, these methods perform minimum distance decoding by computing $\vec{y} = H \cdot \vec{c}'$ of a corrupted codeword $\vec{c}' = \vec{c} + \vec{e}$, where H is a parity-check matrix of $\mathcal{C}$. Notice that

$$H \cdot \vec{c}' = H \cdot (\vec{c} + \vec{e}) = H \cdot \vec{e},$$

hence searching for a low-weight solution to the equation $H \cdot \vec{e} = \vec{y}$ enables retrieving the noise $\vec{e}$, and therefore the original codeword $\vec{c}$. The vector $\vec{y}$ is called a *syndrome* of $\vec{c}'$, and this approach to decoding is referred to as *syndrome decoding*.

However, as of today, all known syndrome decoding algorithms run in time exponential in t. There are even many concrete families of linear codes for which, given a random code from the family, we do not know of any better way to decode corrupted codewords than using these generic exponential-time decoding methods. Coding theorists have long adapted to this bad news by designing concrete families of linear codes (with various useful features) that *do* admit efficient decoding algorithms. But the hardness of solving the general case, or that of finding an efficient decoding algorithm for many concrete families of linear codes, has stood for decades. And when something looks very hard to solve, we cryptographers like to formulate it as an assumption:

Definition 3.6.3 (*Syndrome Decoding Assumption*) Let $\mathbb{F}$ be a finite field, and $(t, k, n) = (t(\lambda), k(\lambda), n(\lambda))$ be polynomials in the security parameter λ with $k, t < n$. Let $m \leftarrow n - k$. Let $\mathcal{S}_t(\mathbb{F}^n)$ denote the set of all t-sparse vectors over $\mathbb{F}^n$. The syndrome decoding assumption over $\mathbb{F}$ with dimension k, codeword length n, and noise t, denoted (t, k, n)-$\mathsf{SD}(\mathbb{F})$, states that for every polynomial-time algorithm $\mathcal{A}$, it holds that

$$\Pr[H \stackrel{\$}{\leftarrow} \mathbb{F}^{m \times n}, \vec{e} \stackrel{\$}{\leftarrow} \mathcal{S}_t(\mathbb{F}^n) : \mathcal{A}(H, H \cdot \vec{e}) = \vec{e}] \leq \mathsf{negl}(\lambda).$$

In the above, H is sampled uniformly at random. This induces the same distribution as picking a uniformly random generator matrix $G \stackrel{\$}{\leftarrow} \mathbb{F}^{n \times k}$ for a linear code, and setting H to be a random parity-check matrix of G. In other words, the assumption above states that syndrome decoding with parameters (t, k, n) is hard to solve for a random linear code.

Coding theorists and cryptographers have a good understanding of which parameters (t, k, n) yield a hard syndrome decoding problem. We will not provide a detailed overview of this aspect to avoid straying too much from our path: the extensive literature on the subject spans multiple research fields, including coding theory (through the information-set decoding algorithms (Prange, 1962; Stern, 1988; Finiasz and Sendrier, 2009; Bernstein et al., 2011a; May et al., 2011; Becker et al., 2012; May and Ozerov, 2015; Esser et al., 2017; Both and May, 2018), and more recently statistical decoding algorithms (Al Jabri, 2001; Fossorier et al., 2006; Overbeck, 2006; Debris-Alazard and Tillich, 2017; Carrier et al., 2022)), constraint satisfaction problems (Feige, 2002; Alekhnovich, 2003; Applebaum et al., 2006), learning theory (through the BKW algorithm and its variants (Blum et al., 2000; Lyubashevsky, 2005)), and cryptography/cryptanalysis (Blum et al., 1994; Wagner, 2002; Kirchner, 2011) (this list gives only a short sample of pointers to the literature). For our target application to pseudorandom correlation generators, we will be more specifically interested in the following parameter setting: $n = \mathsf{poly}(\lambda)$, $k = c \cdot n$ for a constant c (typically $c \in [1/8, 1/2]$), and $t = \Theta(\lambda)$. In this regime of parameters, the best known attacks run in time $2^{\Omega(\lambda)}$. We formulate this parameter setting as a concrete version of the syndrome decoding assumption below:

Definition 3.6.4 (*Syndrome Decoding Assumption, concrete version*) Let $\mathbb{F}$ be a finite field, $0 < c < 1$ be a constant, $n = \text{poly}(\lambda)$, $k = c \cdot n$, and $t = \Theta(\lambda)$. Let $m \leftarrow n - k$. The (t, k, n)-SD($\mathbb{F}$) problem is (T, ε)-hard if for every algorithm $\mathscr{A}$ running in time T, it holds that

$$\Pr[H \xleftarrow{\$} \mathbb{F}^{m \times n}, \vec{e} \xleftarrow{\$} \mathcal{S}_t(\mathbb{F}^n) \; : \; \mathscr{A}(H, H \cdot \vec{e}) = \vec{e}] \leq \varepsilon.$$

Furthermore, the conjecture is believed to hold for $\varepsilon = \text{poly}(T) \cdot 2^{-\Omega(\lambda)}$.

3.6.3   Pseudorandomness from Syndrome Decoding

The (conjectured) hardness of syndrome decoding for random linear codes asserts that given $(H, H \cdot \vec{e})$, it is hard to recover the noise vector $\vec{e}$. For our application to PCGs, however, we want the mapping from (a short description of) $\vec{e}$ to $H \cdot \vec{e}$ to be a pseudorandom generator: that is, $H \cdot \vec{e}$ should be indistinguishable from random, even given $\vec{e}$. Fortunately, it turns out that this stronger assumption is implied by the syndrome decoding assumption (up to some loss in the parameters), a result that is commonly referred to as a search-to-decision reduction. Before we state it, let us formulate the decision version of the syndrome decoding problem (here, specialized to our parameter setting):

Definition 3.6.5 (*Decisional Syndrome Decoding Assumption*) Let $\mathbb{F}$ be a finite field, $0 < c < 1$ be a constant, $n = \text{poly}(\lambda)$, $k = c \cdot n$, and $t = \Theta(\lambda)$. Let $m \leftarrow n - k$. The (t, k, n)-dSD($\mathbb{F}$) problem is (T, ε)-hard if for every algorithm $\mathscr{A}$ running in time T, it holds that

$$|\Pr[H \xleftarrow{\$} \mathbb{F}^{m \times n}, \vec{e} \xleftarrow{\$} \mathcal{S}_t(\mathbb{F}^n) \; : \; \mathscr{A}(H, H \cdot \vec{e})] - \Pr[H \xleftarrow{\$} \mathbb{F}^{m \times n}, \vec{x} \xleftarrow{\$} \mathbb{F}^m \; : \; \mathscr{A}(H, \vec{x})]| \leq \varepsilon.$$

Early search-to-decision reductions (Blum et al., 1994; Katz et al., 2010) had an important loss in the parameters that would not be suitable for our applications. Fortunately, Applebaum et al. (2009) gave a "sample preserving" search-to-decision reduction:

Lemma 3.6.6 (Applebaum et al. (2009)) *Assume that the (t, k, n)-dSD($\mathbb{F}$) problem is not* $(\text{poly}(\lambda), \varepsilon)$-*hard. Then the (t, k, n)-SD($\mathbb{F}$) problem is not* $(\text{poly}(\lambda), \varepsilon^2/8)$-*hard.*

The above lemma shows that, up to a polynomial loss in the runtime (and a quadratic loss in the advantage), the hardness of search and decisional versions of the syndrome decoding problem are equivalent. We note that in practice no faster algorithm is known to solve the decision version of the syndrome decoding problem compared to solving its search version.[8]

Corollary 3.6.7 (a PRG from syndrome decoding) *Let* $0 < c < 1$ *be a constant and* $n = \text{poly}(\lambda)$. *Assume that the* $(\lambda, c \cdot n, n)$-$\textsf{SD}(\mathbb{F})$ *problem is hard. Let* $H \overset{\$}{\leftarrow} \mathbb{F}^{m \times n}$. *Then the map* $G_H : \{0, 1\}^{\lambda \cdot (\log n + \log |\mathbb{F}^*|)} \mapsto \mathbb{F}^{n-k}$ *that, on input the description of a* λ-*sparse vector* $\vec{e}$ *over* $\mathbb{F}^n$ *(given as a list of* λ *pairs* $(i, x) \in [n] \times \mathbb{F}^*$*), outputs* $H \cdot \vec{e}$, *is a pseudorandom generator.*

We note that technically, the above only works with high probability over the choice of H, and hides the use of a small probability lemma called the splitting lemma (that states, roughly, that if sampling $(H, H \cdot \vec{e})$ yields a hard instance of SD with high probability, then when sampling H *once* and fixing it, it holds with high probability that H is *good*, in the sense that sampling $\vec{e}$ yields a hard instance $(H, H \cdot \vec{e})$ of SD with high probability over the choice of $\vec{e}$). We omit further details on these minor technicalities from now on.

Remark 3.6.8 In this book, we will cover several constructions that achieve improved efficiency guarantees by relying on variants of the syndrome decoding assumption, where the matrix H is not sampled from the uniform distribution over $\mathbb{F}^{m \times n}$. It should be noted that, in general, known results on search-to-decision reductions do not carry over to other distributions for H, though some reductions have been established for some other choices of distributions. When using variants of the syndrome decoding assumption, we will therefore typically have to make the stronger decisional assumption.

3.6.4 Wrapping-Up: A PCG for Low-Degree Correlations from Syndrome Decoding

And just like that, we're done! Combining this PRG from syndrome decoding with our FSS construction for the family of functions $F'_{H, \vec{e}}$ whose truth table is $P(H \cdot \vec{e})$, where P is some multi-output low-degree multivariate polynomial, yields a PCG for any low-degree additive correlation.

Theorem 3.6.9 *Let* $0 < c < 1$ *be a constant,* $t = \Theta(\lambda)$, *and* $n = \text{poly}(\lambda)$. *Assume that the* $(\lambda, c \cdot n, n)$-$\textsf{SD}(\mathbb{F})$ *problem is hard, and a PRG* $\textsf{PRG} : \{0, 1\}^\lambda \mapsto \{0, 1\}^{2\lambda+2}$. *Then for any degree-d additive correlation described by a function C over* $\mathbb{F}$, *there exists a pseudorandom correlation generator for C with the following characteristics:*

---

[8] This is almost true, with a slight disclaimer: when the codeword length n becomes very large, the polynomial cost $\Omega(n^\omega)$ with $\omega \in [2.3, 3]$ of solving a system of linear equations (which is required in all algorithms for syndrome decoding) becomes significant, and it can be avoided when solving the decisional version.

- PCG.Gen(1^λ) *outputs keys* (k_0, k_1) *of length* $O(\lambda \cdot t^d \cdot \log n)$;
- PCG.Expand(σ, k_σ) *requires* $O(t^d \cdot n)$ *invocations of* PRG *and* $O(n^2)$ *arithmetic operations over* $\mathbb{F}$, *and outputs vectors of length* $m = (1 - c) \cdot n$.

Again, technically we only get a variant of a pseudorandom correlation generator *with setup*, where the setup algorithm samples the matrix H and passes it as a common reference string to all other algorithms (and security holds over the sampling of H as well).

A concrete example. Before we move on, let us look at a concrete example to get a better intuition: suppose the two parties want to generate $m/2$ Beaver triples—that is, additive shares of pseudorandom triples $(a, b, a \cdot b)$ over some field $\mathbb{F}$. Assume that the common parameters include the description of a matrix $H \in \mathbb{F}^{m \times n}$ (which has been sampled at random in some setup phase), where setting $n = 2m$ is a standard choice. The algorithm PCG.Gen proceeds as follows:

- It samples a uniformly random t-sparse vector $\vec{e}$ ($t = \Theta(\lambda)$ is a parameter, think $t \approx 50$ in case this is helpful). Let $(e_1, \ldots, e_t) \in \mathbb{F}^t$ be the nonzero entries of $\vec{e}$ and $(i_1, \ldots, i_t) \in [n]^t$ be their respective positions.
- It computes $\vec{e} \cdot \vec{e}^\mathsf{T}$ and writes it as a sum of t^2 unit $n \times n$ matrices over $\mathbb{F}$, where each matrix has a single nonzero entry $e_i \cdot e_j$ at position (i_i, i_j).
- It samples a pair of DPF keys for each point function $f_{(i_i,i_j),e_i \cdot e_j}$ over $[n^2]$. It also samples a pair of DPF keys for each point function f_{i_i,e_i} over $[n]$. It outputs all the DPF keys.

Now, given these $t^2 + t$ pairs of DPF keys, the parties can expand them as follows:

- Evaluate each DPF on its entire domain and sum all the results over $\mathbb{F}$. Note that this yields additive shares of the matrix $E = \vec{e} \cdot \vec{e}^\mathsf{T}$, together with shares of $\vec{e}$. Let E_0, E_1 denote the shares of E of the parties P_0, P_1, respectively, and $\vec{e}_0$, $\vec{e}_1$ denote their shares of $\vec{e}$.
- Each party P_σ computes $V_\sigma \leftarrow H \cdot E_\sigma \cdot H^\mathsf{T}$ and $\vec{v}_\sigma \leftarrow H \cdot \vec{e}_\sigma$. Note that $V_0 + V_1 = H \cdot (\vec{e} \cdot \vec{e}^\mathsf{T}) \cdot H^\mathsf{T} = (H \cdot \vec{e}) \cdot (H \cdot \vec{e})^\mathsf{T}$ and that $\vec{v}_0 + \vec{v}_1 = H \cdot \vec{e}$.
- Let us write $\vec{v} = H \cdot \vec{e}$ as a concatenation $\vec{a} || \vec{b}$ of two pseudorandom vectors $(\vec{a}, \vec{b}) \in \mathbb{F}^{m/2} \times \mathbb{F}^{m/2}$ (note that their pseudorandomness follows from the syndrome decoding assumption). For $i = 1$ tp $m/2$, the parties output shares of (a_i, b_i) together with shares of $a_i \cdot b_i$ (which can be "read" from their shares of $(\vec{a} || \vec{b}) \cdot (\vec{a} || \vec{b})^\mathsf{T}$).

Together, these $m/2$ shares of $(a_i, b_i, a_i \cdot b_i)$ form $m/2$ pseudorandom Beaver triples. For concrete parameters, the reader can imagine that $m/2$ is about 2^{30} and $n = 2m = 2^{32}$. Using $\lambda = 128$ and $t = 50$, the keys output by PCG.Gen have length $\approx 2t^2 \cdot \lambda \cdot \log n$ (ignoring low-order terms), which amounts to 2.5 megabytes of keys to generate 128 megabytes worth of triples (here, we used $\mathbb{F} = \mathbb{F}_2$). The construction could have been slightly optimized further by generating $\vec{a} = H \cdot \vec{e}_a$ and $\vec{b} = H \cdot \vec{e}_b$ as two independent pseudorandom vectors (together with their tensor product) instead of viewing them as portions of a single pseudorandom vector $H \cdot \vec{e}$ (we kept the less efficient variant to remain closer to the general construction).

3.7 The Quest for the Right Code

The above numbers might sound attractive: we can generate 128MB worth of Beaver triples from keys of length 2.5 MB. Indeed, using efficient protocols to generate these keys (which we have not described so far, but they exist), one gets silent two-party computation over $\mathbb{F}_2$ using a communication *much below* one bit per Beaver triples for the preprocessing phase—about three orders of magnitudes better than previous IKNP-style approaches to preprocessing, that required a few hundred bits of communication per Beaver triple.

But do not get fooled, wise reader: however appealing it might seem, the constructions we have described so far are *horribly* inefficient. The devil lies not in their communication cost (which is great), but in their *computation* cost. It helps here to think in terms of concrete numbers: to generate 2^{30} Beaver triples, the parties had to first compute shares of E, a matrix with $2^{32} \times 2^{32} = 2^{64}$ entries. We are talking here about *two million terabytes* of storage. Even worse, computing V from E requires about $(2^{32})^{2.7} \approx 2^{86}$ operations, assuming you use Strassen's algorithm to implement the matrix multiplications (and ignoring the constants in Strassen) since asymptotically faster matrix multiplication algorithms have impractical constants. We cannot emphasize how inefficient performing 2^{86} operations is, except perhaps by saying that until quite recently, a cryptosystem that requires 2^{86} operations to be broken could have been deemed secure enough for most use cases.

The two related issues we just mentioned—these millions of Terabytes of storage and this horrendous computational cost—are quite distinct. The first issue, the $\Omega(n^2)$ storage cost, is independent of the matrix distribution H: it appears even before the parity-check matrix H is involved. Looking ahead, overcoming this issue has been done historically on a per-correlation basis: for several specific correlations of interests, it turns out that clever workarounds can be designed to reduce this $\Omega(n^2)$ cost to $O(n \cdot \log n)$, or even $O(n)$.[9] Sections 3.8 and 3.9 will be devoted to these clever workarounds. Even after solving this issue, however, the matrix multiplication cost remains: at the very least, the cost of generating shares of $C(G(r))$ has to scale with the cost of computing G, which itself involves multiplication by the $\Omega(n^2)$-sized matrix H. Overcoming this severe limitation of our template will be the focus of this section.

Let's jump straight ahead on the solution since there is no two ways about it: *we have to pick a different matrix H*. Concretely, the only thing we need from H is

---

[9] In fact, the chronology went the other way around: $O(n)$-cost solutions for a specific correlation—random oblivious transfers—were designed first, before an $O(n \cdot \log n)$ solution was achieved for other ones—OLEs and Beaver triples. Observing that both the optimized instantiations of the generic but inefficient construction that we described in this book came a bit later.

that $H \cdot \vec{e}$, where $\vec{e}$ is a sparse vector, cannot be distinguished from a random vector. Efficiency-wise, what we want from H is that the map $\vec{x} \to H \cdot \vec{x}$ can be computed fast—ideally much faster than the $\Omega(n^2)$ time required when H is a random matrix. When we discussed the syndrome decoding problem, we already hinted at the fact that its apparent hardness extends way beyond random linear codes: there are many concrete families of codes for which no fast syndrome decoding algorithms are known. And for some of them, the map $\vec{x} \to H \cdot \vec{x}$ can be computed much faster. Choosing the *right* map amounts to finding the code that strikes the best possible balance between the security of the associated syndrome decoding assumption, and the efficiency of the map $\vec{x} \to H \cdot \vec{x}$.

3.7.1   The Linear Test Framework

Finding the right code is about finding the best balance between efficiency and security. But how do we know which codes are secure? The traditional answer is that the codes most likely to yield secure variants of syndrome decoding are those that have been studied the most by the community, and for which there is a general agreement of experts that the assumption is solid. However, the reasons that originally motivated the study of some codes—whether in coding theory or cryptography—were removed from the efficiency considerations we are interested in. This is especially true in the PCG setting, where the codeword length n is close to the target length of the correlated randomness we want to generate, which will often be way beyond 2^{20}. From the viewpoint of coding theory, or that of more traditional code-based cryptography, this is an extremely exotic parameter setting, and the design and analysis of standard codes have never been motivated by (or optimized for) this parameter setting. This creates an uncomfortable situation, where we have to choose between using well-studied codes, whose design has not been optimized for use with PCGs and which might be suboptimally efficient for this task, or using seemingly much better codes, but whose underlying assumption lacks extensive study from the research community.

In this section, we cover a folklore approach that provides a rule of thumb to decide whether a new candidate code yields a plausible variant of the syndrome decoding assumption. The ideas underlying this rule of thumb are far from new—they have their roots in the seminal work of Naor and Naor (1990), and these ideas have been used on multiple occasions to provide arguments in favor of syndrome-decoding-style assumptions, including, for example, the work of Zichron (2017), Applebaum et al. (2017). Earlier, it was also employed to study the pseudorandomness of other constructions, such as that of random local functions (see Mossel (2003) and follow-ups).

In short, we know that avoiding short linear dependencies in the output is a necessary condition for the pseudorandomness of variants of syndrome decoding. Assuming that it is a *sufficient* condition for pseudorandomness appears to be a viable heuristic (though one that is known to fail in some settings, see Sect. 3.7.1.3). Formalizing the connection, as we will do afterward, allows us to quantify precisely the security one can hope to reach using this heuristic. Explicitly stating this framework has proven very fruitful in the past few years, and has been used to design and refine new linear codes tailored to PCG applications in several works (Boyle et al., 2020b; Couteau et al., 2021; Boyle et al., 2022; Couteau and Ducros, 2023; Bombar et al., 2023; Raghuraman et al., 2023).

3.7.1.1 Basic Observation

Known attacks against the syndrome decoding assumption and its variants include attacks based on Gaussian elimination and the BKW algorithm (Blum et al., 2000; Lyubashevsky, 2005; Levieil and Fouque, 2006; Esser et al., 2017) and variants based on covering codes (Zhang et al., 2016; Bogos and Vaudenay, 2016; Bogos et al., 2016; Guo et al., 2020), information-set decoding attacks (Prange, 1962; Stern, 1988; Finiasz and Sendrier, 2009; Bernstein et al., 2011a; May et al., 2011; Becker et al., 2012; May and Ozerov, 2015; Esser et al., 2017; Both and May, 2018), statistical decoding attacks (Al Jabri, 2001; Fossorier et al., 2006; Overbeck, 2006; Debris-Alazard and Tillich, 2017), generalized birthday attacks (Wagner, 2002; Kirchner, 2011), linearization attacks (Bellare and Micciancio, 1997; Saarinen, 2007), or on finding correlations with low-degree polynomials (Akavia et al., 2014; Bogdanov and Rosen, 2017). While trying each known attack against each candidate new variant would be excessively cumbersome, the key observation is that most of the above attacks (and more generally, most known attacks against syndrome decoding and its variants) fit in a common framework, which we will call the linear test framework. Concretely, an attack against syndrome decoding in the linear test framework proceeds in two stages:

1. First, a matrix H is sampled, and fed to the (unbounded) adversary $\mathcal{A}$. The adversary returns a (nonzero) *test vector* $\vec{v} = \mathcal{A}(H)$.
2. Second, a noise vector $\vec{e}$ is sampled. The *advantage* of the adversary $\mathcal{A}$ in the linear test game is the bias of the induced distribution $\vec{v} \cdot H \cdot \vec{e}^\mathsf{T}$.

To formalize this notion, we recall the definition of the bias of a distribution:

Definition 3.7.1 (*Bias of a Distribution*) Given a distribution $\mathcal{D}$ over $\mathbb{F}^n$ and a vector $\vec{u} \in \mathbb{F}^n$, the bias of $\mathcal{D}$ with respect to $\vec{u}$, denoted $\mathsf{bias}_{\vec{u}}(\mathcal{D})$, is equal to

$$\mathsf{bias}_{\vec{u}}(\mathcal{D}) = \left| \Pr_{\vec{x} \sim \mathcal{D}} [\vec{u} \cdot \vec{x}^\mathsf{T} = 0] - \Pr_{\vec{x} \sim \mathcal{U}_n} [\vec{u} \cdot \vec{x}^\mathsf{T} = 0] \right| = \left| \Pr_{\vec{x} \sim \mathcal{D}} [\vec{u} \cdot \vec{x}^\mathsf{T} = 0] - \frac{1}{|\mathbb{F}|} \right|,$$

where $\mathcal{U}_n$ denotes the uniform distribution over $\mathbb{F}^n$. The bias of $\mathcal{D}$, denoted $\mathsf{bias}(\mathcal{D})$, is the maximum bias of $\mathcal{D}$ with respect to any nonzero vector $\vec{u}$.

We say that an instance of the syndrome decoding problem is *secure against linear test* if, with very high probability over the sampling of H in step 1, for any possible adversarial choice of $\vec{v} = \mathcal{A}(H)$, the bias of $\vec{v} \cdot H \cdot \vec{e}^\mathsf{T}$ induced by the random sampling of $\vec{e}$ is negligible. Intuitively, the linear test framework captures any attack where the adversary is restricted to computing a linear function of the syndrome $\vec{b}^\mathsf{T} = H \cdot \vec{e}^\mathsf{T}$, but the choice of the linear function itself can depend arbitrarily on the code. Hence, the adversary is restricted in one dimension (it has to be linear in $\vec{b}^\mathsf{T}$), but can run in unbounded time given H.

Resistance against linear test is a property of both the code distribution (this is the "with high probability over the choice of H" part of the statement) and of the noise distribution (this is the "the bias of the distribution induced by the sampling of $\vec{e}$ is low" part of the statement). It turns out that to be secure against all attacks that fit in the linear test framework, it suffices to satisfy the following two simple conditions:

1. (good code) the code generated by H^T has a high minimum distance, and
2. (well-spread noise) for any large enough subset S of coordinates, with high probability over the choice of $\vec{e} \leftarrow \mathcal{D}$, at least one of the coordinates in S of $\vec{e}$ will be nonzero.

The above characterization works for any noise distribution whose nonzero entries are uniformly random over $\mathbb{F}^*$, which is the case for all standard choices of noise distributions. In particular, taking a random sparse vector $\vec{e}$ (as we discussed so far) suffices to satisfy the second condition. The first criterion is therefore the one we should focus on: to resist linear attacks, we need a code with a parity-check matrix H such that H^T generates a code with a large minimum distance. In other words, the code should be chosen such that its *dual code* has a high minimum distance.

To see why these conditions are sufficient, recall that the adversarial advantage is the bias of $\vec{v} \cdot H \cdot \vec{e}^\mathsf{T}$. By condition (2), if the subset S of nonzero entries of $\vec{v} \cdot H$ is sufficiently large, then $\vec{e}$ will "hit" one of these entries with large probabilities, and the output will be uniformly random. But the condition that S is sufficiently large translates precisely to the condition that $\vec{v} \cdot H$ has large Hamming weight for any possible (nonzero) vector $\vec{v}$, which is equivalent to saying that H generates a code with a large minimum distance. We recall the formalization below.

3.7.1.2 Formal Framework

Formally, we will from now on be interested in variants of the syndrome decoding assumption—typically by changing the matrix H, but later on we will also consider changing the distribution of the noise $\vec{e}$. We, therefore, formulate a generalized variant of the (decisional) syndrome decoding assumption, tailored to a given choice of the matrix distribution (denoted $\mathcal{M}$) and the noise distribution (denoted $\mathcal{N}$):

Definition 3.7.2 (*Generalized Decisional Syndrome Decoding Assumption*) Let $\mathbb{F}$ be a finite field, $0 < c < 1$ be a constant, $n = \mathrm{poly}(\lambda)$, $k = c \cdot n$, $m \leftarrow n - k$, and $t = \Theta(\lambda)$. Let $\mathcal{M} = \mathcal{M}_{n,m}(\mathbb{F})$ be a distribution over $\mathbb{F}^{m \times n}$. Let $\mathcal{N} = \mathcal{N}_{n,t}(\mathbb{F})$ denote a distribution over $\mathbb{F}^n$ with $\mathbb{E}_{\vec{e} \sim \mathcal{N}}[\mathsf{HW}(\vec{e})] = t$. The $(\mathcal{M}, \mathcal{N})$-$\mathsf{dGSD}(\mathbb{F})$ problem is (T, ε)-hard if for every algorithm $\mathscr{A}$ running in time T, it holds that

$$|\Pr[H \xleftarrow{\$} \mathcal{M}, \vec{e} \xleftarrow{\$} \mathcal{N} \ : \ \mathscr{A}(H, H \cdot \vec{e})] - \Pr[H \xleftarrow{\$} \mathcal{M}, \vec{x} \xleftarrow{\$} \mathbb{F}^m \ : \ \mathscr{A}(H, \vec{x})]| \leq \varepsilon.$$

Our goal is now to characterize which choices of $\mathcal{M}, \mathcal{N}$ yield plausible flavors of the generalized syndrome decoding assumption. To this end, we formally define below security in the *linear test framework*.

Definition 3.7.3 (*Security against Linear Test*) Let $\mathbb{F}$ be an arbitrary finite field, and let $\mathcal{N} = \mathcal{N}_{n,t}(\mathbb{F})$ denote a noise distributions over $\mathbb{F}^n$. Let $\mathcal{M} = \mathcal{M}_{n,m}(\mathbb{F})$ be a distribution over $\mathbb{F}^{m \times n}$. Let $\varepsilon, \delta : \mathbb{N} \mapsto [0, 1]$ be two functions. We say that the $(\mathcal{M}, \mathcal{N})$-dGSD$(\mathbb{F})$ assumption with dimension k and codeword length n is (ε, δ)-*secure against linear tests* if for any (possibly inefficient) adversary $\mathcal{A}$ that, on input a matrix $H \in \mathbb{F}^{m \times n}$, outputs a nonzero $\vec{v} \in \mathbb{F}^n$, it holds that

$$\Pr[H \xleftarrow{\$} \mathcal{M}, \vec{v} \xleftarrow{\$} \mathcal{A}(A) \; : \; \mathsf{bias}_{\vec{v}}(\mathcal{D}_H) \geq \varepsilon(\lambda)] \leq \delta(\lambda),$$

where $\mathcal{D}_H$ denotes the distribution induced by sampling $\vec{e} \leftarrow \mathcal{N}$, and outputting the syndrome $H \cdot \vec{e}$.

Then, we have the following straightforward lemma:

Lemma 3.7.4 *Let $\mathbb{F}$ be an arbitrary finite field, and let $\mathcal{N} = \mathcal{N}_{n,t}(\mathbb{F})$ denote a noise distributions over $\mathbb{F}^n$. Let $\mathcal{M} = \mathcal{M}_{n,m}(\mathbb{F})$ be a distribution over $\mathbb{F}^{m \times n}$. Then for any integer $d \in \mathbb{N}$, the $(\mathcal{M}, \mathcal{N})$-dGSD$(\mathbb{F})$ problem is (ε_d, η_d)-secure against linear tests, where*

$$\varepsilon_d = \max_{\mathsf{HW}(\vec{u}) > d} \mathsf{bias}_{\vec{u}}(\mathcal{N}), \qquad and \qquad \eta_d = \Pr_{H \xleftarrow{\$} \mathcal{M}} [\mathsf{d}(H) \geq d],$$

where $\mathsf{d}(H)$ denotes the minimum distance of the code generated by the columns of H.

The proof is straightforward: fix any integer d. Then with probability at least δ_d, $\mathsf{d}(H) \geq d$. Consider any (possibly unbounded) adversary $\mathcal{A}$ outputting $\vec{v} \neq \vec{0}$. If $\mathsf{d}(H) \geq d$, denoting $\vec{u} = H \cdot \vec{v}$, it holds that $\mathsf{HW}(\vec{u}) > d$, in which case the advantage of the adversary is bounded by $\max_{\vec{v} \neq \vec{0}} \mathsf{bias}_{\vec{v}}(\mathcal{D}_H) \geq \varepsilon_d = \max_{\mathsf{HW}(\vec{u}) > d} \mathsf{bias}_{\vec{u}}(\mathcal{N})$. We leave it as an interesting exercise for the reader to apply the above lemma to evaluate the security of syndrome decoding against linear tests for random linear codes, with random t-sparse noise.

3.7.1.3 When Security Against Linear Attacks Does Not Suffice

There are two important cases where security against linear tests does not yield security against *all* attacks.

1. When the code is strongly algebraic. For example, Reed–Solomon codes, which have a strong algebraic structure, have a high dual minimum distance but can be decoded efficiently with the Welch–Berlekamp algorithm, hence they do not lead to a secure syndrome decoding instance (and, indeed, Welch–Berlekamp does not fit in the linear test framework).

2. When the noise is structured (e.g., for regular noise) and the code length is close to quadratic in the dimension. This opens the door to algebraic attacks such as the Arora-Ge attack (Arora and Ge, 2011). However, when $n = O(k)$ (which is the case we consider), the Arora-Ge attack and its modern variants (Briaud and Øygarden, 2023) do not apply.

The above are, as of today, the only known cases where security against linear attacks is known to be insufficient. Algebraic decoding techniques have a long history and are only known for very restricted families of codes, and the Arora-Ge type of attack typically never applies in the $n = O(k)$ regime that we usually consider for PCGs. Therefore, a reasonable rule of thumb is that a variant of syndrome decoding yields a plausible assumption if (1) it probably resists linear attacks, and (2) finding an algebraic decoding algorithm is a longstanding open problem.

3.7.2 The Chronology

Finding out which code is the best fit has been a long journey. Initially, in Boyle et al. (2018), the authors suggested relying on LDPC codes: the variant of the syndrome decoding assumption where H is set to be the parity-check matrix of a random LDPC code (i.e. a code with a random sparse generator matrix) dates back to the work of Alekhnovich in 2003 (Alekhnovich, 2003) and has withstood the test of time so far. Furthermore, there is extensive literature on the fast encoding of the dual of LDPC codes (which, by a principle known as the transposition principle, implies a fast $\vec{x} \to H \cdot \vec{x}$ mapping). In later works (Boyle, 2019), the authors switched back to quasi-cyclic codes, for which optimized implementations based on the fast Fourier transform had been designed, and that were generating a lot of interest as a basis for efficient variants of the syndrome decoding assumption in the context of submissions to the NIST post-quantum competitions (e.g., in Aragon et al. (2018)).

In Couteau et al. (2021), the authors advocated a more aggressive choice, building a new concrete linear code highly optimized for correlated randomness generation and where the minimum distance was heuristically estimated using extensive computer simulations, but we stressed that the lack of a provable analysis of the minimum distance required a lot of caution—and indeed, the minimum distance of these codes was later shown to scale poorly to large dimensions (that the computer simulations could not reach) in Raghuraman et al. (2023). Later, the work of Boyle et al. (2022) introduced Expand–Accumulate code, a new type of LDPC code with a very efficient "online–offline" mapping (concretely, computing $\vec{x} \to H \cdot \vec{x}$ boils down to one very fast "offline" accumulation step on $\vec{x}$, followed by an "on-the-fly" sparse mapping) and strong provable guarantees on their minimum distance. In a recent work (Raghuraman et al., 2023), building upon (Boyle et al., 2022), the authors introduced Expand–Convolute codes, a generalization of Expand–Accumulate codes that retain their fast mapping properties, but achieve even better parameters for the minimum distance.

The latest proposals exhibit impressive efficiency performances, where computing $\vec{x} \to H \cdot \vec{x}$ is done in time $O(n)$, with small constants, yet their minimum distance guarantees are essentially as good as that of random linear codes. But are they the best possible? This remains an intriguing and well-motivated question, as any progress in the area yields faster protocols for silent secure computation. As of today, there remain several strong candidates to be investigated, with very appealing efficiency properties and the potential to exhibit good minimum distance properties. The quest continues!

3.8 PCGs for Oblivious Transfers

So far, our focus has been on (1) providing a general framework for pseudorandom correlation generators (with an instantiation for low-degree additive correlations, under the syndrome decoding assumption) and (2) explaining the selection process of the right flavor of the syndrome decoding assumption to make the mapping $\vec{x} \to H \cdot \vec{x}$. If the reader managed to remember everything we said so far,[10] they might remember that making this mapping efficient was only half of the problem: the other, more fundamental problem is that generating a degree-2 correlation in the coordinates of $\vec{v} = H \cdot \vec{e}$ (which is required in all correlations discussed so far in this book, such as random OTs, OLEs, and Beaver triples) requires computing the tensor product $\vec{v} \cdot \vec{v}^{\mathsf{T}}$, which takes time (and space) quadratic in the target amount of correlated randomness.

Fortunately, for all correlations listed so far, it turned out that this cost can be circumvented via dedicated constructions. This was first observed in Boyle et al. (2019) for the OT correlation, then a year later in Boyle et al. (2020a) for the OLE and Beaver triple correlations over a large field $\mathbb{F}$. Eventually, we recently filled the remaining gap, with a construction for OLEs and Beaver triples over all fields $\mathbb{F}$ with $|\mathbb{F}| > 2$ in a recent work (Bombar et al., 2023). In this section, we will focus on the case of the oblivious transfer correlation. The construction described below evolved throughout three papers (Boyle et al., 2018, 2019; Boyle, 2019).

3.8.1 A PCG for Subfield Vector-OLE

We start by describing a PCG for a specific correlation, called the subfield vector-OLE correlation. The OLE correlation distributes many pairs (a_i, b_i) together with additive shares of $a_i \cdot b_i$ over $\mathbb{F}$ to the parties. The vector-OLE (or VOLE) correlation is a variant of the OLE correlation that restricts one of the values, say, the b_i's, to be a single global value x. That is, instead of receiving $(\vec{a}, \vec{b})$ and shares of $\vec{a} \odot \vec{b}$

---

[10] If that's the case, congrats!

(where $\odot$ denotes the component-wise, or Schur, product), the parties receive $\vec{a}$, x, respectively, (where x is a single $\mathbb{F}$-element) together with shares of $x \cdot \vec{a}$. The subfield vector-OLE (or sVOLE) is another variant of the vector-OLE correlation, where $\vec{a}$ is sampled from a subfield $\mathbb{F}'$ of $\mathbb{F}$.

An equivalent way to formulate the *subfield vector-OLE* correlation is as follows: fix $\mathbb{F} = \mathbb{F}_q$ and a subfield $\mathbb{F}_p$ of $\mathbb{F}$ (with $q = p^r$). The correlation samples $(\vec{u}, \vec{v}_0) \xleftarrow{\$} \mathbb{F}_p^n \times \mathbb{F}^n$ and $x \xleftarrow{\$} \mathbb{F}$. It outputs $(\vec{u}, \vec{v}_0)$ to one party P_0, usually called the sender, and $(x, \vec{v}_1 = \vec{u} \cdot x + \vec{v}_0)$ to the second party P_1, usually called the receiver.

From Sect. 3.5.3, we know that (assuming a length-doubling PRG) there exists an FSS scheme for the function class $\mathcal{F} = \{F_{H,\vec{e}}\}$ with leakage $\mathsf{Leak}(F_{H,\vec{e}}) = (t, \mathbb{F}, H)$, with key size $O(t \cdot \lambda \cdot \log n)$, where $F_{H,\vec{e}} : [m] \mapsto \mathbb{F}$ is a function which, given a matrix $H \in \mathbb{F}^{m \times n}$ and a t-sparse vector $\vec{e} \in \mathbb{F}^n$ and on input $i \in [m]$, output the i-th entry of $H \cdot \vec{e}$. The core observation underlying the design of an efficient PCG for this correlation is that the multiplication by an arbitrary field element x is for free in this construction: simply use FSS for the function $F_{H,x \cdot \vec{e}}$. Everything works out because $x \cdot \vec{e}$ is still a t-sparse vector, and because $H \cdot (x \cdot \vec{e}) = x \cdot H \cdot \vec{e}$. The construction also works identically when H, $\vec{e}$ are sampled over the subfield $\mathbb{F}_p$ while x is sampled from the field $\mathbb{F}$. The full construction is given in Fig. 3.4.

Plugging the construction of DPF from Sect. 3.5.2.2 in the construction of Fig. 3.4, we get

---

Parameters. Fix a security parameter λ, a field $\mathbb{F} = \mathbb{F}_q$, and a subfield $\mathbb{F}_p$ of $\mathbb{F}$ (with $q = p^r$). Let m be the target length of the subfield vector-OLE correlation, and $n = m + k$ (in concrete instances, it typically suffices to have $k = m = n/2$). Let t be a noise parameter (typically $t = \Theta(\lambda)$). Let $\mathcal{M} = \mathcal{M}_{n,m}(\mathbb{F}_p)$ be a distribution over $\mathbb{F}_p^{m \times n}$ (choices of the matrix distribution are discussed in Section 3.7). Fix a matrix $H \xleftarrow{\$} \mathcal{M}$. Let $\mathcal{N} = \mathcal{N}_{n,t}(\mathbb{F}_p)$ denote the distribution of random weight-t vectors over $\mathbb{F}_p^n$ (we will discuss alternative distributions later).

Gen. Sample $x \xleftarrow{\$} \mathbb{F}_q$, $\vec{e} \xleftarrow{\$} \mathcal{N}$ and let $(i_1, \cdots, i_t), (e_1, \cdots, e_t)$ denote the positions of the nonzero entries of $\vec{e}$ and their values respectively. For $j = 1$ to t, sample $(k_0^j, k_1^j) \leftarrow \mathsf{DPF.Gen}(1^\lambda, f_{i_j, x \cdot e_j})$ (where $f_{i_j, x \cdot e_j} : [n] \mapsto \mathbb{F}_q$ denotes the point function that evaluates to $x \cdot e_j$ on i_j). Output $k_0 = (i_j, e_j, k_0^j)_{j \leq t}$ and $k_1 = (x, (k_1^j)_{j \leq t})$.

Expand. Let σ be the party index. For $j = 1$ to t, compute $\vec{y}_\sigma^j \leftarrow \mathsf{DPF.FullEval}(\sigma, k_\sigma^j)$ and set $\vec{y}_\sigma \leftarrow \sum_{j=1}^t \vec{y}_\sigma^j$.

- If $\sigma = 0$, set $v_0 \leftarrow H \cdot y_0$, reconstruct $\vec{e}$ from $(i_1, \cdots, i_t), (e_1, \cdots, e_t)$ and output $(\vec{u} = H \cdot \vec{e}, \vec{v}_0)$.

- If $\sigma = 1$, set $v_1 \leftarrow -H \cdot y_1$, and output $(x, \vec{v}_1)$.

Fig. 3.4 Construction of a PCG for the subfield vector-OLE correlation under the generalized syndrome decoding assumption

Theorem 3.8.1 *Fix a security parameter λ, a field $\mathbb{F} = \mathbb{F}_q$, and a subfield $\mathbb{F}_p$ of $\mathbb{F}$ (with $q = p^r$). Let m be the target length of the subfield vector-OLE correlation, and $n = m + k$. Let t be a noise parameter. Let $\mathcal{M} = \mathcal{M}_{n,m}(\mathbb{F}_p)$ be a distribution over $\mathbb{F}_p^{m \times n}$. Let $\mathcal{N} = \mathcal{N}_{n,t}(\mathbb{F}_p)$ denote the distribution of random weight-t vectors over $\mathbb{F}_p^n$. Assume the hardness of the $(\mathcal{M}, \mathcal{N})$-dGSD$(\mathbb{F}_p)$ problem, and that there exists a pseudorandom generator $\mathsf{PRG} : \{0, 1\}^{\lambda} \mapsto \{0, 1\}^{2\lambda+2}$. Then there exists a PCG for the subfield vector-OLE correlation over $(\mathbb{F}_p, \mathbb{F})$ with key size $O(\lambda \cdot t \cdot \log n)$ and where the Expand algorithm boils down to $2 \cdot t \cdot m$ calls to PRG and one computation of the mapping $\vec{v} \to H \cdot \vec{v}$.*

Correctness follows from the fact that $\vec{v}_0 - \vec{v}_1 = H \cdot \sum_{j=1}^{t} (\vec{y}_0^j + \vec{y}_1^j) = H \cdot (x \cdot \vec{e}) = x \cdot H \cdot \vec{e} = x \cdot \vec{u}$ by linearity and correctness of the DPF schemes (the $(-1)^{\sigma}$ term in the construction is just used to get subtractive secret sharing, in line with how we define subfield VOLE). Security follows from the security of the DPF scheme (here again, we omit a formal security analysis—the interested reader can check (Boyle et al., 2018)).

3.8.2 From Subfield VOLE to OT

We now explain how to turn a PCG for the subfield VOLE correlation into a PCG for the random OT correlation. At the heart of this transformation is a technique from Ishai et al. (2003) that relies on the observation that a VOLE correlation can be seen, by reversing the roles of the sender and the receiver, as an OT correlation with correlated OTs—OTs where the pairs of sender messages differ by a fixed offsets. Then, the correlation among the OT instances (the fixed offset) can be removed using a hash function satisfying a suitable security notion, called *correlation-robustness*.

3.8.2.1 Reversing the Roles of the Parties

Fix $p = 2$ and $r = \lambda$, so that $\mathbb{F} = \mathbb{F}_{2^{\lambda}}$ is an extension field of $\mathbb{F}_2$. When instantiating the construction of Fig. 3.4 with these fields, the sender receives $(\vec{u}, \vec{v}_0) \in \mathbb{F}_2^m \times \mathbb{F}_2^m$ and the receiver receives $(x, \vec{v}_1 = \vec{u} \cdot x + \vec{v}_0) \in \mathbb{F}_2^m \times \mathbb{F}_2^m$. Since $\vec{u} \in \mathbb{F}_2^m$, we can alternatively view this construction the other way around: reversing the roles of the receiver and the sender, observe that for any $i \leq m$, it holds that $v_{0,i} = v_{1,i}$ if $u_i = 0$, and $v_{0,i} = v_{1,i} + x$ otherwise. Hence, we can view this construction as distributing m *correlated* oblivious transfers between a sender with correlated pairs of inputs $(v_{1,i}, v_{1,i} - x)$, where the $v_{1,i}$ are pseudorandom, and a receiver with pseudorandom selection bits u_i.

3.8.2.2   Breaking Correlations with a Correlation-Robust Hash

Let $H : \mathbb{F}_{2^\lambda} \mapsto \{0, 1\}^\lambda$ be a hash function. In the last step of the transformation, the sender computes $r^i \leftarrow H(v_{0,i})$ and the receiver computes $(s_0^i, s_1^i) \leftarrow (H(v_{1,i}), H(v_{1,i} + x))$ for $i = 1$ to m. The tuples (u_i, r^i) and (s_0^i, s_1^i) satisfy the OT correlation, and by the security of the subfield VOLE, the u_i's are pseudorandom. To finish the proof, it remains to argue that even knowing the values $v_{0,i}$ for $i = 1$ to m, the values $H(v_{0,i} + x)$ should all look *simultaneously random* to the receiver, where x is a truly random element of $\mathbb{F}_{2^\lambda}$. This is precisely what the notion of correlation-robust hashing captures:

Definition 3.8.2 (*Correlation-Robust Hash* (Ishai et al., 2003)) A hash function $H : \mathbb{F}_{2^\lambda} \mapsto \{0, 1\}^\lambda$ is *m*-correlation-robust if for *every* sequence $(v^1, \ldots, v^m)$ of distinct elements of $\mathbb{F}_{2^\lambda}$, the following distributions are indistinguishable:

$$\mathcal{D}_0 = \{H(v^1 + x), \ldots, H(v^m + x) \mid x \xleftarrow{s} \mathbb{F}_{2^\lambda}\}, \text{ and } \mathcal{D}_1 = \mathcal{U}_\lambda^n,$$

where $\mathcal{U}_\lambda$ denotes the uniform distribution over $\{0, 1\}^\lambda$.

In our application to OT from sVOLE, the requirement that the v^i's are all distinct holds with overwhelming probability $\approx m \cdot 2^{-\lambda}$. Plugging the construction of Fig. 3.4 into this transformation, we get

Theorem 3.8.3 *Fix a security parameter λ. Let m be the target number of pseudorandom OTs, and $n = m + k$. Let t be a noise parameter. Let $\mathcal{M} = \mathcal{M}_{n,m}(\mathbb{F}_2)$ be a distribution over $\mathbb{F}_2^{m \times n}$. Let $\mathcal{N} = \mathcal{N}_{n,t}(\mathbb{F}_2)$ denote the distribution of random weight-t vectors over $\mathbb{F}_2^n$. Assuming the hardness of the $(\mathcal{M}, \mathcal{N})$-dGSD$(\mathbb{F}_2)$ problem and using the following tools:*

- *a pseudorandom generator* $\mathsf{PRG} : \{0, 1\}^\lambda \mapsto \{0, 1\}^{2\lambda+2}$,
- *an m-correlation-robust hash function* $\mathsf{H} : \mathbb{F}_{2^\lambda} \mapsto \{0, 1\}^\lambda$,

there exists a PCG for the OT correlation (with λ-bit sender messages) with key size $O(\lambda \cdot t \cdot \log n)$ and where the Expand *algorithm is dominated by $2 \cdot t \cdot n$ calls to* PRG*, one computation of the mapping $\vec{v} \to H \cdot \vec{v}$ (where $H \in \mathbb{F}_2^{m \times n}$ denotes the parity-check matrix sampled from $\mathcal{M}$), and m calls to H for the receiver (resp. $2m$ for the sender).*

We note that unlike our generic construction of PCG for low-degree additive correlations, the construction captured by Theorem 3.8.3 is really efficient: if an appropriate parity-check matrix H is chosen (such that there is a linear-time algorithm computing the mapping $\vec{v} \to H \cdot \vec{v}$), the computation boils down to $O(m)$ arithmetic operations, $2n$ calls to a PRG, and ≈ 1.5 m calls to a correlation-robust hash function. Over modern hardware, a standard practice is to instantiate both the PRG and the hash function using the AES block cipher (with a fixed key), to benefit from the Intel AES-NI set of hardware instructions for AES. These are insanely fast:

about 20 CPU cycles to encrypt 128 bits (Münch et al., 2021). With such hardware support, the construction enables the generation of millions of OTs per second on one core of a standard machine, and the key size for 2^{30} OTs is below 40kB. While these are impressive numbers, we can do even better! In the next two sections, we cover two standard ways to improve the construction of PCG for OTs, which have been described, respectively, in Boyle et al. (2018) and Boyle (2019).

3.8.3   Improvement I: Using a Regular Noise Distribution

Here, we consider a variant of the construction where the noise distribution is changed, from random t-sparse vectors to random *regular* vectors. For simplicity, assume that t divides n. We let $\mathcal{N} = \mathcal{N}_{n,t}(\mathbb{F}_2)$ denote the following distribution: $\mathcal{N}$ samples t uniformly random unit (i.e. weight-1) vectors over $\mathbb{F}_2^{n/t}$, and outputs their concatenation. Compared to random t-sparse vectors, this corresponds to dividing the noise vector $\vec{e}$ into t equal-length blocks and adding a single random noisy coordinate to each block.

3.8.3.1   Security Considerations

The first and most important aspect to deal with is whether this change hurts security. Changing the noise distribution to regular noise amounts to changing the syndrome decoding assumption; the variant of syndrome decoding with regular noise is called *regular syndrome decoding*. We will not cover extensively the impact of using this noise distribution in the cryptanalysis of syndrome decoding. But let us just mention a few important points:

- Regular syndrome decoding is not a new assumption: It is a well-established variant of syndrome decoding whose introduction dates back to 2003, where it was introduced in Augot et al. (2003) as the assumption underlying the FSB candidate to the NIST hash function competition. It was subsequently analyzed in Finiasz et al. (2007), Meziani et al. (2011), Bernstein et al. (2011b), Hazay et al. (2018), among others (of course, it was also used and analyzed in many works on silent secure computation, but they are posterior to the first use of regular noise for PCGs).
- Regularity is a two-edged sword for cryptanalysis: It reduces the search space (which improves syndrome decoding algorithms), but puts constraints on the shape of the solution (which makes it more difficult to satisfy).[11] As of today, for the

---

[11] This statement holds when solving the *search* RSD problem, but not necessarily when solving its decisional counterpart. However, as of today, the fastest known attacks on decisional RSD rely on information-set decoding (Esser and Santini, 2023) and actually solve the search variant.

range of parameters of interest in PCG applications, there are no known syndrome
decoding algorithms that perform better against regular syndrome decoding compared to "traditional" syndrome decoding.[12]
• Eventually, it is easy to check that the regular noise distribution satisfies the criteria
  outlined in Lemma 3.7.4: for every large enough subset S of coordinates, with very
  high probability over the choice of $\vec{e} \xleftarrow{\$} \mathcal{N}$, at least one of the coordinates in S of $\vec{e}$
  will be nonzero. A quick calculation shows that this probability is asymptotically
  identical for regular noise and the more standard t-sparse noise: from the viewpoint
  of linear tests, the regular noise distribution offers the same security as the random
  t-sparse noise.

3.8.3.2 Efficiency Considerations

Let us now switch to *why* we want to use regular noise instead of random t-sparse
noise. Remember that to succinctly share the noise vector $\vec{e}$, we wrote $\vec{e}$ as a sum
of t unit vectors of length m and interpreted each of these unit vectors as the truth
table of a point function with domain $[n]$ that we can share with a DPF of size
$O(\lambda \cdot \log m)$. Switching to regular noise makes things much easier: now, $\vec{e}$ is directly
a *concatenation* of t unit vectors of length m/t each, and each of the blocks of $\vec{e}$ can
therefore be shared with a DPF of size $O(\lambda \cdot \log(m/t))$.

This already yields a slight improvement in the key length (from $O(t \cdot \lambda \cdot \log m)$
to $O(t \cdot \lambda \cdot \log(m/t))$), but the most important effect is on *computation*. When representing $\vec{e}$ as a sum of t unit vectors, the PCG.Expand algorithm had to run FullEval
t times in parallel on an m-sized domain, requiring about $2tn$ calls to the PRG.
Instead, when $\vec{e}$ is a concatenation of t unit vectors, the PCG.Expand algorithm
runs FullEval t times in parallel on an n/t-sized domain that requires $2t(n/t) = 2n$
calls to the PRG: a t-fold reduction of the number of calls to our PRG! When using
a flavor of syndrome decoding where the mapping $\vec{v} \to H \cdot \vec{v}$ is very efficient (as
modern constructions do), calling the PRG $2tn$ times is by far the dominant cost of
the computation, and using a regular noise yields one to two orders of magnitude of
improvement.

---

[12] There is a very recent exception in the work of Briaud and Øygarden (2023) that tailors algebraic
cryptanalysis techniques to the regular syndrome decoding problem. However, they have a very
moderate impact on their security and only apply to very specific parameter settings used in so-
called "primal" PCG constructions, which we did not cover at all in this book and are typically less
efficient than the approach we cover here.

3.8.4 Improvement II: Using a Puncturable Pseudorandom Function

Upon closer inspection, using FSS to compress shares of $x \cdot \vec{e}$ in our PCG construction for sVOLE is an overkill. Indeed, FSS guarantees that $x \cdot \vec{e}$ remains hidden to both parties, but the construction reveals x to the receiver and $\vec{e}$ to the sender anyway. It would suffice to rely on a variant of DPF for point functions $f_{\alpha,\beta}$ where the *position* α is revealed to one party (the sender, since it corresponds to a position of a nonzero entry in $\vec{e}$) and the *value* β is revealed to the other party (the receiver, since it corresponds to x). It turns out that this functionality can be achieved using a primitive known as a puncturable pseudorandom function.

3.8.4.1 Definition of PPRFs

Pseudorandom functions (PRF), introduced in Goldreich et al. (1986), are keyed functions that are indistinguishable from truly random functions. More formally,

Definition 3.8.4 A pseudorandom function (PRF) with key space $\{0, 1\}^\lambda$, domain $[n]$, and range $\mathbb{F}_{2^\lambda}$ is a keyed family of functions $\{F_K\}_{K \in \{0,1\}^\lambda}$ such that for every polynomial-time adversary $\mathcal{A}$, it holds that

$$\left| \Pr_{F \xleftarrow{\$} \mathcal{F}} [\mathcal{A}^F(1^\lambda) = 1] - \Pr_{K \xleftarrow{\$} \{0,1\}^\lambda} [\mathcal{A}^{F_K}(1^\lambda) = 1] \right| \leq \mathsf{negl}(\lambda),$$

where $\mathcal{F}$ denotes the space of all functions from $[n]$ to $\mathbb{F}_{2^\lambda}$, and $\mathcal{A}^F$ indicates that $\mathcal{A}$ is given oracle access to F. If the above holds for adversaries $\mathcal{A}$ restricted to querying only uniformly random inputs $x \xleftarrow{\$} [n]$ to the oracle, we say that F_K is a *weak* pseudorandom function (WPRF).

A puncturable pseudorandom function (PPRF) is a PRF F such that given an input x, and a PRF key k, one can generate a *punctured* key, denoted $k\{x\}$, that allows evaluating F at every point except for x and does not reveal any information about the value $F.\mathsf{Eval}(k, x)$. PPRFs have been introduced in Kiayias et al. (2013), Boneh and Waters (2013), Boyle et al. (2014). Below, we directly define PPRFs for the range of parameters of interest in our construction of PCG for OTs.

Definition 3.8.5 (*t-Puncturable Pseudorandom Function*) A *puncturable pseudorandom function* (PPRF), with key space $\{0, 1\}^\lambda$, domain $[n]$, and range $\mathbb{F}_{2^\lambda}$, is a pseudorandom function F with three probabilistic polynomial-time algorithms ($F.\mathsf{KeyGen}, F.\mathsf{Puncture}, F.\mathsf{Eval}$) such that

- $F.\mathsf{KeyGen}(1^\lambda)$ outputs a random key $K \in \{0, 1\}^\lambda$;
- $F.\mathsf{Puncture}(K, \{S\})$, on input a key $K \in \{0, 1\}^\lambda$, and a subset $S \subset [n]$ of size t, outputs a punctured key $K\{S\}$;

Experiment Exp-PPRF

Setup Phase. The adversary $\mathcal{A}$ sends a size-t subset $S^* \in [n]$ to the challenger. When it receives S^*, the challenger picks $K \overset{\$}{\leftarrow} F.\mathsf{KeyGen}(1^\lambda)$ and a random bit $b \overset{\$}{\leftarrow} \{0,1\}$.

Challenge Phase. The challenger sends $K\{S^*\} \leftarrow F.\mathsf{Puncture}(K, S^*)$ to $\mathcal{A}$. If $b = 0$, the challenger additionally sends $(F(K, x))_{x \in S^*}$ to $\mathcal{A}$; otherwise, if $b = 1$, the challenger picks t random values $(y_x \overset{\$}{\leftarrow} \mathbb{F}_{2^\lambda}$ for every $x \in S^*)$ and sends them to $\mathcal{A}$.

Fig. 3.5 Selective security game for puncturable pseudorandom functions. At the end of the experiment, $\mathcal{A}$ sends a guess b' and wins if $b' = b$

- $F.\mathsf{Eval}(K\{S\}, x)$, on input a key $K\{S\}$ punctured at all points in S, and a point x, outputs $F(K, x)$ if $x \notin S$, and $\perp$ otherwise,

such that no probabilistic polynomial-time adversary wins the experiment Exp-PPRF represented in Fig. 3.5 with a non-negligible advantage over the random guess.

3.8.4.2   Puncturable PRFs from Length-Doubling PRGs

Here, we recall how a PPRF can be constructed from any length-doubling pseudorandom generator G, using the GGM tree-based construction (Goldreich et al., 1986; Kiayias et al., 2013; Boneh and Waters, 2013; Boyle et al., 2014). For simplicity, assume that n is a power of two; we write $n = 2^d$. The construction proceeds as follows: On input a key $K \in \{0, 1\}^\lambda$ and a point $x \in [n]$ (viewed as a bitstring $x_1 \cdots x_d \in \{0, 1\}^d$), set $K^{(0)} \leftarrow K$ and perform the following iterative evaluation procedure: for $i = 1$ to $\ell \leftarrow d$, compute $(K_0^{(i)}, K_1^{(i)}) \leftarrow G(K^{(i-1)})$, and set $K^{(i)} \leftarrow K_{x_i}^{(i)}$. Output $K^{(\ell)}$. This procedure creates a complete binary tree with edges labeled by keys and 2^d leaves. The output of the PRF on an input x is the key labeling the leaf at the end of the path defined by x from the root of the tree.

- $F.\mathsf{KeyGen}(1^\lambda)$: output a random seed for G.
- $F.\mathsf{Puncture}(K, z)$: on input a key $K \in \{0, 1\}^\lambda$ and a point $x = x_1 \cdots x_d$, for $i = 1$ to $\ell \leftarrow d$, compute $(K_0^{(i)}, K_1^{(i)}) \leftarrow G(K^{(i-1)})$, and set $K^{(i)} \leftarrow K_{x_i}^{(i)}$. Return $K\{x\} = (K_{1-x_1}^{(1)}, \ldots, K_{1-x_\ell}^{(\ell)})$.
- $F.\mathsf{Eval}(K\{x\}, x')$, on input a punctured key $K\{x\}$ and a point x, if $x = x'$, output $\perp$. Otherwise, parse $K\{x\}$ as $(K_{1-x_1}^{(1)}, \ldots, K_{1-x_\ell}^{(\ell)})$ and start the iterative evaluation procedure from the first $K_{1-x_i}^{(i)}$ such that $x_i' = 1 - x_i$.

To obtain a t-puncturable PRF with input domain $[n]$, one can simply run t instances of the above PPRF and set the output of the PRF to be the bitwise XOR of the output of each instance; when the t punctured points are in distinct n/t-sized blocks (as in our construction based on regular syndrome decoding), it suffices instead to use a separate PPRF on domain $[n/t]$ for each block. With this construction, the length of a key punctured at t points is $t\lambda\log n$ (resp. $t\lambda\log(n/t)$), where λ is the seed size of the PRG.

3.8.4.3 Sharing the Noise Vector Using a PPRF

Let $F = (F.\mathsf{KeyGen}, F.\mathsf{Puncture}, F.\mathsf{Eval})$ be a PPRF with domain $[n/t]$. When evaluating t instances of this PPRF on its full domain (with keys $K_1, \ldots, K_t$), the receiver gets a t-fold concatenation of length-n/t pseudorandom vectors. Furthermore, denoting $i_1, \ldots, i_t \in [n/t]$ the nonzero entries of $\vec{e}$, we can reveal the entire pseudorandom vector *except for the t positions indexed by the i_j's* to the sender. For the remaining t positions, we simply give to the sender the values $F(K_j, i_j) + x$ for $j = 1$ to t, and the sender places each value at position i_j in the j-th block of the pseudorandom vector.

The two vectors obtained this way form pseudorandom shares of a length-m vector over $\mathbb{F}_{2^\lambda}$ that is equal to 0 everywhere, except the entry i_j of each block j, where it is equal to x. This is the same as saying that the vector form shares of $x \cdot \vec{e}$. Hence, we achieved the same result as with FSS for point functions but using a much simpler construction, leveraging the fact that the sender knows the positions i_j of the nonzero entries of $\vec{e}$. Beyond the simplicity of the construction, it has two main advantages:

- A smaller receiver key. In this construction, the key of the receiver is compressed to $t \cdot \lambda$ bits (to store the punctured PPRF keys $(K_1, \ldots, K_t)$) that can be further compressed to just λ bits by generating them from a short seed using a pseudorandom generator. This reduces the size of the entire receiver key to be as small as 128 bits (the sender key is also slightly reduced, but of size comparable to its size in the FSS-based construction).
- A better key distribution protocol. This touches on an aspect that we have not discussed so far, and won't have the space to discuss much, but briefly: when using PCGs to do secure computation in the silent preprocessing model, the parties need to distributively and securely generate the keys of the PCG using an interactive protocol (see Fig. 3.1). It turns out that the PPRF-based construction of PCG for OT has a much better key distribution protocol that uses only two rounds of interaction and $t \cdot \log(n/t)$ OT instances. The low number of rounds is a major advantage over high-latency networks, but also has the independent advantage of enabling various useful forms of *non-interactive secure computation*, an area that we will not discuss any further here—but the interested reader should check (Boyle, 2019) to read more about it!

3.8.5 Concrete Efficiency

Using all the improvements discussed above, we get

Theorem 3.8.6 *Fix a security parameter λ. Let m be the target number of pseudorandom OTs, and $n = m + k$. Let t be a noise parameter. Let $\mathcal{M} = \mathcal{M}_{n,m}(\mathbb{F}_2)$ be a distribution over $\mathbb{F}_2^{m \times n}$. Let $\mathcal{N} = \mathcal{N}_{n,t}(\mathbb{F}_2)$ denote the distribution of random t-regular vectors over $\mathbb{F}_2^n$. Then, assuming the hardness of the $(\mathcal{M}, \mathcal{N})$-$\mathsf{dGSD}(\mathbb{F}_2)$ problem and the following tools:*

- *a pseudorandom generator $\mathsf{PRG} : \{0, 1\}^\lambda \mapsto \{0, 1\}^{2\lambda+2}$;*
- *an m-correlation-robust hash function $\mathsf{H} : \mathbb{F}_{2^\lambda} \mapsto \{0, 1\}^\lambda$,*

there exists a PCG for the OT correlation (with λ-bit sender messages) with sender key size $\lambda \cdot t \cdot \log(n/t)$, receiver key size λ, and where the cost of the Expand algorithm is dominated by $2 \cdot n$ calls to PRG, one computation of the mapping $\vec{v} \to H \cdot \vec{v}$ (where $H \in \mathbb{F}_2^{m \times n}$ denotes the parity-check matrix sampled from $\mathcal{M}$), and m calls to H for the receiver (resp. $2m$ for the sender).

To give some perspective on this theorem, let us derive a few concrete numbers. The exact choice of t depends on the concrete cryptanalysis of the syndrome decoding assumption with the parameters used in the construction. Among many works on the subject, the recent work of Liu et al. (2022) provides precise security estimations tailored to the parameters used in PCG constructions. Concretely, to generate $m = 2^{22}$ instances of λ-bit OTs and setting $n = 4m$, they estimate that using a value as low as $t = 34$ suffices to get 128 bits of security (see Table 5 in their work). With these numbers, setting $\lambda = 128$ yields a sender key size of about 10kB (and 16 Bytes for the receiver key).

As for computation, instantiating the PRG and the hash using the AES block cipher, it boils down to $\approx 2^{25}$ calls to AES[13] and one computation of the mapping $\vec{v} \to H \cdot \vec{v}$. Concretely, modern implementations can generate about 10 million pseudorandom λ-bit OTs per second with these approaches, on one core of a standard laptop (using more cores multiplies the number of OTs since everything parallelizes optimally).

3.9 Beyond Oblivious Transfers: PCGs for Complex Correlations

The construction of PCG for OT described in Sect. 3.8 circumvents the (impractical) $\Omega(n^2)$ computational cost of the generic PCG construction (for degree-2 additive correlations) using a two-step construction that first produces a subfield VOLE

---

[13] Recent works (Boyle et al., 2022; Guo et al., 2023) show how to further halve this cost, but we will not cover these recent techniques here.

correlation, and then uses a correlation-robust hash function to turn it into an OT correlation. Unfortunately, this approach is strictly tailored to the OT correlation. Even though OT is essentially just an OLE over $\mathbb{F}_2$, the approach does not extend to OLEs over larger fields. More precisely, the subfield VOLE part of the construction extends easily (after all, we directly described over general fields), but the hashing technique does not generalize. To make it clear, let us look at the case of $\mathbb{F}_3$: here, the receiver would hold some $u_i \in \mathbb{F}_3$, and one of $(v_i, v_i + x, v_i - x) = (v_i, z_i, t_i)$. However, hashing these values does not yield an OLE over $\mathbb{F}_3$: it yields a 1-out-of-3 OT. Getting an OLE would require preserving the property that $z_i + t_i = 2v_i$—but, of course, hashing breaks this correlation as well!

As of today, we do not know of a construction for OLEs with performances as impressive as those we have for OTs. The case of OLEs is known to be much harder to handle—we have had efficient OT extension protocols for more than two decades (Ishai et al., 2003), and no efficient OLE extension protocols (while OLE extensions have been demonstrated in Applebaum et al. (2017) in the semi-honest setting, their concrete efficiency remains unclear). However, we can still do much better than paying the unaffordable $\Omega(n^2)$ cost of the general solution by relying on a variant of the syndrome decoding problem with considerably more algebraic structure.

3.9.1 High-Level Intuition

The key insight of the construction is that some structured degree-2 correlations can be obtained without computing the full tensor product of $H \cdot \vec{e}$ with itself. Instead, the idea will be to use a structured matrix H to embed $H \cdot \vec{e}$ into a polynomial ring. Over this ring, the tensor product can be replaced by a polynomial product that can be computed in time $O(n \cdot \log^2 n)$, or even just $O(n \cdot \log n)$ when using cyclotomic rings. Then, the construction leverages the fact that if the polynomial splits entirely, the product of two polynomials can be projected back to the component-wise product of the two pseudorandom vectors they encode, which will exactly yield the OLE correlation.

3.9.2 A PCG for Ring-OLE

We start by explaining how to compress the generation of a *single* OLE correlation over a large polynomial ring $\mathcal{R} = \mathbb{F}_p[X]/(P)$, where P is some degree-n split polynomial (i.e., a polynomial that splits into n linear factors), and $\mathbb{F}_p$ is a finite field. Let us call ring-OLE this correlation:

Definition 3.9.1 In a ring-OLE correlation each party P_σ receives $(x_\sigma, y_\sigma) \in \mathcal{R}^2$ for $\sigma = 0, 1$ that are random conditioned on $x_0 + x_1 = y_0 \cdot y_1$. Given an integer t, a t-sparse ring-OLE correlation is a correlation in which each party P_σ receives $(x_\sigma, y_\sigma) \in \mathcal{R}^2$ for $\sigma = 0, 1$, where y_0, y_1 are random t-sparse polynomials over $\mathcal{R}$, and x_0, x_1 random conditioned on $x_0 + x_1 = y_0 \cdot y_1$.

Looking ahead, the degree n of the polynomial will translate afterward to the number of OLEs produced over the base field $\mathbb{F}_p$. The construction follows our FSS-based template and proceeds in two steps: we show how to use FSS to obtain a PCG for t-sparse ring-OLE correlations, and then use a syndrome decoding assumption to turn it into a PCG for the ring-OLE correlation.

3.9.2.1 Distributing Sparse Ring-OLE Correlations

First, using an FSS for multipoint functions allows to succinctly distribute a *sparse* ring-OLE correlation: sample two random t-sparse polynomials y_0, y_1 (i.e. polynomials with t nonzero coefficients in the standard basis), and define f to be the t^2-point function whose truth table is the coefficients of $y_0 \cdot y_1$ (over $\mathbb{F}_p[X]$—i.e., without reduction modulo P). Each party P_σ receives $\mathsf{k}_\sigma = (y_\sigma, f_\sigma)$, where $(f_0, f_1) = \mathsf{FSS.Gen}(f)$. With the construction of multipoint FSS discussed in Sect. 3.5.3, the size of k_σ is $O(t^2 \cdot \lambda \cdot \log n)$.

3.9.2.2 Distributing Ring-OLE Correlations

Then, to turn this sparse ring-OLE correlation into a pseudorandom ring-OLE correlation, we will compress two instances of the correlation using the mapping $(u, v) \to (u + a \cdot v)$, where $a \xleftarrow{s} \mathcal{R}$ is a random (fixed) polynomial. Looking ahead, this will correspond to relying on the security of a variant of the syndrome decoding assumption over a polynomial ring, with a random systematic-form parity-check matrix $(1, a)$. Let $(x_\sigma^0, y_\sigma^0)_{\sigma \in \{0,1\}}$ and $(x_\sigma^1, y_\sigma^1)_{\sigma \in \{0,1\}}$ be two instances of a sparse ring-OLE correlation. Fix a random element $a \xleftarrow{s} \mathcal{R}$. Each party P_σ defines

$$y_\sigma \leftarrow (1, a) \cdot (y_\sigma^0, y_\sigma^1)^\mathsf{T} = y_\sigma^0 + a \cdot y_\sigma^1 \bmod P(X).$$

The assumption that y_σ is indistinguishable from random is the *ring syndrome decoding* assumption. Using FFT, the mapping can be computed in $O(n \cdot \log^2 n)$ $\mathbb{F}_p$-operations over general rings (or even $O(n \cdot \log n)$ over cyclotomic rings), where n is the degree of the polynomials. Then, observe that we have

$$y_0 y_1 = (y_0^0 + a \cdot y_0^1) \cdot (y_1^0 + a \cdot y_1^1) = y_0^0 \cdot y_1^0 + a \cdot (y_1^0 \cdot y_0^1 + y_0^0 \cdot y_1^1) + a^2 \cdot (y_0^1 \cdot y_1^1),$$

where the polynomials $y_0^0 \cdot y_1^0, y_1^0 \cdot y_0^1, y_0^0 \cdot y_1^1$, and $y_0^1 \cdot y_1^1$ are all t^2-sparse. Hence, each of these four polynomials can be succinctly shared using FSS for a t^2-point function. Therefore, shares of y_0y_1 can be reconstructed using a local linear combination of shares of sparse polynomials with public coefficients $(1, a, a^2)$, and the shares of the sparse polynomials can be distributed succinctly using FSS for multi-point functions.

Wrapping-Up. The final PCG looks as follows: each party P_σ gets (y_σ^0, y_σ^1) together with four FSS shares of t^2-point functions whose domain corresponds to these four terms. The PCG key size scales as $O(\lambda t^2 \log n)$ overall, where n is the degree of the polynomials over $\mathcal{R}$. Expanding the keys amounts to locally computing the shares of the sparse polynomial products (four evaluations of the FSS on their entire domain, using $O(t \cdot n)$ calls to a pseudorandom generator, or even $O(n)$ when relying on the regular ring syndrome decoding assumption—see Sect. 3.8.3 for the discussions on regular noise) and a few polynomial multiplications (computed using $\tilde{O}(n)$ arithmetic operations) with a and a^2 (which are public parameters).

3.9.3 From Ring-OLE to OLEs

When P splits into n linear factors over $\mathbb{F}_p[X]$ (that is, in particular, the case over a suitable cyclotomic ring), a single pseudorandom ring-OLE correlation as above can be locally transformed into n instances of pseudorandom OLEs over $\mathbb{F}_p$, by evaluating the polynomials on n fixed distinct points. Furthermore, this entire evaluation can be performed in time $O(n \cdot \log n)$ using fast multipoint polynomial evaluation. This yields a PCG for generating n instances of the OLE correlation, with keys of size $O(\lambda t^2 \log n)$, and runtime $O(n \cdot \log n)$ when assuming the regular syndrome decoding assumption over a cyclotomic ring where P splits entirely.

This construction is significantly less efficient than our PCG for OT: its key size has a t^2 factor instead of a factor t, and the computation scales as $O(n \cdot \log n)$ instead of n. In practice, this translates to a construction with a key size in the $2 \sim 10$ megabytes range for generating 2^{20} to 2^{35} OLEs. As for runtime, implementations using FFTs over cyclotomic rings can generate about a million OLEs in 10 s over one core of a standard laptop. This is quite efficient, but still two orders of magnitude slower than the runtime achieved by fast PCGs for OTs.

3.9.4 From OLEs to Other Correlations

Using the same reduction as in Sect. 2.7.2.2, a PCG for OLEs immediately yields a PCG for Beaver triples (with a key size twice larger). Furthermore, given any element $\Delta \in \mathbb{F}$, the protocol from the previous section can be easily modified to yield shares of a Beaver triple $(\vec{a}, \vec{b}, \vec{a} \odot \vec{b})$ together with *authenticated* shares $(\Delta \cdot \vec{a}, \Delta \cdot \vec{b}, \Delta \cdot \vec{a} \odot \vec{b})$ of this Beaver triple. This variant is particularly useful because, while Beaver triple is the natural resource to use in the semi-honest secure computation of arithmetic circuits in the correlated randomness model, its authenticated counterpart is the natural resource that enables efficient malicious secure computation of arithmetic circuits in the correlated randomness model. We refer the reader to Boyle et al. (2020a) for more details on these generalizations.

3.9.5 Historical Notes

The study of the ring syndrome decoding assumption dates back to Heyse et al. (2012) and has received some (limited) attention from the cryptography community (Bernstein and Lange, 2012; Damgård and Park, 2012; Lipmaa and Pavlyk, 2015; Guo et al., 2015). For an appropriate choice of the polynomial P, it is also equivalent to the well-studied quasi-cyclic syndrome decoding assumption used in NIST submissions such as BIKE (Aragon et al., 2017) and HQC (Melchor et al., 2018).

The construction sketched in this section was introduced by Boyle et al. (2020a). Because it requires P to split entirely over $\mathbb{F}$, it is restricted to OLEs over a large field $\mathbb{F}$ of size $|\mathbb{F}| \geq n$. This limitation was circumvented in 2023, in a work by Bombar et al. (2023), achieving PCGs for OLEs (with comparable efficiency features) for all fields of size $|\mathbb{F}| > 2$. The construction is more mathematically involved; it uses quasi-abelian codes, but it follows a similar template (and additionally benefits from a heuristic security argument in the linear test framework). At a high level, it can be viewed as a generalization of the approach to multivariate polynomial rings (multivariate polynomials can have many roots over a small field, which circumvents the issue) that carefully picks $P = P(X_1, \ldots, X_d)$ as a multivariate polynomial, so that $\mathbb{F}[X_1, \ldots, X_d]/P(X_1, \ldots, X_d)$ forms a group algebra. In turn, the group algebra structure allows preserving important features of the template (for example, the product of sparse elements remains sparse over a group algebra) and relating the underlying assumption to a well-studied problem in coding theory. Somewhat intriguingly, the construction falls short of handling all fields, the case of $\mathbb{F}_2$ remaining out of reach of this method. Nevertheless, in 2025, Li et al. (2025) finally completed the picture and extended the construction to work over $\mathbb{F}_2$ by making a clever use of the trace polynomial.

References

Akavia, A., Bogdanov, A., Guo, S., Kamath, A., & Rosen, A. (2014). Candidate weak pseudorandom functions in AC^0 o MOD_2. In M. Naor (Ed.) *ITCS 2014* (pp. 251–260). ACM, Jan. 2014. https://doi.org/10.1145/2554797.2554821.

Al Jabri, A. (2001). A statistical decoding algorithm for general linear block codes. In 2001.

Alekhnovich, M. (2003). More on average case vs approximation complexity. In *44th FOCS*, Oct. 2003 (pp. 298–307). IEEE Computer Society Press. https://doi.org/10.1109/SFCS.2003.1238204.

Applebaum, B., Damgård, I., Ishai, Y., Nielsen, M., & Zichron, L. (2017). Secure Arithmetic Computation with Constant Computational Overhead. In J. Katz & H. Shacham (Ed.) *CRYPTO 2017, Part I* (Vol. 10401, pp. 223–254). LNCS, Aug. 2017. https://doi.org/10.1007/978-3-319-63688-7_8.

Applebaum, B., Ishai, Y., & Kushilevitz, E. (2006). On pseudorandom generators with linear stretch in NC0. In *International Workshop on Approximation Algorithms for Combinatorial Optimization* (pp. 260–271). Springer.

Applebaum, B., Ishai, Y., & Kushilevitz, E. (2009). Cryptography with constant input locality. *Journal of Cryptology, 22*(4), 429–469. https://doi.org/10.1007/s00145-009-9039-0.

Aragon, N., Barreto, P., Bettaieb, S., Bidoux, L., Blazy, O., Deneuville, J. -C., Gaborit, P., Gueron, S., Guneysu, T., Aguilar-Melchor, C., Misoczki, R., Persichetti, E., Sendrier, N., Tillich, J. -P., Zémor, G., Vasseur, V., & Ghosh, S. (2020). *BIKE.* Tech. rep. available at https://csrc.nist.gov/projects/post-quantum-cryptography/post-quantum-cryptography-standardization/round-3-submissions. National Institute of Standards and Technology.

Aragon, N., Barreto, P., Bettaieb, S., Bidoux, L., Blazy, O., Deneuville, J.-C., Gaborit, P., Gueron, S., Guneysu, T., Melchor, C. A., et al. (2017). Bike: Bit flipping key encapsulation. In: (2017).

Arora, S., & Ge, R. (2011). New algorithms for learning in presence of errors. In *ICALP 2011.* Earlier version: Learning Parities with Structured Noise, ECCC 2010 (pp. 403–415).

Augot, D., Finiasz, M., & Sendrier, N. (2003). *A Fast Provably Secure Cryptographic Hash Function.* Cryptology ePrint Archive, Report 2003/230. https://eprint.iacr.org/2003/230.

Baum, C., Braun, L., Munch-Hansen, A., & Scholl, P. (2022). Moz$\mathbb{Z}_{2^k}$arella: Efficient vector-OLE and zero-knowledge proofs over $\mathbb{Z}_{2^k}$. In Y. Dodis & T. Shrimpton (Ed.) *CRYPTO 2022, Part IV,* Aug. 2022 (Vol. 13510, pp. 329–358). LNCS. https://doi.org/10.1007/978-3-031-15985-5_12.

Baum, C., Dittmer, S., Scholl, P., & Wang, X. (2023). Sok: Vector OLE-based zero-knowledge protocols. In (Vol. 91(11), pp. 3527–3561). https://doi.org/10.1007/s10623-023-01292-8.

Beaver, D. (1996). Correlated pseudorandomness and the complexity of private computations. In *28th ACM STOC,* May 1996 (pp. 479–488). ACM Press. https://doi.org/10.1145/237814.237996.

Becker, A., Joux, A., May, A., & Meurer, A. (2012). Decoding random binary linear codes in $2^{n/20}$: How $1 + 1 = 0$ improves information set decoding. In D. Pointcheval & T. Johansson (Ed.) *EUROCRYPT 2012,* Apr. 2012 (Vol. 7237, pp. 520–536). LNCS. https://doi.org/10.1007/978-3-642-29011-4_31.

Bellare, M., & Micciancio, D. (1997). A new paradigm for collision-free hashing: Incrementality at reduced cost. In: W. Fumy (Ed.) *EUROCRYPT'97* (Vol. 1233, pp. 163–192). LNCS, May 1997. https://doi.org/10.1007/3-540-69053-0_13.

Bernstein, D. J., & Lange, T. (2012). Never trust a bunny. In *International Workshop on Radio Frequency Identification: Security and Privacy Issues* (pp. 137–148). Springer.

Bernstein, D. J., Lange, T., & C. Peters. (2011a). Smaller decoding exponents: Ball-collision decoding. In P. Rogaway (Ed.) *CRYPTO 2011,* Aug. 2011 (Vol. 6841, pp. 743–760). LNCS. https://doi.org/10.1007/978-3-642-22792-9_42.

Bernstein, D. J., Lange, T., Peters, C., & Schwabe, P. (2011b). Really fast syndrome-based hashing. In A. Nitaj & D. Pointcheval (Eds.) *AFRICACRYPT 11* (Vol. 6737, pp. 134–152). LNCS, July 2011. https://doi.org/10.1007/978-3-642-21969-6_9.

Blum, A., Furst, M. L., Kearns, M. J., & Lipton, R. J. (1994). Cryptographic primitives based on hard learning problems. In D. R. Stinson (Eds.) *CRYPTO'93* (Vol. 773, pp. 278–291). LNCS, Aug. 1994. https://doi.org/10.1007/3-540-48329-2_24.

Blum, A., Kalai, A., & Wasserman, H. (2000). Noise-tolerant learning, the parity problem, and the statistical query model. In *32nd ACM STOC,* May 2000 (pp. 435–440). ACM Press. https://doi.org/10.1145/335305.335355.

Bogdanov, A., & Rosen, A. (2017). *Pseudorandom Functions: Three Decades Later.* Cryptology ePrint Archive, Report 2017/652. https://eprint.iacr.org/2017/652.

Bogos, S., & Vaudenay, S. (2016). Optimization of LPN solving algorithms. In J. Hee Cheon & T. Takagi (Eds.) *ASIACRYPT 2016, Part I* (Vol. 10031, pp. 703–728). LNCS, Dec. 2016. https://doi.org/10.1007/978-3-662-53887-6_26.

Bogos, S., Tramer, F., & Vaudenay, S. (2016). On solving LPN using BKW and variants. In (2016).

Bombar, M., Bui, D., Couteau, G., Couvreur, A., Ducros, C., & Servan-Schreiber, S. (2024). FOLEAGE: $\mathbb{F}_4$OLE-based multi-party computation for Boolean circuits. In LNCS, Dec. 2024 (pp. 69–101). https://doi.org/10.1007/978-981-96-0938-3_3.

Bombar, M., Couteau, G., Couvreur, A., & Ducros, C. (2023). Correlated pseudorandomness from the hardness of quasi-abelian decoding. In *CRYPTO 2023, Part IV* (Aug. 2023, pp. 567–601). LNCS. https://doi.org/10.1007/978-3-031-38551-3_18.

Boneh, D., & Waters, B. (2013). Constrained pseudorandom functions and their applications. In K. Sako & P. Sarkar (Eds.) *ASIACRYPT 2013, Part II* (Vol. 8270, pp. 280–300). LNCS, Dec. 2013. https://doi.org/10.1007/978-3-642-42045-0_15.

Both, L., & May, A. (2018). Decoding linear codes with high error rate and its impact for LPN security. In T. Lange & R. Steinwandt (Eds.) *Post-Quantum Cryptography - 9th International Conference, PQCrypto 2018* (pp. 25–46). https://doi.org/10.1007/978-3-319-79063 3_2.

Bouillaguet, C., Delaplace, C., Hamdad, M., & Vergnaud, D. (2025). Practical cryptanalysis of pseudorandom correlation generators based on quasi-Abelian syndrome decoding. In *Cryptology ePrint Archive* .

Boyle, E., Couteau, G., Gilboa, N., Ishai, Y. (2018). Compressing vector OLE. In D. Lie, M. Mannan, M. Backes, & X.F. Wang (Ed.) *ACM CCS 2018*, Oct. 2018 (pp. 896–912). ACM Press. https://doi.org/10.1145/3243734.3243868.

Boyle, E., Couteau, G., Gilboa, N., Ishai, Y., & Orrù, M. (2017). Homomorphic secret sharing: Optimizations and applications. In B. M. Thuraisingham, D. Evans, T. Malkin, & D. Xu (Ed.) *ACM CCS 2017* (pp. 2105–2122). ACM Press. https://doi.org/10.1145/3133956.3134107.

Boyle, E., Couteau, G., Gilboa, N., Ishai, Y., Kohl, L., & Scholl, P. (2019). Efficient pseudorandom correlation generators: Silent OT extension and more. In A. Boldyreva & D. Micciancio (Ed.) *CRYPTO 2019, Part III*, Aug. 2019 (Vol. 11694, pp. 489–518). LNCS. https://doi.org/10.1007/978-3-030-26954-8_16.

Boyle, E., Couteau, G., Gilboa, N., Ishai, Y., Kohl, L., & Scholl, P. (2020a). Efficient pseudorandom correlation generators from ring-LPN. In D. Micciancio & T. Ristenpart (Ed.) *CRYPTO 2020, Part II* (Vol. 12171, pp. 387–416). LNCS. https://doi.org/10.1007/978-3-030-56880-1_14.

Boyle, E., Couteau, G., Gilboa, N., Ishai, Y., Kohl, L., & Scholl, P. (2020b). Correlated pseudo-random functions from variable-density LPN. In *61st FOCS*, Nov. 2020 (pp. 1069–1080). IEEE Computer Society Press. https://doi.org/10.1109/FOCS46700.2020.00103.

Boyle, E., Couteau, G., Gilboa, N., Ishai, Y., Kohl, L., Resch, N., & Scholl, P. (2022). Correlated pseudorandomness from expand-accumulate codes. In Y. Dodis & T. Shrimpton (Ed.) *CRYPTO 2022, Part II* (Vol. 13508, pp. 603–633). LNCS. Aug. 2022. https://doi.org/10.1007/978-3-031-15979-4_21.

Boyle, E., Couteau, G., Gilboa, N., Ishai, Y., Kohl, L., Rindal, P., & Scholl, P. (2019). Efficient two-round OT extension and silent non-interactive secure computation. In L. Cavallaro, J. Kinder, X.F. Wang, & J. Katz (Ed.) *ACM CCS 2019*, Nov. 2019 (pp. 291–308). ACM Press. https://doi.org/10.1145/3319535.3354255.

Boyle, E., Gilboa, N., & Ishai, Y. (2015). Function secret sharing. In E. Oswald, M. Fischlin (Ed.) *EUROCRYPT 2015, Part II*, Apr. 2015 (Vol. 9057, pp. 337–367). LNCS. https://doi.org/10.1007/978-3-662-46803-6_12.

Boyle, E., Gilboa, N., & Ishai, Y. (2016). Function secret sharing: Improvements and extensions. In E. R. Weippl, S. Katzenbeisser, C. Kruegel, A. C. Myers, & S. Halevi (Ed.) *ACM CCS 2016*, Oct. 2016 (pp. 1292–1303). ACM Press. https://doi.org/10.1145/2976749.2978429.

Boyle, E., Goldwasser, S., & Ivan, I. (2014). Functional signatures and pseudorandom functions. In H. Krawczyk (Eds.) *PKC 2014* (Vol. 8383, pp. 501–519). LNCS, Mar. 2014. https://doi.org/10.1007/978-3-642-54631-0_29.

Briaud, P., & Øygarden, M. (2023). A new algebraic approach to the regular syndrome decoding problem and implications for PCG constructions. In LNCS, June 2023 (pp. 391–422). https://doi.org/10.1007/978-3-031-30589-4_14.

Bui, D., Couteau, G., Meyer, P., Passelègue, A., & Riahinia, M. (2024). Fast public-key silent OT and more from constrained Naor-Reingold. In LNCS, June 2024 (pp. 88–118). https://doi.org/10.1007/978-3-031-58751-1_4.

Carrier, K., Debris-Alazard, T., Meyer-Hilfiger, C., & Tillich, J.-P. (2022). Statistical decoding 2.0: Reducing decoding to LPN. In S. Agrawal & D. Lin (Eds.) *ASIACRYPT 2022, Part IV* (Vol. 13794, pp. 477–507). LNCS, Dec. 2022. https://doi.org/10.1007/978-3-031-22972-5_17.

Couteau, G., & Ducros, C. (2023). Pseudorandom correlation functions from variable-density LPN, revisited. In *PKC 2023, Part II*. LNCS, May 2023 (pp. 221–250). https://doi.org/10.1007/978-3-031-31371-4_8.

Couteau, G., Devadas, L., Devadas, S., Koch, A., & Servan-Schreiber, S. (2024). QuietOT: Lightweight oblivious transfer with a public-key setup. In *ASIACRYPT 2024, Part II*. LNCS, Dec. 2024 (pp. 197–231). https://doi.org/10.1007/978-981-96-0888-1_7.

Couteau, G., Meyer, P., Passelègue, A., & Riahinia, M. (2023). Constrained pseudorandom functions from homomorphic secret sharing. In *EUROCRYPT 2023, Part III*, June 2023 (pp. 194–224). LNCS. https://doi.org/10.1007/978-3-031-30620-4_7.

Couteau, G., Rindal, P., & Raghuraman, S. (2021). Silver: silent VOLE and oblivious transfer from hardness of decoding structured LDPC codes. In T. Malkin & C. Peikert (Ed.) *CRYPTO 2021, Part III* (Vol. 12827, pp. 502–534). LNCS. Virtual Event, Aug. 2021. https://doi.org/10.1007/978-3-030-84252-9_17.

Damgård, I., Park, S. (2012). *How Practical is Public-Key Encryption Based on LPN and Ring-LPN?* Cryptology ePrint Archive, Report 2012/699. https://eprint.iacr.org/2012/699.

Debris-Alazard, T., & Tillich, J.-P. (2017). Statistical decoding. In: 2017.

Dittmer, S., Ishai, Y., & Ostrovsky, R. (2021). Line-point zero knowledge and its applications. In LIPIcs. Schloss Dagstuhl, 5:1–5:24. https://doi.org/10.4230/LIPIcs.ITC.2021.5.

Esser, A., & Santini, P. (2023). Not just regular decoding: Asymptotics and improvements of regular syndrome decoding attacks. In *Cryptology ePrint Archive*.

Esser, A., Kübler, R., & May, A. (2017). LPN decoded. In J. Katz & H. Shacham (Ed.) *CRYPTO 2017, Part II* (Vol. 10402, pp. 486–514). LNCS. Aug. 2017. https://doi.org/10.1007/978-3-319-63715-0_17.

Feige, U. (2002). Relations between average case complexity and approximation complexity. In *34th ACM STOC*, May 2002 (pp. 534–543). ACM Press. https://doi.org/10.1145/509907.509985.

Finiasz, M., & Sendrier, N. (2009). Security bounds for the design of code-based cryptosystems. In Mitsuru Matsui (Ed.) *ASIACRYPT 2009*, Dec. 2009 (Vol. 5912, pp. 88–105). LNCS. https://doi.org/10.1007/978-3-642-10366-7_6.

Finiasz, M., Gaborit, P., & Sendrier, N. (2007). Improved fast syndrome based cryptographic hash functions. In *Proceedings of ECRYPT Hash Workshop* (Vol. 2007). Citeseer. 2007 (p. 155).

Fossorier, M. P. C., Kobara, K., & Imai, H. (2006). Modeling bit flipping decoding based on nonorthogonal check sums with application to iterative decoding attack of McEliece cryptosystem. *IEEE Transactions on Information Theory, 53*(1), 402–411.

Gilboa, N., & Ishai, Y. (1999). Compressing cryptographic resources. In M. J. Wiener (Ed.) *CRYPTO '99*, Aug. 1999 (Vol. 1666, pp. 591–608). LNCS. https://doi.org/10.1007/3-540-48405-1_37.

Gilboa, N., & Ishai, Y. (2014). Distributed point functions and their applications. In P. Q. Nguyen & E. Oswald (Ed.) *EUROCRYPT 2014*, May 2014 (Vol. 8441, pp. 640–658). LNCS. https://doi.org/10.1007/978-3-642-55220-5_35.

Goldreich, O., Goldwasser, S., & Micali, S. (1986). How to construct random functions. *Journal of the ACM, 33*(4), 792–807. https://doi.org/10.1145/6490.6503.

Guo, Q., Johansson, T., & Löndahl, C. (2015). A new algorithm for solving Ring-LPN with a reducible polynomial. *IEEE Transactions on Information Theory, 61*(11), 6204–6212.

Guo, Q., Johansson, T., & Löndahl, C. (2020). Solving LPN using covering codes. *Journal of Cryptology, 33*(1), 1–33. https://doi.org/10.1007/s00145-019-09338-8.

Guo, X., Yang, K., Wang, X., Zhang, W., Xie, X., Zhang, J., & Liu, J. (2023). Half-tree: Halving the cost of tree expansion in COT and DPF. In *EUROCRYPT 2023, Part I*. LNCS, June 2023 (pp. 330–362). https://doi.org/10.1007/978-3-031-30545-0_12.

Hazay, C., Orsini, E., Scholl, P., & Soria-Vazquez, E. (2018). TinyKeys: A new approach to efficient multi-party computation. In H. Shacham & A. Boldyreva (Eds.) *CRYPTO 2018, Part III* (Vol. 10993, pp. 3–33). LNCS, Aug. 2018. https://doi.org/10.1007/978-3-319-96878-0_1.

Heyse, S., Kiltz, E., Lyubashevsky, V., Paar, C., & Pietrzak, K. (2012). Lapin: An efficient authentication protocol based on ring-LPN. In A. Canteaut (Ed.) *FSE 2012*, Mar. 2012 (Vol. 7549, pp. 346–365). LNCS. Heidelberg: Springer. https://doi.org/10.1007/978-3-642-34047-5_20.

Ishai, Y., Kilian, J., Nissim, K., & Petrank, E. (2003). Extending oblivious transfers efficiently. In D. Boneh (Ed.) *CRYPTO 2003* (Vol. 2729, pp. 145–161). LNCS, Aug. 2003. https://doi.org/10.1007/978-3-540-45146-4_9.

Katz, J., Shin, J. S., & Smith, A. (2010). Parallel and concurrent security of the HB and HB+ protocols. *Journal of Cryptology, 23*(3), 402–421. https://doi.org/10.1007/s00145-010-9061-2.

Kiayias, A., Papadopoulos, S., Triandopoulos, N., & Zacharias, T. (2013). Delegatable pseudorandom functions and applications. In A.-R. Sadeghi, V. D. Gligor, & M. Yung (Eds.) *ACM CCS 2013*. ACM Press, Nov. 2013 (pp. 669–684). https://doi.org/10.1145/2508859.2516668.

Kirchner, P. (2011). *Improved Generalized Birthday Attack*. Cryptology ePrint Archive, Report 2011/377. https://eprint.iacr.org/2011/377.

Levieil, É., & Fouque, P.-A. (2006). An improved LPN algorithm. In R. De Prisco & M. Yung (Ed.) *SCN 06* (Vol. 4116, pp. 348–359). LNCS, Sept. 2006. https://doi.org/10.1007/11832072_24.

Li, Z., Xing, C., Yao, Y., & Yuan, C. (2025). Efficient pseudorandom correlation generators for any finite field. In LNCS, June 2025 (pp. 145–175). https://doi.org/10.1007/978-3-031-91092-0_6.

Lipmaa, H., & Pavlyk, K. (2015). Analysis and implementation of an efficient ring-LPN based commitment scheme. In M. Reiter & D. Naccache (Eds.) *CANS 15*. LNCS, Dec. 2015 (pp. 160–175). https://doi.org/10.1007/978-3-319-26823-1_12.

Liu, H., Wang, X., Yang, K., & Yu, Y. (2022). *The Hardness of LPN over Any Integer Ring and Field for PCG Applications*. Cryptology ePrint Archive, Report 2022/712. https://eprint.iacr.org/2022/712.

Liu, H., Wang, X., Yang, K., & Yu, Y. (2024). The hardness of LPN over any integer ring and field for PCG applications. In LNCS (pp. 149–179). https://doi.org/10.1007/978-3-031-58751-1_6.

Lyubashevsky, V. (2005). The parity problem in the presence of noise, decoding random linear codes, and the subset sum problem. In 2005.

May, A., & Ozerov, I. (2015). On computing nearest neighbors with applications to decoding of binary linear codes. In E. Oswald & M. Fischlin (Ed.) *EUROCRYPT 2015, Part I*, Apr. 2015 (Vol. 9056, pp. 203–228). LNCS. https://doi.org/10.1007/978-3-662-46800-5_9.

May, A., Meurer, A., & Thomae, E. (2011). Decoding random linear codes in $\tilde{O}(2^{0.054n})$. In D. Hoon Lee & X. Wang (Ed.) *ASIACRYPT 2011*, Dec. 2011 (Vol. 7073, pp. 107–124). LNCS. https://doi.org/10.1007/978-3-642-25385-0_6.

Melchor, C. A., Blazy, O., Deneuville, J. -C., Gaborit, P., & Zémor, G. (2018). Efficient encryption from random quasi-cyclic codes. *IEEE Transactions Information Theory, 64*(5), 3927–3943. https://doi.org/10.1109/TIT.2018.2804444.

Meziani, M., Dagdelen, Ö., Cayrel, P. -L., & El Yousfi Alaoui, S. M. (2011). S-FSB: An improved variant of the FSB hash family. In: *International Conference on Information Security and Assurance*. Springer (pp. 132–145).

Mossel, E., Shpilka, A., & Trevisan, L. (2003). On e-biased generators in NC0. In *44th FOCS*, Oct. 2003 (pp. 136–145). IEEE Computer Society Press. https://doi.org/10.1109/SFCS.2003.1238188.

Münch, J. -P., Schneider, T., & Yalame, H. (2021). *VASA: Vector AES Instructions for Security Applications*. Cryptology ePrint Archive, Report 2021/1493. https://eprint.iacr.org/2021/1493.

Naor, J., & Naor, M. (1990). Small-bias probability spaces: Efficient constructions and applications. In *22nd ACM STOC*, May 1990 (pp. 213–223). ACM Press. https://doi.org/10.1145/100216.100244.

Orlandi, C., Scholl, P., & Yakoubov, S. (2021). The rise of Paillier: Homomorphic secret sharing and public-key silent OT. In A. Canteaut & F.-X. Standaert (Ed.) *EUROCRYPT 2021, Part I,* Oct. 2021 (Vol. 12696, pp. 678–708). LNCS. https://doi.org/10.1007/978-3-030-77870-5_24.

Overbeck, R. (2006). Statistical decoding revisited. In L. Margaret Batten and R. Safavi-Naini (Eds.) *ACISP 06* (Vol. 4058, pp. 283–294). LNCS, July 2006. https://doi.org/10.1007/11780656_24.

Prange, E. (1962). The use of information sets in decoding cyclic codes. In (1962).

Raghuraman, S., Rindal, P., & Tanguy, T. 2023. Expand-convolute codes for pseudorandom correlation generators from LPN. In *CRYPTO 2023, Part IV.* LNCS. Aug. 2023 (pp. 602–632). https://doi.org/10.1007/978-3-031-38551-3_19.

Saarinen, M. -J. O. Linearization attacks against syndrome based hashes. In K. Srinathan, C. Pandu Rangan, & Moti Yung (Eds.) *INDOCRYPT 2007* (Vol. 4859, pp. 1–9). LNCS, Dec. 2007. https://doi.org/10.1007/978-3-540-77026-8_1.

Schoppmann, P., Gascón, A., Reichert, L., & Raykova, M. (2019). Distributed vector-OLE: Improved constructions and implementation. In L. Cavallaro, J. Kinder, X.F. Wang, & J. Katz (Ed.) *ACM CCS 2019* Nov. 2019 (pp. 1055–1072). ACM Press. https://doi.org/10.1145/3319535.3363228.

Stern, J. (1988). A method for finding codewords of small weight. In 1988.

Wagner, D. (2002). A generalized birthday problem. In M. Yung (Ed.) *CRYPTO 2002* (Vol. 2442, pp. 288–303). LNCS, Aug. 2002. https://doi.org/10.1007/3-540-45708-9_19.

Weng, C., Yang, K., Katz, J., & Wang, X. (2021). Wolverine: Fast, scalable, and communication-efficient zero-knowledge proofs for Boolean and arithmetic circuits. In *2021 IEEE Symposium on Security and Privacy*, May 2021 (pp. 1074–1091). IEEE Computer Society Press. https://doi.org/10.1109/SP40001.2021.00056.

Yang, K., Sarkar, P., Weng, C., & Wang, X. (2021). QuickSilver: Efficient and affordable zero-knowledge proofs for circuits and polynomials over any field. In G. Vigna & E. Shi (Ed.) *ACM CCS 2021*, Nov. 2021 (pp. 2986–3001). ACM Press. https://doi.org/10.1145/3460120.3484556.

Yang, K., Weng, C., Lan, X., Zhang, J., & Wang, X. (2020). Ferret: Fast extension for correlated OT with small communication. In J. Ligatti, X. Ou, J. Katz, & G. Vigna (Ed.) *ACM CCS 2020*, Nov. 2020 (pp. 1607–1626). ACM Press. https://doi.org/10.1145/3372297.3417276.

Zhang, B., Jiao, L., & Wang, M. (2016). Faster algorithms for solving LPN. In M. Fischlin & J.-S. Coron (Ed.) *EUROCRYPT 2016, Part I* (Vol. 9665, pp. 168–195). LNCS, May 2016. https://doi.org/10.1007/978-3-662-49890-3_7.

Zichron, L. (2017). *Locally Computable Arithmetic Pseudorandom Generators.*

Chapter 4
Advanced Topics in Silent Secure Computation

In this chapter, we cover more advanced developments in silent secure computation. We warn the reader that some of the material discussed here is much more recent than the results covered in the previous chapters, and might become outdated as the research if and when the area stabilizes. In particular, the last section provides an overview of open problem, targets for future works, and possible directions to investigate, but the area is evolving fast—parts of this section required significant adaptations to account for new results that appeared between the first draft of the book and the current version. The first two sections cover distributed setup protocols and pseudorandom correlation functions: while more advanced, they remain fundamental topics in silent secure computation.

4.1 Distributing the Setup

Even though PCGs and PCFs are the cornerstone of silent secure computation, they do not suffice alone to yield silent protocols: to use them, one also needs to interactively and securely execute the Gen algorithm of the PCG/PCF. While in theory, the fact that Gen outputs short keys suffices to guarantee the existence of a low-communication protocol to securely distribute them, it might not translate to a concretely efficient protocol *in practice*.

Designing efficient protocols for distributing PCG keys has been an important research topic with non-trivial challenges on its own, especially in the setting of security against malicious adversaries. What makes this challenge particularly well motivated is that (1) we have very efficient MPC protocols in the correlated randomness model with security against malicious adversaries, and (2) a nice byproduct of the silent generation of pseudorandom correlations is that, when using a maliciously secure MPC protocol in the correlated randomness model, it suffices to use a

G. Couteau, *An Introduction to Silent Secure Computation*,
SpringerBriefs in Information Security and Cryptography,
https://doi.org/10.1007/978-3-032-07089-0_4

maliciously secure protocol to distribute the PCG keys for the resulting silent protocol to be maliciously secure! In theory, this permits achieving malicious security at
a minimal overhead—and an important research effort has been devoted to turning
this nice theoretical feature into a reality. In particular, the use of PPRFs has been
key to achieving more efficient malicious distributed setup protocols.

4.1.1 Distributing PPRF Keys

In Sect. 3.8.4.2, we describe a classical construction of PPRF from a length-doubling
pseudorandom generator. It helps to view this construction as generating a full binary
tree: the root is labeled with the key. Then, for each node labeled with a string s, the
two children of this node are labeled with s_0 and s_1, respectively, where $(s_0, s_1) =$
$G(s)$ are obtained by parsing the output of the length-doubling PRG on s as a pair of
equal-length strings. If the PPRF inputs are d-bit long, the full binary tree has $n = 2^d$
leaves, and the labels on the leaves correspond to the 2^d evaluations of the PPRF on
all possible inputs. Each input is associated with a leaf via the path it determines: in
the illustration given in Fig. 4.1, the path "right-right-left-left" in blue corresponds
to the input 0011, and the corresponding value is the label of the green-colored leaf.
Given (the label of) any node of the tree, one can reconstruct the subtree rooted at
this node using the PRG G. Then, the punctured key is given by the labels of the
nodes on the co-path to the punctured leaf (the red-colored nodes in Fig. 4.1): they
allow reconstructing all leaves, except for the punctured leaf.

  Given this PPRF, there is an extremely simple but ingenious protocol to securely
distribute the keys. The protocol assumes that the two parties can run an OT protocol

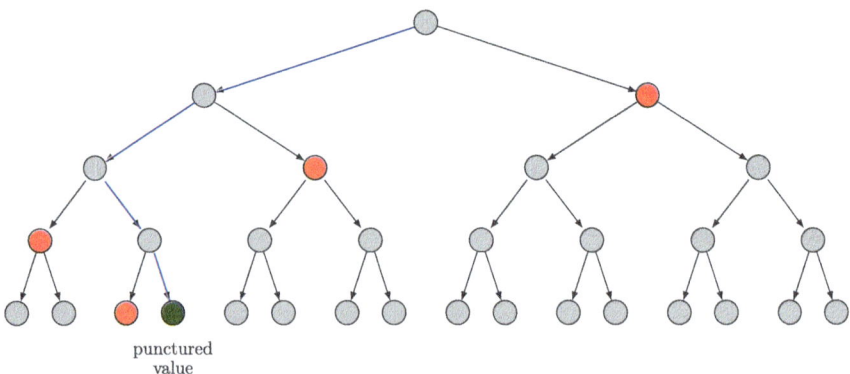

          punctured
            value

Fig. 4.1 The Goldreich–Goldwasser–Micali PPRF construction. The node in green corresponds
to the punctured value, and the edges in blue are the edges on the path from the root to this node,
corresponding to the input 0011 (right-right-left-left) on the example above. The nodes in red
form the co-path to the punctured point, and allow recomputing the full binary tree except for the
punctured point

with λ-bit inputs, e.g., using the method described in Sect. 2.3.2 (or any more modern variant thereof). In this protocol, the party with the PPRF key will play the role of the sender, while the party with the punctured key will play the role of the receiver. We describe the protocol below; the receiver initially holds an input $x \in \{0, 1\}^d$ corresponding to the value at which the PPRF should be punctured.

- The sender samples a root key $K \overset{s}{\leftarrow} \{0, 1\}^\lambda$ and creates the full binary tree, as in Fig. 4.1. We call $(K_1, \ldots, K_d)$ the labels of the nodes on the co-path—that is, the punctured key that should be securely revealed to the receiver (without revealing the value at the punctured point, and without revealing x to the sender).
- For each level $i \in \{1, \cdots, d\}$ of the tree, the sender computes the XOR of all the left children of nodes of the previous level, denoted s_0^i, and the XOR of all the right children of nodes of the previous level, denoted s_1^i.
- For each level $i \in \{1, \cdots, d\}$ of the tree, the sender and the receiver engage in an oblivious transfer protocol where the sender inputs (s_0^i, s_1^i), and the receiver inputs the opposite of the i-th bit of x, denoted $\bar{x}_i$. All OTs are executed in parallel, and the receiver learns $s_{\bar{x}_i}^i$ for $i = 1$ to d.
- From the values $s_{\bar{x}_i}^i$, the receiver reconstructs the keys on the co-path to x:

  - The first key is simply $s_{\bar{x}_1}^1$.
  - The value $s_{\bar{x}_2}^2$ is the XOR of two values that are the left (if $x_2 = 1$) or right (if $x_2 = 0$) children of the root node. Assume that $x_2 = 0$ for simplicity (as in Fig. 4.1). The key observation is that $s_{\bar{x}_2}^2 = K_2 \oplus v_1$, where K_2 is the sought-after punctured key for the level $i = 2$ (in red in Fig. 4.1), and $(v_0, v_1) = G(s_{\bar{x}_1}^1) - G(K_1)$ are the children of the level-1 punctured key K_1 that the receiver already knows. Hence, the receiver can recompute v_1 and "unmask" K_2.
  - Similarly, at each level i, the value $s_{\bar{x}_i}^i$ will be the XOR of K_i with $2^{i-1} - 1$ other values that the receiver can recompute from the keys $(K_1, \ldots, K_{i-1})$.

The above protocol is extremely efficient: it involves only d OTs to securely distribute a PPRF punctured key on an input $x \in \{0, 1\}^d$. On top of the OTs, the cost is dominated by the $2^d - 1$ PRG evaluations, and the $\approx 2^i$ XORs at each level. However, recall that using the PPRF to share noise vectors as in Sect. 3.8.4.3 involves evaluating the PPRF on its entire domain anyway (hence, the PRG evaluations are "for free" during the distributed setup since they are required at a later point anyway), and the added cost of the 2^{d+1} XORs is essentially negligible, since a PRG evaluation is typically much more costly than an XOR.

Security. The protocol is secure in the semi-honest model. The proof of security is a classical exercise in game-based proofs and involves a sequence of d hybrids, one per level of the tree. Here is a sketch: we are going to progressively replace values in the tree (including the punctured point itself) with truly random and independent values. We describe the following sequence of hybrids below; for the sake of readability, we assume $d = 4$ that $x = 0011$ is as in the example of Fig. 4.1 (the general proof can be inferred immediately).

0-th hybrid.   This is the original protocol as described above.

1-st hybrid.   We replace the left and right children of the root key K with truly random and independent values. Let us denote (K_1', K_1) these two values (K_1 is the level-1 punctured key, the first red node on the example, and K_1' is its sibling, the level-1 node on the blue path). As K (used here as the seed of the PRG) is random, this change is unnoticeable by the receiver under the security of the PRG.

2-nd hybrid.   We replace the left and right children of K_1' with truly random and independent values. Here, proving indistinguishability involves a sequence of two arguments: first, by the OT security, K_1' (corresponding to $s_{x_1}^1$, the input *not* selected by the receiver in the first OT) remains fully hidden (in formal terms, the transcript of the OT protocol can be simulated without knowing K_1'). Second, because K_1' is truly random and never leaked to the receiver, we can invoke the pseudorandomness of the PRG G to replace its output with a pair of random strings.

i-th hybrid.   Similarly, as above, we replace the left and right children of the $(i - 1)$-th node on the blue path with random values. Indistinguishability with the previous hybrid requires invoking the OT sender security notion to guarantee that no information about this node is ever revealed, then invoking the PRG security.

d-th hybrid.   In this last hybrid, the children of the $(d - 1)$-th node on the blue path are replaced with random. This makes the punctured point truly random and independent of the values on the co-path, which completes the proof.

Note that in the above proof, we directly "embedded" the proof of security of the underlying protocol inside the analysis of the distributed protocol. Alternatively, one can define a stronger security property for the PPRF in the first place (saying, in essence, that the values on the path from the root to the punctured point are indistinguishable from random) and prove it from the security of G directly, and then prove security of the above protocol using only the security of the OT and invoking the (stronger) PPRF security in a "black-box" way.

Efficiency considerations. While the above protocol is extremely efficient, it suffers from one important downside: as we mentioned, distributing the keys requires evaluating the full GGM tree. We claimed earlier that this is not an issue as the full tree will be evaluated anyway during the noise generation, but this should be toned down a bit for two reasons:

- First, to avoid redoing the full tree expansion from scratch, the parties should store all the leaves at the end of the distributed protocol. However, this can be inconvenient: in the template that we introduced in Sect. 3.2.2, the distributed protocol corresponds to the one-time short interaction that the participants run ahead of time. But then, the silent computation phase must now take place at the same time as the distributed setup, and not anymore in a subsequent offline phase!

- Second, the initial interaction can happen long before the actual protocol (the online phase) takes place. This means that the parties must dedicate a large amount of space to storing the expanded trees over a possibly long duration. Alternatively, the parties can instead only store the PPRF key, but then, they will have to redo the entire tree evaluation later on, losing the benefit of having already completed the tree evaluation.
- Third, as we will cover in the next section, it can be highly desirable to strengthen the PCG notion to allow for a virtually unbounded amount of correlated randomness, where any amount of correlated randomness can be generated on the fly by the participants. This stronger notion comes with a lot of challenges in its own right—we will discuss them next—but it should be noted that the above distributed setup will completely fail in this setting: in this scenario, the tree has an exponential number of leaves and it becomes impossible to fully generate it and store it. Once the root key and punctured key have been generated, this is not necessarily an issue, as each leaf can be generated on the fly, using an amount of work logarithmic in the tree size (d PRG evaluations). But this makes distributing the setup much more challenging, and, in fact, as of the time of the writing of this book, no satisfying solution is known in this setting.

4.1.2 Extension I: DPFs

So far, we have restricted ourselves to semi-honest protocols for distributing PPRFs; this protocol immediately implies a distributed setup for the PCG for subfield VOLE and for OT described in Sects. 3.8.1 and 3.8.2, respectively, as the Gen algorithm boils down to distributing several PPRF keys between the parties. However, some of our PCG constructions cannot rely on PPRFs: this is the case, for example, of the PCG for the OLE correlation introduced in Sect. 3.9. For this PCG, one must instead rely on distributed point functions. Nevertheless, the state-of-the-art distributed point function from (Boyle et al., 2016) has a structure very similar to the above PPRF. A slightly more involved but similar distributed setup protocol can be constructed to distribute the setup of this DPF. While the structure is similar, there is an important difference: in the DPF setting, a "correction word" must be applied at each level to ensure that Alice and Bob maintain shares of 0 when the corresponding node is on the blue path. These correction words are computed iteratively throughout the distributed protocol, and the sender inputs to the i-th level OT are computed from the "corrected" values from the previous level. The consequence is that the d OTs can no longer be executed in parallel: they must be executed sequentially. The total communication remains roughly the same, but the number of rounds now becomes $\Omega(d)$. In a high-latency setting, this can incur a significant slowdown.

4.1.3   Extension II: Malicious Security

The distributed protocol for the PPRF only provides security against semi-honest participants. This is not just a limitation of our analysis: for example, a malicious sender can mount a type of attack called *selective failure attack*. Consider a sender that, in the first OT (that takes as input the left and right children of K), replaces the left input with random. Then, if no failures occur at a later point during the protocol, the sender deduces that the left child was not selected; else, they deduce that the right child was not selected. In both cases, they reconstruct x_1 from this information. Another, more subtle issue is that malicious security of the PPRF protocol in isolation does not suffice: recall that the protocol from Sect. 3.8.4 requires additionally giving $F(K^{(j)}, x^{(j)}) + \Delta$ to the receiver, where Δ is a value known to the sender, $F(K^{(j)}, x^{(j)})$ is the PPRF evaluation with the j-th root key $K^{(j)}$, and $x^{(j)}$ is the j-th punctured point (j ranges from 1 to t, where t is the Hamming weight of the noise vector). In the distributed protocol, this is done by asking the sender to send $\sum_{x \in \{0,1\}^d} F(K^{(j)}, x) + \Delta$: because the receiver can compute $\sum_{x \neq x^{(j)}} F(K^{(j)}, x)$, this lets her retrieve $F(K^{(j)}, x^{(j)}) + \Delta$. However, when the sender is malicious, this introduces an additional attack vector: the sender could send incorrect values, which is virtually identical to sending values $\sum_{x \in \{0,1\}^d} F(K^{(j)}, x) + \Delta_j$ where the Δ_j might not necessarily equal.

   We will not cover further the issue of malicious security in this book, but confine ourselves to observing that these issues can be circumvented by adding some careful checks. In the original work of Boyle et al. (2019), this was done by making the tree one layer deeper, defining the left children in the last layer to be the PPRF values, and using a random linear combination of the right children to let the verifier check that the received material was correctly computed. This check itself is sensitive to a form of selective failure attack, but the attack can be shown to have no impact on the security of the PCG, provided that the underlying syndrome decoding problem remains secure given a small amount of leakage, an assumption that remains plausible and reasonably conservative. A refined but similar checking mechanism was later introduced by Weng et al. (2021), which reduces the concrete overhead of achieving malicious security to a small fraction of the cost of the semi-honest protocol.

4.1.4   Historical Notes and Open Problems

The original distributed protocol for DPFs was introduced by Doerner and shelat in Doerner and Shelat (2017). The specialization to the PPRF setting, which is more round efficient, was introduced concurrently by Boyle et al. (2019) and by Schoppmann et al. (2019). Malicious versions of the protocol were introduced in Boyle et al. (2019) and later refined in Weng et al. (2021).

   The protocol of Doerner and Shelat (2017) requires $\Omega(d)$ rounds. Distributing a DPF using several rounds that does not grow with d is an important research question.

While heavy-hammer solutions exist, using high-end cryptographic primitives, they do not provide more than a feasibility result and, in particular, cannot be based on minimal assumptions. The first constant-round protocol for a DPF based on the minimal assumption of pseudorandom generators was introduced by Boyle et al. (2022). While it represents a significant step forward, the DPF remains significantly less efficient than the one from Boyle et al. (2016) (for which a constant-round distributed setup is not known). Obtaining a constant-round protocol for a DPF of efficiency comparable to that of Boyle et al. (2016) remains an important open question.

All the protocols discussed in this section have a computational cost that scales with the number of leaves of the tree. When the aim is to generate a very large amount of correlation, computing all these leaves at setup time can be prohibitively expensive. Another important research question is to find a distributed protocol whose cost only scales with d, and not 2^d. Such a protocol can always be obtained by evaluating the DPF key generation procedure inside a generic MPC protocol. However, this requires using generic MPC to securely evaluate d calls to a pseudorandom generator, which can be complex and expensive: for example, the AES blockcipher—the most standard choice for instantiating the PRG due to the availability of hardware support for AES instructions—has a circuit with 6800 multiplication gates. For $d = 30$ (corresponding to a target number of 2^{30} correlations) and using $t = 50$, this translates to about 10^6 secure multiplications in the semi-honest setting: this is feasible, but very costly. A work by Bui et al. (2024) introduced a new PPRF that admits a very efficient distributed setup: it requires d parallel OTs and $O(d)$ additional arithmetic operations. However, it relies on relatively non-standard assumptions (a variant of the decision Diffie–Hellman assumption, the hardness of a recent candidate low-complexity weak pseudorandom function) and requires a scalar multiplication over an elliptic curve for each evaluation, which is significantly more costly than the d calls to AES per evaluations required by the GGM PPRF. Furthermore, it only provides a PPRF: obtaining a DPF with a similarly efficient distributed setup remains an open problem.

4.2 Beyond PCGs: Pseudorandom Correlation Functions

In Sects. 3.2.1.2 and 3.2.1.3, we drew a parallel between secure computation in the correlated randomness model and secure communication via the one-time pad: in both cases, pre-distributed random strings satisfying some appropriate relations enable an information-theoretic realization of the target functionality. Then, we explained how pseudorandom generators (or stream ciphers) can be used to compress the one-time pad, yielding efficient secure communication from short keys, to motivate the search for a similar primitive targeting secure computation, which led us to pseudorandom correlation generators.

A few sections later, here we are, equipped with super-efficient PCGs for the OT correlation, and with relatively efficient PCGs for the OLE correlation (and more). However, in a sense that we will make precise very soon, these constructions do not fully mimic the features of stream-cipher-based protocols for secure communication. A useful feature of secure communication protocols is that, after securely exchanging a short key, two parties can *continuously* communicate. Concretely, this means that at any time, the two parties can exchange messages, without having to decide ahead of time on a bound on the amount of communication or to store long keys in advance for later use.

In practice, this can be done by replacing the pseudorandom generator in the construction of Sect. 3.2.1.2 by a pseudorandom function F_K: following their one-time generation of a shared random key $K \in \{0, 1\}^\lambda$, the two parties can publicly agree on a unique nonce x for the session and use the sequence $F_K(x)$, $F_K(x + 1)$, $F_K(x + 2)$, $\cdots$ of pseudorandom strings to mask messages of arbitrary length. This allows the parties, given only K, to generate on the fly and upon need arbitrarily long shared pseudorandom strings to use in the one-time pad protocol. Alternatively, this can also be achieved using a simple PRG in *stream-cipher mode*: after using $G(K) = (k_0, \ldots, k_n)$ to generate n λ-bit pseudorandom strings (assuming G is a PRG from $\{0, 1\}^\lambda$ to $\{0, 1\}^{(n+1)\cdot\lambda}$), the parties can use $(k_1, \ldots, k_n)$ to mask an $n \cdot \lambda$-bit message M, and keep k_0 as a new "fresh" PRG seed to be used in the next communication session.

Switching back to PCGs, it turns out that there are no obvious incremental approaches to silent secure computation using any of the constructions we described so far. A natural approach, similar to the re-keying approach for secure communication that we just sketched, would be to use a portion of the pseudorandom correlations generated so far to run a secure computation protocol for re-generating fresh PCG seeds. However, unlike with secure communication, this approach requires the participants to interact online before they can compute their fresh PCG seeds. In practice, this means that whenever two participants execute a secure computation, they would have to anticipate a bound on the amount of correlations they will need in their next interaction (of course, they can always pick a very large bound, but this comes at a strong cost as we will see next). A much better solution would allow them to decide the amount of correlated randomness they need on the fly, without having to interact first.

Unfortunately, all the PCGs we constructed come with a major limitation: The expansion of the correlated seeds is an "all-or-nothing" procedure, where the target correlation is produced *all at once* without enabling fast random access to the long output. Furthermore, existing PCG constructions do not even support the type of (stateful) incremental evaluation enabled by standard PRGs in stream-cipher mode, because the correlation of the PCG outputs is distinct from the correlation between the PCG keys (while for PRG, the correlation is preserved: equal seeds yield equal pseudorandom strings). This limits the use of PCGs to a monolithic form of silent preprocessing that requires parties to generate one for all and to store big amounts of correlated randomness that they might want to use in the future, or to re-interact to generate fresh PCG seeds whenever they anticipate that they might need to run a secure protocol.

4.2.1 Defining Pseudorandom Correlation Functions

Without further ado, we introduce the notion of pseudorandom correlation functions to capture the ability to perform silent secure computation protocols where, after a one-time short interaction, the parties can on-demand and on the fly generate an a-priori arbitrary amount of pseudorandom correlated strings. A PCF is a pair (PCF.Gen, PCF.Eval) of algorithms where

- PCF.Gen outputs a pair of short correlated keys (k_0, k_1),
- PCF.Eval(k_σ, x) is a deterministic polynomial-time algorithm.

We require the following properties of a PCF: First, the joint distribution of outputs of Eval has to be computationally indistinguishable from truly random outputs satisfying the target correlation. Second, we require that for $\sigma = 0, 1$, when given the key $k_{1-\sigma}$, the outputs of PCF.Eval$(k_\sigma, \cdot)$ are indistinguishable from random outputs of the target correlation when sampled conditioned on the partial outputs from PCF.Eval$(k_{1-\sigma}, x)$.

Preliminaries. To formally define a PCF, we use the notion of reverse-sampleable correlation generator given in Definition 3.3.2. However, we will use a slightly different semantics: when building PCGs, we typically consider the correlation generator $\mathcal{C}$ as generating directly, on input 1^n, an "n-fold" instance of a target correlation (e.g., n copies of an OLE). Here, we will think of our correlation generator $\mathcal{Y}$ as outputting "single-instances" of a target correlation (e.g., a single OLE), and we give it a different name to clarify the semantics. We will also assume a slightly generalized syntax for correlation generators compared with Definition 3.3.1:

Definition 4.2.1 (*Reverse-sampleable correlation generators, modified*) We define a reverse-sampleable correlation generator $\mathcal{Y}$ as in Definitions 3.3.1 and 3.3.2, except that we assume that $\mathcal{Y}(1^\lambda)$ returns a pair of string in $\{0, 1\}^{\tau_0(\lambda)} \times \{0, 1\}^{\tau_1(\lambda)}$ (rather than $\{0, 1\}^\lambda \times \{0, 1\}^\lambda$), where τ_0, τ_1 are output length functions, and pass 1^λ as additional argument to RSample (to cover the case where $\tau_\sigma(\lambda)$ is much smaller than λ).

Note also that the definition of reverse-sampleable correlation generators does not capture correlations with a global parameter that remains the same across samples, as in the sVOLE correlation. This is captured by the notion of reverse-sampleable correlation with setup, which allows all algorithms to depend on a fixed global secret, ensuring consistency across different invocations, formally defined in Boyle et al. (2020a) (we omit it there to avoid overcomplicating an already cumbersome definition).

Definition. We introduce the formal definition of PCFs for a reverse-sampleable correlation generator $\mathcal{Y}$ in Definition 4.2.2. The experiments for the two properties of a PCF, pseudorandom $\mathcal{Y}$-correlated outputs and internal security, are given in Figs. 4.2 and 4.3, respectively. In these experiments, N denotes a bound on the number

$\mathsf{Exp}^{\mathsf{pr}}_{\mathcal{A},N,0}(\lambda):$
for $i = 1$ to $N(\lambda)$:
  $x^{(i)} \xleftarrow{\$} \{0,1\}^{n(\lambda)}$
  $(y_0^{(i)}, y_1^{(i)}) \leftarrow \mathcal{Y}(1^\lambda)$
$b \leftarrow \mathcal{A}(1^\lambda, (x^{(i)}, y_0^{(i)}, y_1^{(i)})_{i \in [N(\lambda)]})$
return b

$\mathsf{Exp}^{\mathsf{pr}}_{\mathcal{A},N,1}(\lambda):$
$(\mathsf{k}_0, \mathsf{k}_1) \leftarrow \mathsf{PCF.Gen}(1^\lambda)$
for $i = 1$ to $N(\lambda)$:
  $x^{(i)} \xleftarrow{\$} \{0,1\}^{n(\lambda)}$
  for $\sigma \in \{0,1\}$:
    $y_\sigma^{(i)} \leftarrow \mathsf{PCF.Eval}(\sigma, \mathsf{k}_\sigma, x^{(i)})$
$b \leftarrow \mathcal{A}(1^\lambda, (x^{(i)}, y_0^{(i)}, y_1^{(i)})_{i \in [N(\lambda)]})$
return b

Fig. 4.2 Pseudorandom $\mathcal{Y}$-correlated outputs of a PCF

$\mathsf{Exp}^{\mathsf{sec}}_{\mathcal{A},N,\sigma,0}(\lambda):$
$(\mathsf{k}_0, \mathsf{k}_1) \leftarrow \mathsf{PCF.Gen}(1^\lambda)$
for $i = 1$ to $N(\lambda)$:
  $x^{(i)} \xleftarrow{\$} \{0,1\}^{n(\lambda)}$
  $y_{1-\sigma}^{(i)} \leftarrow \mathsf{PCF.Eval}(1-\sigma, \mathsf{k}_{1-\sigma}, x^{(i)})$
$b \leftarrow \mathcal{A}(1^\lambda, \sigma, \mathsf{k}_\sigma, (x^{(i)}, y_{1-\sigma}^{(i)})_{i \in [N(\lambda)]})$
return b

$\mathsf{Exp}^{\mathsf{sec}}_{\mathcal{A},N,\sigma,1}(\lambda):$
$(\mathsf{k}_0, \mathsf{k}_1) \leftarrow \mathsf{PCF.Gen}(1^\lambda)$
for $i = 1$ to $N(\lambda)$:
  $x^{(i)} \xleftarrow{\$} \{0,1\}^{n(\lambda)}$
  $y_\sigma^{(i)} \leftarrow \mathsf{PCF.Eval}(\sigma, \mathsf{k}_\sigma, x^{(i)})$
  $y_{1-\sigma}^{(i)} \leftarrow \mathsf{RSample}(1^\lambda, \sigma, y_\sigma^{(i)})$
$b \leftarrow \mathcal{A}(1^\lambda, \sigma, \mathsf{k}_\sigma, (x^{(i)}, y_{1-\sigma}^{(i)})_{i \in [N(\lambda)]})$
return b

Fig. 4.3 Internal security of a PCF. Here, $\mathsf{RSample}$ is the algorithm for reverse sampling $\mathcal{Y}$ as in Definition 3.3.2

of evaluations of the PCF made by the adversary $\mathcal{A}$, and the bit b distinguishes between the real-world experiment ($b = 0$) and the simulated experiment ($b = 1$). The definition below captures a notion of weak pseudorandom functions, which are secure when all queries to the function are uniformly random.

Definition 4.2.2 (*Pseudorandom correlation function (PCF)*) Let $\mathcal{Y}$ be a reverse-sampleable correlation with output length functions $\tau_0(\lambda)$, $\tau_1(\lambda)$ and let $\lambda \le n(\lambda) \le \mathrm{poly}(\lambda)$ be an input length function. A PCF ($\mathsf{PCF.Gen}, \mathsf{PCF.Eval}$) is a pair of algorithms with the following syntax:

- $\mathsf{PCF.Gen}(1^\lambda)$ is a probabilistic polynomial-time algorithm that on input 1^λ, outputs a pair of keys ($\mathsf{k}_0, \mathsf{k}_1$); we assume that λ can be inferred from the keys.
- $\mathsf{PCF.Eval}(\sigma, \mathsf{k}_\sigma, x)$ is a deterministic polynomial-time algorithm that on input $\sigma \in \{0,1\}$, key k_σ and input value $x \in \{0,1\}^{n(\lambda)}$, outputs a value $y_\sigma \in \{0,1\}^{\tau_\sigma(\lambda)}$.

Let N denote a bound on the number of PCF evaluations, B denote a bound on the size of the adversaries, and ε a bound on their success probability. We say ($\mathsf{PCF.Gen}, \mathsf{PCF.Eval}$) is a (weak) (N, B, ε)-*secure pseudorandom correlation function (PCF) for* $\mathcal{Y}$, if the following conditions hold:

- **Pseudorandom $\mathcal{Y}$-correlated outputs.** For every $\sigma \in \{0, 1\}$ and non-uniform adversary $\mathcal{A}$ of size $B(\lambda)$, it holds

$$\left| \Pr[\mathsf{Exp}^{\mathsf{pr}}_{\mathcal{A},N,0}(\lambda) = 1] - \Pr[\mathsf{Exp}^{\mathsf{pr}}_{\mathcal{A},N,1}(\lambda) = 1] \right| \le \varepsilon(\lambda)$$

for all sufficiently large λ, where $\mathsf{Exp}^{\mathsf{pr}}_{\mathcal{A},N,b}(\lambda)$ for $b \in \{0, 1\}$ is as defined in Fig. 4.2. In particular, the adversary is given access to $N(\lambda)$ samples.

- **Internal security.** For each $\sigma \in \{0, 1\}$ and non-uniform adversary $\mathcal{A}$ of size $B(\lambda)$, it holds

$$\left| \Pr[\mathsf{Exp}^{\mathsf{sec}}_{\mathcal{A},N,\sigma,0}(\lambda) = 1] - \Pr[\mathsf{Exp}^{\mathsf{sec}}_{\mathcal{A},N,\sigma,1}(\lambda) = 1] \right| \leq \varepsilon(\lambda)$$

for all sufficiently large λ, where $\mathsf{Exp}^{\mathsf{sec}}_{\mathcal{A},N,\sigma,b}(\lambda)$ for $b \in \{0, 1\}$ is as defined in Fig. 4.3 (again, with $N(\lambda)$ samples).

We say that (PCF.Gen, PCF.Eval) is a *PCF for* $\mathcal{Y}$ if it is a $(p, 1/p, p)$-secure PCF for $\mathcal{Y}$ for every polynomial p. If $B = N$, we will write (B, ε)-secure PCF for short.

The definition above can be strengthened to the notion of strong PCFs. Informally, a strong PCF is defined as in Definition 4.2.2, except that in the experiments for pseudorandom $\mathcal{Y}$-correlated outputs and internal security (given in Figs. 4.2 and 4.3), the PCF inputs $x^{(i)}$ are not sampled uniformly from $\{0, 1\}^{n(\lambda)}$. Instead, they are adaptively chosen by the adversary $\mathcal{A}$ which is given oracle access to PCF.Eval$(1 - \sigma, \mathsf{k}_{1-\sigma}, \cdot)$ for up to N queries. We focus here on weak PCFs for two reasons:

- The constructions we will describe in this write-up are only weak PCFs. This is somewhat inherent to the limitations of our template; we will elaborate on this later.
- Any weak PCF can be heuristically transformed into a strong PCF by hashing the input before feeding it to the function. This heuristic transformation is provably secure if the hash function is modeled as a (programmable) random oracle.

Let us clarify that the distinction between weak and strong PCFs plays a role in secure computation. When using (weak) PCFs to generate N instances of a pseudorandom correlation for a secure computation protocol, the two parties must (without interaction) agree on the N random inputs $x^{(1)}, \ldots, x^{(N)}$. Concretely, this amounts to assuming access to a very long common reference string. A strong PCF, on the other hand, allows for generating the correlations using an arbitrary sequence of distinct inputs (typically a counter, setting $x^{(i)} = i$ for $i = 1, \cdots N$), which does not require any setup assumption. Then, the general transformation of a weak PCF into a strong PCF via a hash function modeled as a random oracle becomes equivalent to the well-known fact that a random oracle H can be used to setup a long common random string $(x^{(1)}, \ldots, x^{(N)})$ by setting $x^{(i)} \leftarrow \mathsf{H}(i)$ for $i = 1$ to N.

Equipped with a proper definition of PCFs, we now turn our attention to the question of constructing them. So, let us go back to our template, shall we?

4.2.2 A Template for Pseudorandom Correlation Functions

Earlier in this book (in Sect. 3.4.2.3), we introduced a template for PCGs for an additive correlation C which combines a pseudorandom generator G with a function secret sharing for the class of functions $C \circ G_k$, where $G_k(i)$ returns the i-th component of $G(k)$. Adapting this template to PCFs is straightforward: to get a PCF for an additive correlation C, we combine a PRF $F = \{F_K\}_{K \in \{0,1\}^*}$ with an FSS scheme for the class of functions $\mathcal{F} = \{C \circ F_K\}_{K \in \{0,1\}^*}$. That's it!

Theorem 4.2.3 *For any* $\lambda \in \mathbb{N}$, *let* $C_\lambda : \mathbb{F}_{2^\lambda} \mapsto \mathbb{G}_\lambda$ *be a function whose range is an Abelian group* $\mathbb{G}_\lambda$, *and let* $m = m(\lambda) \in \text{poly}(\lambda)$. *Let* $F = \{F_{K_\lambda} : [m] \mapsto \mathbb{F}_{2^\lambda}\}_{\lambda \in \mathbb{N}, K_\lambda \in \{0,1\}^\lambda}$ *be a PRF with key space* $\{0,1\}^\lambda$. *Let* $\mathcal{F} = \{C_\lambda \circ F_{K_\lambda} : [m] \mapsto \mathbb{G}_\lambda\}_{\lambda \in \mathbb{N}, K_\lambda \in \{0,1\}^\lambda}$. *Let* (FSS.Gen, FSS.Eval) *be a two-party function secret sharing for the class of functions* $\mathcal{F}$. *Consider the following construction:*

- PCF.Gen(1^λ): *sample* $K \xleftarrow{\$} \{0,1\}^\lambda$ *and output* $(k_0, k_1) \leftarrow$ FSS.Gen($1^\lambda, C_\lambda \circ F_K$).
- PCG.Eval(σ, k_σ, x): *on input* $x \in [m]$, *return* FSS.Eval(σ, k_σ, x).

The construction (PCG.Gen, PCG.Eval) *is a secure PCF for the two-party additive correlation of length 1 defined by* C_λ.

In the above theorem, we view C and F as public information, and the PRF key K_λ as the secret description of $C_\lambda \circ F_{K_\lambda}$. We remind the reader that an additive correlation of length 1 is a correlation defined by a function C_λ that outputs additive shares of $C_\lambda(r)$ to the parties, where r is a random input (see Definition 3.4.1). The proof of security proceeds through a sequence of straightforward game hops. Fix a party index σ:

1. First, using the secrecy property of the FSS, replace the key k_σ in the experiment $\text{Exp}^{\text{sec}}_{\mathcal{A},N,\sigma,0}(\lambda)$ with a simulated key $k_\sigma \leftarrow \text{Sim}(1^\lambda, \text{Leak}(C \circ F_K))$, where here $\text{Leak}(C_\lambda \circ F_{K_\lambda})$ returns (m, C_λ, F). Observe that from this game onward, k_σ does not depend on the PRF key K_λ anymore.
2. Using the pseudorandomness of the PRF F_{K_λ}, replace each evaluation of F_{K_λ} made in PCF.Eval($1 - \sigma, k_{1-\sigma}, x$) by a call to a uniformly random function.
3. At this stage, the samples $y^{(i)}_{1-\sigma}$ from the correlation are truly random. Replace the sampling of $(y^{(i)}_0, y^{(i)}_1)$ by a sampling of $y^{(i)}_\sigma$ followed by $y^{(i)}_{1-\sigma} \leftarrow$ RSample($1^\lambda, \sigma, y^{(i)}_\sigma$). This last game corresponds exactly to the experiment $\text{Exp}^{\text{sec}}_{\mathcal{A},N,\sigma,1}(\lambda)$.

For a detailed formal proof, we refer the reader to Boyle et al. (2020a).

4.2.3 Instantiating the Template: Challenges

We know from Sect. 3.5 that, assuming only a length-doubling PRG, there is an FSS scheme for every function that we can represent as a linear combination of point functions. From there, we can pick one of two paths:

- (1) finding an appropriate pseudorandom function F_K such that $C \circ F_K$ fits within this class or
- (2) if the above does not work out, or does not yield sufficiently satisfying instances, further expanding the class of functions for which we have efficient FSS until it captures $C \circ F_K$.

Looking ahead, we are going to describe two constructions, each of which follows one of the two paths above. But before we delve into the details of these two constructions, it is interesting to take a step back and understand why our construction of PCG from syndrome decoding does not directly work here.

4.2.3.1 What Goes Wrong with Syndrome Decoding

In short, we constructed PCGs as $\mathsf{FSS}(C \circ G_k)$, where k is (a short description of) a sparse vector $\vec{e}$, and $G : k \to H \cdot \vec{e}$ with a public compressive matrix H. Then, G_k computes $H \cdot \vec{e}$ and outputs the i-th entry of this vector. The key hurdle of this construction can be described in one sentence:

Even to evaluate G_k at a single point i, one must compute the entire mapping $\vec{v} \to H \cdot \vec{v}$ before outputting its i-th entry.

Here, the reader might be raising an eyebrow: aren't we computing $H \cdot \vec{e}$ for a very sparse vector $\vec{e}$, say, with $t \approx 50$ nonzero entries? And if so, does this not require summing t columns of H? This is true, but recall that in the PCG construction, the parties will not manipulate $\vec{e}$ directly: rather, using FSS for point functions, they will first construct pseudorandom shares $(\vec{e}_0, \vec{e}_1)$ of $\vec{e}$ (which, unlike $\vec{e}$, are dense vectors!), and compute $(H \cdot \vec{e}_0, H \cdot \vec{e}_1)$.

Anyway, for our application to PCGs, this was no trouble: the PCG.Expand algorithm will, in any case, evaluate the PRG on its entire domain. But when we switch to PCFs, the *entire point* is to enable an incremental evaluation of the primitive, where each output $\mathsf{FSS}(C \circ F_K(i))$ can be computed independently of the others. With our syndrome-decoding-based PRG, the cost of evaluating $G_k(i)$ scales (at best linearly if there is a very fast mapping $\vec{v} \to H \cdot \vec{v}$) with the size of the *entire domain* of G_k. But a pseudorandom function should look random even given arbitrary polynomial access to its evaluations, hence the entire domain of a pseudorandom function F_K must have superpolynomial size![1]

---

[1] While a PRF can be defined over a polynomial-size domain, in this work, we typically focus on PRFs and PCFs which allow an arbitrary polynomial number of queries since our goal is to let the parties generate an arbitrary (polynomial) number of correlations.

4.2.4 Instantiating the Template I: Variable-Density Syndrome Decoding

If we want to follow a similar approach to build PCFs, we will need a few crucial tweaks:

1. The matrix H and noise vector $\vec{e}$ should have superpolynomially large dimensions, yet $\vec{e}$ and the rows of H should admit a compact (polynomial-size) representation. This is easy for $\vec{e}$, which can be represented with $t \cdot \log n$ bits, which remains polynomial even for exponentially large n, but highly non-trivial for H: none of the candidates used for PCG construction satisfy this.
2. There should be an efficiently computable algorithm which, given an index i and (the compact description of) H and $\vec{e}_\sigma$ (party P_σ's FSS share of $\vec{e}$), outputs the i-th entry of $H \cdot \vec{e}_\sigma$.

We stress that we need both conditions above to hold, while simultaneously having the property that $H \cdot \vec{e}$ looks pseudorandom (to any polynomial-time algorithm that gets arbitrary access to the entries of this superpolynomially large vector).

4.2.4.1 Key Idea: A Sparse but Variable-Density H

A natural way to satisfy the two conditions above would be to set H to have exponentially sparse rows, i.e., rows of exponential length $n(\lambda)$ with only $\text{poly}(\lambda)$ nonzero entries: this way, its rows could be described succinctly (or even sampled on the fly). Furthermore, computing the i-th entries of $H \cdot \vec{e}_\sigma$ could be done by computing only the $\text{poly}(\lambda)$ entries of $\vec{e}_\sigma$ corresponding to the nonzero entries $(i_1, \ldots, i_{\text{HW}(h_i)})$ in the i-th row h_i of H, which translates to evaluating $\mathsf{FSS.Eval}(\sigma, \mathsf{k}_\sigma, i_j)$ for $j = 1$ to $\text{HW}(h_i)$ and summing the $\text{poly}(\lambda)$ outputs.

However, there is an apparent contradiction with the property that $H \cdot \vec{e}$ looks pseudorandom: if each h_i is exponentially sparse, and $\vec{e}$ is exponentially sparse as well, how could the inner products $\langle h_i, \vec{e} \rangle$ look pseudorandom? This is where the second idea comes in: we choose h_i and $\vec{e}$ with a *varying density* of nonzero entries. Concretely, by setting h_i and $\vec{e}$ to be dense at the beginning, and more sparse toward the end, we ensure that $\Pr_{h_i}[\langle h_i, \vec{e} \rangle = 0] \approx 1/2$. This does of course not suffice in itself to guarantee security. Nevertheless, we show that, by carefully balancing the varying densities in the vectors, it is possible to simultaneously reduce their Hamming weight to $\text{poly}(\lambda)$ (enabling compact representation and evaluation of $\langle h_i, \vec{e}_\sigma \rangle$) while obtaining a variant of the syndrome decoding problem that is provably secure against all attacks from the linear test framework, which we covered in Sect. 3.7.1. At a high level, the variable density we choose is a regular distribution where each row h_i is divided into D blocks. The j-th block $h_{i,j}$ is sampled as a concatenation of λ unit vectors of length 2^j (observe that each block $h_{i,j}$ has exactly λ nonzero entries and a density of ones equal to $1/2^j$). The noise vector $\vec{e}$ is sampled from the same distribution as each of the rows h_i. The total number of nonzero entries per row is exactly $\lambda \cdot D$, while the length of a row is $O(\lambda \cdot 2^{2D})$. The formal definition follows.

4.2.4.2 Variable-Density Syndrome Decoding

Fix parameters $\mathsf{pp} = (\lambda, D, N = 2^D)$. Let $\mathcal{R}_{\lambda,i}$ be the distribution of random λ-regular vectors over $\mathbb{F}_2^{\lambda \cdot 2^i}$: that is, a sample from $\mathcal{R}_{\lambda,i}$ is obtained by concatenating λ independent length-2^i unit vectors. We let $\mathcal{M}_{\mathsf{vd}}^i(\mathsf{pp})$ denote the distribution over $N \times (\lambda \cdot 2^i)$ matrices over $\mathbb{F}_2$ where each row is sampled independently from $\mathcal{R}_{\lambda,i}$, and $\mathcal{M}_{\mathsf{vd}}(\mathsf{pp})$ denote the distribution over $\mathbb{F}_2^{N \times 2N}$ obtained by sampling $H_i \xleftarrow{\$} \mathcal{M}_{\mathsf{vd}}^i(\mathsf{pp})$ for $i = 1$ to D and outputting $H = H_1 || \cdots || H_D$. Eventually, we denote by $\mathcal{N}_{\mathsf{vd}}(\mathsf{pp})$ the noise distribution obtained by sampling $\vec{e}_i^\mathsf{T} \xleftarrow{\$} \mathcal{R}_{\lambda,i}$ and outputting $\vec{e} \leftarrow (\vec{e}_1 // \cdots // \vec{e}_D) \in \mathbb{F}_2^{2N}$ (that is, $\vec{e}^\mathsf{T}$ is distributed as a row of H).

Definition 4.2.4 (VDSD(λ, D, N)) The *variable-density syndrome decoding* assumption with VDSD λ, D blocks, and number of samples N, denoted VDLPN(λ, D, N), states that

$$\{(H, \vec{b}) \mid H \xleftarrow{\$} \mathcal{M}_{\mathsf{vd}}(\mathsf{pp}), \vec{e} \xleftarrow{\$} \mathcal{N}_{\mathsf{vd}}(\mathsf{pp}), \vec{b} \leftarrow H \cdot \vec{e}\} \overset{c}{\approx} \{(H, \vec{b}) \mid H \xleftarrow{\$} \mathcal{M}_{\mathsf{vd}}(\mathsf{pp}), \vec{b} \xleftarrow{\$} \mathbb{F}_2^N\}.$$

In other words, using the terminology of Definition 3.7.2, VDSD corresponds to the $(\mathcal{M}_{\mathsf{vd}}(\mathsf{pp}), \mathcal{N}_{\mathsf{vd}}(\mathsf{pp}))$-dGSD$(\mathbb{F}_2)$ assumption. In Boyle et al. (2020a), Couteau and Ducros (2023), it was shown that the VDSD assumption is secure against all attacks from the linear test framework (Definition 3.7.3):

Theorem 4.2.5 ((Boyle et al., 2020a; Couteau and Ducros, 2023), informal) *The* VDSD$(\lambda, D, 2^D)$ *assumption with* $D = \Omega(\lambda)$ *is* $(2^{-\Omega(\lambda)}, 2^{-\Omega(\lambda)})$-*secure against linear tests.*

The VDSD assumption parametrized with any $D = \text{poly}(\lambda)$ immediately yields a weak PRF F:

- The vector $\vec{e} \xleftarrow{\$} \mathcal{N}_{\mathsf{vd}}(\mathsf{pp})$ defines the secret key of F.
- Given a string $x \in \{0, 1\}^{\lambda \cdot \sum_{i \leq D} i}$, parse x into D blocks x_i of $\lambda \cdot i$ bits, each divided into λ strings $x_{i,j} \in \{0, 1\}^i$. Map each $x_{i,j}$ to the length-2^i unit vector which has a 1 at $x_{i,j}$. Let $\mathsf{map}(x)$ denote the concatenation of all these unit vectors. Output $F_{\vec{e}}(x) = \mathsf{map}(x)^\mathsf{T} \cdot \vec{e}$.

For a random x, by construction, $\mathsf{map}(x)$ is distributed as a uniformly random column of H. Therefore, breaking the security of the above weak PRF after receiving N samples is equivalent to breaking the VDSD assumption.

4.2.4.3 From VDSD to PCFs

Using FSS for point functions, two parties can compute shares of the evaluation of the weak PRF $F_K : x \to \mathsf{map}(x)^\mathsf{T} \cdot \mathsf{map}(K)$ by summing $\lambda \cdot D = \mathsf{poly}(\lambda)$ evaluations of distributed point functions with respective domains $[\lambda \cdot 2^i]$. To obtain a PCF for some target additive correlation C from there, we have two options:

- For general degree-d additive correlations, we can use the Observation 3.5.5 which lets us extend the class of functions supported by our FSS constructions to handle any degree-d multivariate polynomial evaluated on each of the entries of $H \cdot \vec{e}$. Here, since $H \cdot \vec{e}$ is exponentially large, the transformation works as long as the multivariate polynomial is limited to taking a polynomial number of entries of $H \cdot \vec{e}$ as input. For example, we gave a step-by-step explanation of how to apply this observation to the Beaver triple correlation in Sect. 3.6.4. In this case, we get PCFs for Beaver triples with key size $O(\lambda' \cdot (\lambda \cdot D)^2 \cdot \log D)$ (where λ' denotes a security parameter for the distributed point function—we use a different one because it can typically be smaller than λ). While theoretically interesting, this yields much larger keys than for PCGs: using parameters computed in Couteau and Ducros (2023), we can set $\lambda' = 128$, $\lambda = 350$, and $D = 40$ (recall that the construction allows for up to 2^D pseudorandom instances of the correlation), this yields PCF keys of size 240 Gigabytes: that's not a very practical construction!
- Alternatively, if we only want PCFs for subfield VOLE or for OT, we can follow the much more efficient path outlined in Sect. 3.8, which applies equally well to PCFs. This yields a PCF for OT under the VDSD assumption with key size $O(\lambda' \cdot \lambda \cdot D \cdot \log D)$, which translates to a few megabytes using concrete parameters.

4.2.4.4 Historical Notes

The variable-density syndrome decoding assumption has been introduced in Boyle et al. (2020a) under the name *variable-density learning parity with noise* (VDLPN). In the context of PCGs, LPN and syndrome decoding are two different names for the same assumption, which reflect the emergence of related assumptions from within different communities (the learning theory community for LPN, and the coding theory community for syndrome decoding). Because we make heavy use of the coding-theoretic notions and formalism in this write-up, we decided to present all assumptions as being flavors of a generalized syndrome decoding assumption dGSD.

The security of VDSD was initially proven against attacks from the linear test framework in Boyle et al. (2020a). Later, Couteau and Ducros identified a flaw in the analysis and introduced a corrected proof Couteau and Ducros (2023). This follow-up work also describes a variant of the VDSD assumption that enjoys the same features as the original assumption, but also benefits from a much tighter proof of security against linear tests, allowing one to derive concrete provably secure parameters (the analysis in Boyle et al. (2020a) was purely asymptotic).

4.2.5 Instantiating the Template II: Expand-Accumulate Syndrome Decoding

The construction from variable-density syndrome decoding induces a much larger overhead compared to PCG constructions, mainly because of the $\lambda \cdot D$ factor in the key length (and number of FSS evaluations per output) which is directly inherited from the use of a variable-density distribution (together with the constraints imposed by the security in the linear test framework). In this section, we will briefly cover a more recent and much more efficient construction that circumvents the limitations of the previous construction. The key insight underlying this improved construction lies in using more advanced FSS constructions for predicates such as the greater-than predicates, and their generalization to multi-dimensional rectangles. That is, unlike all other constructions described in this book so far, *this new* PCF *cannot be based on a distributed point function in a black-box way*. Below, we sketch both the more advanced FSS schemes used in the construction and the new variant of syndrome decoding tailored to these advanced FSS. In the spirit of not making this book much longer than it already is, we will stick to relatively high-level sketches of the ideas here. The construction outlined in this section was described in Boyle et al. (2022).

4.2.5.1 Intuition

As before, we want to build a suitable "FSS-friendly" PRF using a syndrome decoding variant, where the noise $\vec{e}$ will be specified by the PRF key, and a random input x will define a random row from the parity-check matrix H. The goal is to define H and $\vec{e}$ such that (1) succinct shares of $\vec{e}$ can be efficiently distributed using and efficient function secret sharing scheme, and (2) obtaining shares of $\langle \vec{h}, \vec{e}_\sigma \rangle$ for a random row $\vec{h}$ of H and a (pseudo)random shares of $\vec{e}$ (computed via FSS) can be done efficiently (i.e., in polynomial time), even when the vectors $\vec{h}, \vec{e}$ have length exponential in λ.

The key idea underlying the construction is to replace the sparse noise $\vec{e}$ by an *interval noise*. A t-interval noise is filled with $t/2$ randomly placed all-1 strings. More precisely, $\vec{e}$ is sampled as follows: first, sample a random t-sparse $\vec{e}'$. Next, *accumulate* $\vec{e}'$ into $\vec{e}$: set $e_1 \leftarrow e_1'$, $e_2 \leftarrow e_1' \oplus e_2'$, $e_3 \leftarrow e_1' \oplus e_2' \oplus e_3'$, and so on. The resulting distribution has the same entropy as the distribution of t-sparse vectors (since accumulating is a bijective mapping), but (crucially) it produces vectors whose proportion of zeroes and ones is balanced. Then, the expand-accumulate syndrome decoding assumption, which we introduce afterward, essentially says that $(M, M \cdot \vec{e})$ is indistinguishable from $(M, \vec{b})$, where $\vec{b}$ is a random vector, M is a random *sparse* matrix, and $\vec{e}$ is a random t-interval noise. Because $\vec{e}$ is not sparse, this assumption can hold even when H is very sparse, and we provide heuristic support for its security using the linear test framework. The second core observation underlying the result from Boyle et al. (2022) is that t-interval noise can be written as a sum of t vectors of the form $(11 \cdots 1 \| 00 \cdots 0)$, and such vectors can be succinctly shared using function secret sharing for *interval functions* $f_{<\alpha}$ which map every $x < \alpha$ to 1, and every $x \geq \alpha$ to 0.

The presentation below follows the outline of the intuition above, with the following modifications:

- The rate of the code is fixed to $1/5$ (that is, H is an N-by-$5N$ matrix) for concreteness. This choice strikes a reasonable balance between efficiency and achieving good security bounds against linear tests.
- Observe that one can write a t-interval noise $\vec{e}$ as $\Delta_N \cdot \vec{e}'$, where $\vec{e}'$ is a t-sparse noise, and Δ_N is a $5N$-by-$5N$ lower triangular matrix filled with ones. In the definition below, we absorb the accumulation into the parity-check matrix: that is, we view $H = M \cdot \Delta_N$ as the parity-check matrix, and the t-sparse vector $\vec{e}'$ as the noise (the two views are equivalent because Δ_N is a public invertible matrix). This presentation is more in line with describing expand-accumulate syndrome decoding as a variant of syndrome decoding over a standard noise distribution (but our description with t-interval noise matches more closely the intuition that motivated the approach).
- Eventually, we let $\vec{e}'$ be a *regular* t-sparse noise as in previous constructions, since it yields much more efficient constructions and provides the same security guarantees against linear tests (and does heuristically not seem to reduce security).

4.2.5.2 Expand-Accumulate Syndrome Decoding

Fix parameters $\mathsf{pp} = (t, c, N)$. $N = N(\lambda)$ is the number of samples (typically exponential in λ, $c = c(\lambda)$ is a matrix sparsity parameter (typically $c = \Theta(\log N)$ or $\omega(\log N)$), and $t = t(\lambda)$ is the Hamming weight of the noise (typically $t = \Omega(\lambda)$). Let Δ_N denote a $5N$-by-$5N$ lower triangular matrix filled with ones. We let $\mathcal{M}_{\mathsf{ea}}(\mathsf{pp})$ denote the distribution obtained by sampling an N-by-$5N$ matrix M whose entries are independent Bernoulli samples equal to 1 with probability $c/2N$, and outputting $H = M \cdot \Delta_N$. Let $\mathsf{Ber}_{c/2N}^{5N}$ denote the distribution of the rows of M (that is, the rows are sampled as $5N$ independent Bernoulli samples). We denote by $\mathcal{N}_{\mathsf{ea}}(\mathsf{pp})$ the distribution obtained by concatenating t random unit vectors of length $5N/t$.

Definition 4.2.6 (EASD(t, c, N)) The *expand-accumulate syndrome* assumption with noise weight t, matrix sparsity c, and number of samples N, denoted EASD(t, c, N), states that

$$\{(H, \vec{b}) \mid H \overset{\$}{\leftarrow} \mathcal{M}_{\mathsf{ea}}(\mathsf{pp}), \vec{e} \overset{\$}{\leftarrow} \mathcal{N}_{\mathsf{ea}}(\mathsf{pp}), \vec{b} \leftarrow H \cdot \vec{e}\} \overset{c}{\approx} \{(H, \vec{b}) \mid H \overset{\$}{\leftarrow} \mathcal{M}_{\mathsf{ea}}(\mathsf{pp}), \vec{b} \overset{\$}{\leftarrow} \mathbb{F}_2^N\}.$$

The security of EASD against attacks from the linear test framework is directly stated as a theorem about the minimum distance of the code spanned by H in Boyle et al. (2022):

Lemma 4.2.7 (Boyle et al. (2022), Theorem 3.10) *Fix a parameter $c = \omega(\log N)$. The code generated by the rows of $H = M \cdot \Delta_N$ has minimum distance at least $\Omega(N)$, with probability at least $1 - N^{-\omega(1)}$ over the choice of H.*

We now explain how to get a weak PRF from the EASD assumption. Let $\vec{e}_1, \ldots, \vec{e}_t$ denote the t unit blocks of $\vec{e}$, and let $i_1, \ldots, i_t$ denote the indices of their nonzero entries. Observe that $\vec{v} \leftarrow \Delta_N \cdot \vec{e}$ can be decomposed into t blocks $\vec{v}_1, \ldots, \vec{v}_t$ such that each block $\vec{v}_j$ for j odd is of the form:

$$(0, \ldots, 0, 1, \ldots, 1),$$

where the index of the first 1 is i_j. When j is even, the block is similar, but in reverse order: $(1, \ldots, 1, 0, \ldots, 0)$, with a first 0 at position i_j. This is more easily observed by noting that the operator $\vec{u} \rightarrow \Delta_N \cdot \vec{u}$ is the *accumulator* operator, which outputs a vector $\vec{v}$ whose j-th entry is the XOR of all entries of $\vec{u}$ from 1 to j. Now, each of these blocks can be seen as the truth table of a greater-than predicate, either $f_{i_j}^{\geq}(\ell)$ which outputs 1 iff $\ell \geq i_j$ (for odd j), or $f_{i_j}^{\leq}(\ell)$ which outputs 1 iff $\ell \leq i_j$ (for even j). This observation is what allows to compute the i-th entry of $M \cdot \Delta_N \cdot \vec{e}$ without computing the full vector, by evaluating $\approx c$ greater-than predicates on inputs defined by the i-th row of H (whose Hamming weight is close to c with high probability).

- As for VDSD, the vector $\vec{e} \xleftarrow{\$} \mathcal{N}_{\mathsf{ea}}(\mathsf{pp})$ defines the secret key of F. Let K denotes its compressed description ($K \in \{0, 1\}^{t \cdot \log(5N/t)}$).
- On input a random x,

  - Use x as the randomness to sample a length-$5N$ vector $h \leftarrow \mathsf{Ber}_{c/2N}^{5N}(x)$ from the distribution $\mathsf{Ber}_{c/2N}^{5N}$.
  - Let c' be the Hamming weight of h and let $(\ell_1, \ldots, \ell_{c'})$ denote the positions of the nonzero entries in h. Divide h into t equal-length blocks. For $j = 1$ to c', retrieve the index j' of the block where ℓ_j falls, and compute y_j as $f_{i_{j'}}^{\geq}(\ell_j)$ (if j' is odd) or as $f_{i_{j'}}^{\leq}(\ell_j)$ (if j' is even).
  - Output $F_K(x) = \bigoplus_{j=1}^{t} y_j$.

The function is indeed efficient, as it requires sampling a vector of average density c and XORing the outputs of t greater-than predicates. We will let the reader check that the value $F_K(x)$ corresponds exactly to $h \cdot \Delta_N \cdot \vec{e}$, where $h = \mathsf{Ber}_{c/2N}^{5N}(x)$ is sampled as a uniformly random row of H. Therefore, distinguishing F_K from a random function using at most N calls entails distinguishing $H \cdot \Delta_N \cdot \vec{e}$ from random, which contradicts the EASD assumption.

4.2.5.3 Function Secret Sharing for Intervals

As we just saw, EASD also yields a weak PRF. But where the PRF obtained from VDSD could be written as an XOR of point functions that is not the case anymore:

rather, we have a weak PRF which can be written as an XOR of *greater-than pred-icates*. Fortunately, it turns out that there also exist efficient constructions FSS for greater-than predicates (called *distributed comparison functions*, or DCFs (Boyle et al., 2016, 2021)), assuming only a length-doubling pseudorandom generator. The construction, while more involved, follows an approach similar to the construction of distributed point functions. Informally, a DCF allows one to efficiently share a comparison function $f_{<\alpha}^{\beta} : [N] \to \mathbb{F}$ which maps every $x < \alpha$ to β and every $x \geq \alpha$ to 0.

4.2.5.4   From EASD to PCFs

Using FSS for the greater-than predicate, two parties can compute shares of the eval-uation of the weak PRF F_K defined above. To obtain a PCF for some target additive correlation C from there, we have again two options:

General construction for degree-d correlations. For general degree-d additive correlations, use the Observation 3.5.5. But there is a catch: while the product of point functions is still a point function (with quadratically larger domain), the product of two greater-than predicates is not a greater-than predicate anymore, but rather a predicate defined by a "two-dimensional rectangle." Fortunately, the constructions described in the work of Boyle et al. (2016) extend to predicates defined by multi-dimensional rectangles, as a particular case of the general construction of PRG-based FSS for predicates defined by an arbitrary decision tree. Concretely, if we target the Beaver triple correlation (a degree-2 correlation), we must rely on the function class of two-dimensional $5N/t \times 5N/t$ intervals over a ring $\mathcal{R}$, where each function in the class is specified by a pair of indices $\alpha_1, \alpha_2 \in [5N/t]$ and $\beta \in \mathcal{R}$, and defined by

$$f_{\alpha_1, \alpha_2, \beta} : [5N/t] \times [5N/t] \to \mathcal{R}$$
$$(x_1, x_2) \mapsto \begin{cases} \beta & \text{if } x_1 < \alpha_1 \text{ and } x_2 < \alpha_2 \\ 0 & \text{otherwise.} \end{cases}$$

The FSS construction from Boyle et al. (2016) has a key size bounded by $2|V|(\lambda + 1)$ bits, where V is the set of nodes in the binary decision tree. A $5N/t \times 5N/t$ interval function can be expressed as a decision tree with $2\log(5N/t)(\log(5N/t) + 1) + 1$ nodes, giving a key size of roughly $4\log^2 5N/t\lambda$ bits for the FSS scheme. Plugging this FSS in our construction for Beaver triples yields a PCF with a key size of roughly $4 \cdot (t \cdot \log(5N/t))^2 \lambda$ bits. Using the parameter estimations from Boyle et al. (2022), this translates to keys of size about 200 megabytes.

Specialized construction for OT correlations. Alternatively, if we only want PCFs for subfield VOLE or for OT, we can again follow the much more efficient path outlined in Sect. 3.8. In fact, for the same reason that we could replace the DPF with a PPRF when tailoring the template to the OT correlation, it turns out that a relaxed notion of distributed comparison function suffices, and that this notion can be realized more efficiently. Let me skip the details at this stage and refer the reader to Boyle et al. (2022) to discover in more detail what relaxed DCFs are, and how they can be constructed. We will just note that using this approach, the EASD assumption yields a very efficient PCF, with keys in the 200-kilobyte range, and the ability to generate around 10^5 pseudorandom OTs per second on one core of a standard laptop (e.g., any modern laptop with a processor that has the AES-NI instruction set).

4.3 Beyond Pseudorandom Correlation Functions

We are now reaching the end of this book, which we hope conveys some useful intuitions about pseudorandom correlation generators and their variants: how to build them, how efficient they are, and what challenges lie on the road to better PCGs and PCFs. Before we leave you, let us briefly mention a few more thrilling directions and topics, some of which we briefly mentioned in passing in this write-up.

4.3.1 Multi-party PCGs

We touched on this very briefly in Sect. 3.9.5. In short, all constructions we have described throughout this entire book are restricted to the two-party setting, and as such, they only enable two-party silent secure computation. The more general setting of n-party silent MPC requires a generalization of PCGs to n-party PCGs. And the reason we have not introduced the notion is... We do not know how to construct it yet!

This is not entirely true. For degree-2 correlations, n-party PCGs can be obtained via the notion of programmable PCG, which we will discuss below. For more general correlations, it is known that n-party PCGs follow from high-end cryptographic primitives, such as indistinguishability obfuscation (Boyle et al., 2015) or spooky encryption (Dodis et al., 2016) (the latter being known from the LWE assumption). However, none of these constructions are anywhere near practical, leaving a wide gap between the two-party setting, where we can base concretely efficient protocols on coding-theoretic assumptions, and the n-party setting for $n > 2$, where only feasibility results using "heavy-hammer" cryptography are known. The issue lies not in the template itself, which extends immediately to the n-party setting, but in the FSS component: in fact, the two works we mentioned above (Boyle et al., 2015; Dodis et al., 2016) construct multi-party FSS, and the application to n-party PCGs follows by plugging these FSS into the template.

4.3.1.1 The Challenge of Multi-party DPFs

Now, to instantiate the template from coding-theoretic assumptions, when targeting low-degree additive correlations, it would suffice to have an n-party FSS for point functions only. Unfortunately, while two-party FSS for point functions with domain size m is known with key size $O(\lambda \cdot \log m)$, the best known three-party constructions have key size $O(\lambda \cdot \sqrt{m})$. This construction is achieved using a slight tweak on the construction which we described in Sect. 3.5.2.1:

- To deal "compressed shares of zero" to three parties, the dealer distributes unordered pairs of PRG seeds $\{a, b\}$, $\{a, c\}$, and $\{b, c\}$ to the three parties, who expend them by XORing the outputs of the PRG on each of them. This works, because $(\mathsf{PRG}(a) \oplus \mathsf{PRG}(b)) \oplus (\mathsf{PRG}(a) \oplus \mathsf{PRG}(c)) \oplus (\mathsf{PRG}(b) \oplus \mathsf{PRG}(c)) = 0$.
- For the α_0-th row, the dealer distributes instead unordered pairs of the form $\{a, b\}$, $\{a, c\}$, and $\{a, d\}$. Observe now that $(\mathsf{PRG}(a) \oplus \mathsf{PRG}(b)) \oplus (\mathsf{PRG}(a) \oplus \mathsf{PRG}(c)) \oplus (\mathsf{PRG}(a) \oplus \mathsf{PRG}(d))$ is pseudorandom from the viewpoint of any pair of parties (for example, it looks pseudorandom to the first two parties because of the $\mathsf{PRG}(d)$ term). Yet, no pair of parties can distinguish their seeds from three-party compressed shares of zeroes: they always just see a pair of unordered sets with a single common element.

Unfortunately, unlike the two-party construction, there is no known variant of this technique that opens itself to recursive composition, hence the method is stuck at $O(\sqrt{m})$-sized keys (ignoring terms depending on λ). This is still a non-trivial key size, but when using the template for degree-d additive correlation, there is a power-of-d blowup in the seed size, which becomes already linear in m for $d = 2$!

When targeting only three-party Beaver triples, this limitation can be circumvented by using the more efficient PCG for OLEs which we covered in Sect. 3.9, since it avoids this quadratic overhead. This approach yields three-party PCGs for Beaver triples from the ring syndrome decoding assumption with non-trivial key size $O(t^2 \cdot \lambda \cdot \sqrt{m})$, which have found some interesting applications in recent works Abram and Scholl (2022) but are still considerably less efficient than their two-party counterpart.

4.3.1.2 Nesting to the Rescue

To circumvent the limitations of the PRG-based construction of FSS for point functions, one possible direction is to rely on a nesting technique. At a high level, the idea of nesting is to combine an external FSS scheme within an internal FSS scheme. Concretely, suppose you have a two-party FSS scheme $\mathsf{FSS}_{\mathsf{in}} = (\mathsf{FSS}_{\mathsf{in}}.\mathsf{Gen}, \mathsf{FSS}_{\mathsf{in}}.\mathsf{Eval})$ for some class of functions $\mathcal{F}_{\mathsf{in}}$, and an outer two-party FSS scheme $\mathsf{FSS}_{\mathsf{out}} = (\mathsf{FSS}_{\mathsf{out}}.\mathsf{Gen}, \mathsf{FSS}_{\mathsf{out}}.\mathsf{Eval})$ for the class of functions $\mathcal{F}_{\mathsf{out}} = \{x \to \mathsf{FSS}_{\mathsf{in}}.\mathsf{Eval}(\mathsf{k}, f(x)) \mid f \in \mathcal{F}_{\mathsf{in}}\}$ (that is, the outer scheme supports a class of function that evaluates $\mathsf{FSS_{in}.Eval}$ on top of functions from $\mathcal{F}_{in}$). Then one directly gets a four-party FSS scheme for the class $\mathsf{FSS_{in}}$:

- Generate 4 keys by running $(k_0, k_1) \leftarrow \mathsf{FSS_{in}.Gen}(f)$, and then

$$(k_{\sigma,0}, k_{\sigma,1}) \leftarrow \mathsf{FSS_{out}.Gen}(k_\sigma, f)$$

  for $\sigma = 0, 1$.
- To evaluate shares of $f(x)$, each pair of parties $(P_{\sigma,0}, P_{\sigma,1})$ runs $\mathsf{FSS_{out}.Eval}(k_{\sigma,b}, x)$ for $\sigma, b = 0, 1$ to obtain additive shares of $\mathsf{FSS_{in}.Eval}((k_\sigma, f), x)$. The terms $\mathsf{FSS_{in}.Eval}((k_\sigma, f), x)$ for $\sigma = 0, 1$ form themselves additive shares of $f(x)$, as expected.

The main downside of nesting is that the cost of the evaluation algorithm blows up: for a single level of nesting, we already require homomorphically evaluating the evaluation algorithm $\mathsf{FSS_{in}.Eval}$ within $\mathsf{FSS_{out}.Eval}$. A direct use of this strategy gets stuck at a single level of nesting. Boyle et al. (2023) used this direct nesting approach to obtain four-party PCGs for a non-trivial class of correlations (those that can be computed by a very low-depth circuit). A more involved nesting strategy was later introduced by Couteau and Kumar (2024), which allowed them to push the number of nesting levels to 2 and to get an eight-party PCG for low-depth circuits (where "low" means doubly logarithmic here). Eventually, Couteau et al. (2025) built upon this method to enable an arbitrary number of nesting, and obtained as a result n-party PCGs for any constant-degree correlation for any n. Their construction relies on standard cryptographic assumptions (LPN and MQ) but is purely of theoretical interest.

4.3.1.3 Programmability to the Rescue

A much more practical solution is offered by the notion of *programmable* PCGs. At a high level, a programmable PCG has the feature that multiple instances of the two-party PCG can be combined into a single instance of an n-party PCG. This is easier to see if the reader remembers the construction of n-party Beaver triples from two-party Beaver triples from Sect. 2.7.2.1: one can view an n-party Beaver triple as a linear combination of $O(n^2)$ "correlated" two-party Beaver triples. Programmable PCGs for Beaver triples allow precisely to correlate two instances in the following way: given a pair of keys (k_0, k_1) generating shares of pseudorandom vectors $(\vec{a}, \vec{b})$ and of their component-wise product $\vec{a} \odot \vec{b}$, one can generate a related pair of keys (k_0, k_1) generating shares of pseudorandom vectors $(\vec{a}, \vec{c})$ and their component-wise product $\vec{a} \odot \vec{c}$, with a new pseudorandom vector $\vec{c}$, but the same $\vec{a}$ as before.

The notion of programmable PCGs has been introduced in Boyle et al. (2019), and a programmable PCG for Beaver triples was described in Boyle et al. (2020b). It offers a practical way to achieve n-party PCGs, with two main caveats:

- It is not compatible with the technique that lets one generate PCG keys for *authenticated* Beaver triples, which we mentioned in Sect. 3.9.4. Concretely, this means that we do not have an efficient strategy, as of today, to generate (silently) the type of n-party correlated randomness used in malicious secure computation.
- The cost of sharing an n-party correlation scales as n^2, while a "direct" FSS-based construction (obtained by plugging an n-party FSS in the template) would have keys of size scaling linearly with n. This makes the construction efficient only for a relatively small number of parties.

4.3.2   Public-Key PCFs

Eventually, the notion of PCF, which we covered in Sect. 4.2, is still not the perfect counterpart to the efficient protocols we have for the easier setting of secure communication. The reader might remember that we described PCF as a means to emulate a property similar to what one gets from stream ciphers, but in the secure computation setting: a way to continuously and on-demand generate the appropriate shared material to be used in a two-party secure computation protocol.

Now, PCFs like stream ciphers require a distributed setup phase, where the two parties will interact to generate short keys. Over a large network, say, with n users, this means that if n parties want to be able to do pairwise secure computations at any point in the future, they will need to run $\Omega(n^2)$ pairwise distributed setup protocols among themselves, to let each pair of parties obtain shared PCF keys. For secure communication, however, this can be circumvented using public-key cryptography: in modern secure communication protocols, each participant simply uploads a short public key online and stores a short associated secret key. Now, whenever two parties P_i, P_j want to communicate, they can directly derive a shared key K from $(\mathsf{pk}_j, \mathsf{sk}_i)$ and $(\mathsf{pk}_i, \mathsf{sk}_j)$, respectively. This means that only $O(n)$ communications are required to enable secure communication between every pair of nodes in the network—a fundamental property over a very large network such as the Web.

A strengthening of the notion of PCF, dubbed *public-key PCF*, was described in Orlandi et al. (2021) to emulate precisely these features. Informally, a public-key PCF enables all parties to publish online a short public key and store a short secret key, such that each pair (P_i, P_j) of parties can later run a key derivation algorithm (without further communication) $\mathsf{k}_i \leftarrow \mathsf{KeyDer}(\mathsf{pk}_j, \mathsf{sk}_i, i)$ and $\mathsf{k}_j \leftarrow \mathsf{KeyDer}(\mathsf{pk}_i, \mathsf{sk}_j, j)$ so that the key pair $(\mathsf{k}_i, \mathsf{k}_j)$ is a PCF key pair (from which the parties can later derive an arbitrary amount of correlated pseudorandomness). None of the constructions described in this book achieves the stronger notion of public-key PCF. The work of Orlandi et al. (2021) described the first "reasonably efficient" construction using clever and elegant ideas, but their construction is still about five orders of magnitude slower than, for example, the PCF based on Expand-Accumulate codes. A more recent construction by Bui et al. (2024) achieves much greater efficiency (about 40k evaluations per second on one core of a modern laptop) at the cost of relying on less standard assumptions. However, their construction is limited exclusively to the OT correlation. Countless open problems remain: can we obtain even faster public-key PCFs? Can we design efficient public-key PCFs for other correlations, such as OLE or vector-OLE? Can we build *post-quantum* public-key PCFs? All of these questions are fascinating open problems.

References

Abram, D., & Scholl, P. (2022). Low-communication multiparty triple generation for SPDZ from ring-LPN. In G. Hanaoka, J. Shikata, & Y. Watanabe (Eds.) *PKC 2022, Part I* (Vol. 13177, pp. 221–251). LNCS, Mar. 2022. https://doi.org/10.1007/978-3-030-97121-2_9.

Boyle, E., Chandran, N., Gilboa, N., Gupta, D., Ishai, Y., Kumar, N., & Rathee, M. (2021). Function secret sharing for mixed-mode and fixed-point secure computation. In A. Canteaut & F.-X. Standaert (Eds.) *EUROCRYPT 2021, Part II* (Vol. 12697, pp. 871–900). LNCS, Oct. 2021. https://doi.org/10.1007/978-3-030-77886-6_30.

Boyle, E., Couteau, G., & Meyer, P. (2023). Sublinear-communication secure multiparty computation does not require FHE. In *EUROCRYPT 2023, Part II*. LNCS. June 2023 (pp. 159–189). https://doi.org/10.1007/978-3-031-30617-4_6.

Boyle, E., Couteau, G., Gilboa, N., Ishai, Y., Kohl, L., & Scholl, P. (2019). Efficient pseudorandom correlation generators: Silent OT extension and more. In A. Boldyreva & D. Micciancio (Eds.) *CRYPTO 2019, Part III* (Vol. 11694, pp. 489–518). LNCS, Aug. 2019. https://doi.org/10.1007/978-3-030-26954-8_16.

Boyle, E., Couteau, G., Gilboa, N., Ishai, Y., Kohl, L., & Scholl, P. (2020a). Correlated pseudorandom functions from variable-density LPN. In *61st FOCS*. IEEE Computer Society Press, Nov. 2020 (pp. 1069–1080). https://doi.org/10.1109/FOCS46700.2020.00103.

Boyle, E., Couteau, G., Gilboa, N., Ishai, Y., Kohl, L., & Scholl, P. (2020b). Efficient pseudorandom correlation generators from ring-LPN. In D. Micciancio & T. Ristenpart (Eds.) *CRYPTO 2020, Part II* (Vol. 12171, pp. 387–416). LNCS, Aug. 2020. https://doi.org/10.1007/978-3-030-56880-1_14.

Boyle, E., Couteau, G., Gilboa, N., Ishai, Y., Kohl, L., Resch, N., & Scholl, P. (2022). Correlated pseudorandomness from expand-accumulate codes. In Y. Dodis & T. Shrimpton (Eds.) *CRYPTO 2022, Part II* (Vol. 13508). LNCS, Aug. 2022 (pp. 603–633). https://doi.org/10.1007/978-3-031-15979-4_21.

Boyle, E., Couteau, G., Gilboa, N., Ishai, Y., Kohl, L., Rindal, P., & Scholl, P. (2019). Efficient two-round OT extension and silent non-interactive secure computation. In L. Cavallaro, J. Kinder, X.F. Wang, & J. Katz (Eds.) *ACM CCS 2019*. ACM Press, Nov. 2019 (pp. 291–308). https://doi.org/10.1145/3319535.3354255.

Boyle, E., Gilboa, N., & Ishai, Y. (2015). Function secret sharing. In E. Oswald & M. Fischlin (Eds.) *EUROCRYPT 2015, Part II* (Vol. 9057, pp. 337–367). LNCS, Apr. 2015. https://doi.org/10.1007/978-3-662-46803-6_12.

Boyle, E., Gilboa, N., & Ishai, Y. (2016). Function secret sharing: Improvements and extensions. In E. R. Weippl, S. Katzenbeisser, C. Kruegel, A. C. Myers, & S. Halevi (Eds.) *ACM CCS 2016*. ACM Press, Oct. 2016 (pp. 1292–1303). https://doi.org/10.1145/2976749.2978429.

Boyle, E., Gilboa, N., Ishai, Y., & Kolobov, V. I. (2022). Programmable distributed point functions. In Y. Dodis & T. Shrimpton (Eds.) *CRYPTO 2022, Part IV* (Vol. 13510, pp. 121–151). LNCS, Aug. 2022. https://doi.org/10.1007/978-3-031-15985-5_5.

Bui, D., Couteau, G., Meyer, P., Passelègue, A., & Riahinia, M. (2024). Fast public-key silent OT and more from constrained Naor-Reingold. In LNCS, June 2024 (pp. 88–118). https://doi.org/10.1007/978-3-031-58751-1_4.

Couteau, G., & Ducros, C. (2023). Pseudorandom correlation functions from variable-density LPN, Revisited. In *PKC 2023, Part II*. LNCS. May 2023 (pp. 221–250). https://doi.org/10.1007/978-3-031-31371-4_8.

Couteau, G., & Kumar, N. (2024). 10-party sublinear secure computation from standard assumptions. In LNCS, Aug. 2024 (pp. 39–73). https://doi.org/10.1007/978-3-031-68400-5_2.

Couteau, G., Kumar, N., & Ye, X. (2025). Multiparty homomorphic secret sharing and more from LPN and MQ. In *Cryptology ePrint Archive*.

Dodis, Y., Halevi, S., Rothblum, R. D., & Wichs, D. (2016). Spooky encryption and its applications. In M. Robshaw & J. Katz (Eds.) *CRYPTO 2016, Part III* (Vol. 9816, pp. 93–122). LNCS, Aug. 2016. https://doi.org/10.1007/978-3-662-53015-3_4.

Doerner, J., & Shelat, A. (2017). Scaling ORAM for secure computation. In B. M. Thuraisingham, D. Evans, T. Malkin, & D. Xu (Eds.) *ACM CCS 2017*. ACM Press, Oct. 2017 (pp. 523–535). https://doi.org/10.1145/3133956.3133967.

Orlandi, C., Scholl, P., & Yakoubov, S. (2021). The rise of paillier: Homomorphic secret sharing and public-key silent OT. In A. Canteaut & F.-X. Standaert (Eds.) *EUROCRYPT 2021, Part I* (Vol. 12696, pp. 678–708). LNCS, Oct. 2021. https://doi.org/10.1007/978-3-030-77870-5_24.

Schoppmann, P., Gascón, A., Reichert, L., & Raykova, M. (2019). Distributed vector-OLE: Improved constructions and implementation. In L. Cavallaro, J. Kinder, X. F. Wang, & J. Katz (Eds.) *ACM CCS 2019*. ACM Press, Nov. 2019 (pp. 1055–1072). https://doi.org/10.1145/3319535.3363228.

Weng, C., Yang, K., Katz, J., & Wang, X. (2021). Wolverine: Fast, scalable, and communication-efficient zero-knowledge proofs for Boolean and arithmetic circuits. In *2021 IEEE Symposium on Security and Privacy*. IEEE Computer Society Press, May 2021 (pp. 1074–1091). https://doi.org/10.1109/SP40001.2021.00056.

The manufacturer's authorised representative in the EU is Springer
Nature Customer Service Centre GmbH, Europaplatz 3, 69115 Heidelberg,
Germany. If you have any concerns regarding our products, please
contact ProductSafety@springernature.com

Printed and bound by CPI Group (UK) Ltd, Croydon, CR0 4YY

27/04/2026

02097578-0003